C000092406

The Welsh Pony

The Welsh Pony

WYNNE DAVIES

J. A. ALLEN

ACKNOWLEDGEMENTS

I wish to thank: Mr David Blair of the Welsh Part-bred Pony Group for collating much of the material in chapter 4; the photographers who have been acknowledged and have given their permission for the photographs to be incorporated in the book; Ruth who proof read the manuscript and put the text on disk; all the family who have put up with my preoccupation during the three years taken to compile this book.

Wynne Davies

Published in Great Britain in 2006 by
J.A. Allen
An imprint of Robert Hale Ltd
Clerkenwell House
45-47 Clerkenwell Green
London EC1R 0HT

A catalogue record for this book is available from the British Library

ISBN-10: 0-85131-870-3
ISBN-13: 978-0-85131-870-7

Edited by Lesley Young
Design and typesetting by Bridgewater Book Company
Photographs by the author, except for those reproduced with permission as detailed on the individual photographs

Colour separation by Tenon & Polert Colour Scanning Limited, Hong Kong
Printed by New Era Printing Co. Limited, China

Contents

Preface

THIS BOOK is a companion volume to *The Welsh Cob* (Wynne Davies, J. A. Allen, 1998) which deals with the current section D of the Welsh Stud Book (WSB). *The Welsh Pony* encompasses the current sections A, B and C of the WSB, namely the Welsh Mountain pony (A), the Welsh pony (B) and the Welsh pony of Cob-type (C), but caution is advised when adopting the symbols (A), (B) and (C) prior to volume 33 (1949) of the WSB because, although section A has always referred to the Welsh Mountain pony, until the Welsh pony of Riding-type (B) was 'invented' in the 1930s, the home of the pony of Cob-type was in section B from 1901 until volume 30 (1931–34) and, to confuse matters further, section C of volume 32 (1939–48) contained both Welsh ponies of Cob-type and Welsh Cobs ranging from 123 cm to 163 cm.

At the time when section B was allocated to the pony of Riding-type (1930), the fortunes of ponies and cobs (and agriculture in general) were at a very low ebb; volume 29 of the WSB mustering only 96 registrations in total (compared with 8,580 in 1995), while the section C ponies of Cob-type totalled only two stallions and five mares. There were still only two Cob-type stallions registered in volume 32 (1939–48) and three in volume 43 (1960). This meant that until numbers warranted separate classes at shows, ponies of Riding-type and Cob-type competed against one another. One example of this was at the 1930 Royal Welsh Show when the Welsh pony stallion class contained only four entries, headed by Royal Welsh Jack (Cob-type) and followed by the four-year-old Ceulan Comet (Cob-type, owned and bred by my father and champion in 1931, 1932 and 1934 when he was sold to Australia), Mab-y-Brenin (Cob-type, owned by my grandfather and sire of the famous Mathrafal) and Tanybwlch Berwyn (Riding-type, who can be regarded as the 'Abraham' of the current section B).

It is interesting to see how the proportions of the various sections have varied in popularity and demand. For example:

Year	Section A	Section D	Ratio	Total registrations
Females				
1902	273	180	1.5:1	609
1970	3135	142	22:1	5628
1995	1163	1216	1:1	8580
Males				
1995	522	1037	0.5:1	8580

Nowadays, the Welsh part-breds (WP-B) occupy an equally important role within the WSB; e.g. WP-B registrations in 2001 were 984 compared with totals of 790 section Bs and 658 section Cs. When the part-bred register was introduced in 1950 the rules were ponderously complicated, there was very little enthusiasm or advantage in registration and only nine were recorded in ten years. The P-B section was reconstituted and the regulations simplified in 1960 and immediately 21 animals were registered during that first year (which increased dramatically to 640 in 1965) with 25 per cent registered Welsh blood as a total accumulated from sire or dam side. As from 1 January 2003, animals with a total of 12.5 per cent Welsh blood, again from either side (or both), were accepted into the part-bred register.

CHAPTER ONE

The Welsh Mountain Pony

PONIES HAVE roamed the hills and marshes of Wales since time immemorial. Fragments of harness and chariots found in North Wales (Llyn Cerrig Bach hoard) from the Bronze Age (*circa* 1500 to 500 BC) suggest that ponies, rather than horses, were used for harness work. In the two years that Julius Caesar spent in Britain, during which time he established a stud near Bala, he is reported to have been so impressed with the speed of the Welsh chariot ponies that he took some back with him to Rome. Roman horses were small – remains of the average cavalry mounts dug up at Roman forts such as Newsead were around 12 hands – but those owned by emperors, e.g. Incitatus owned by the emperor Caligula Caesar around AD 37, were up to 14 hands 2 in. There is no mention of 'ponies' in the Welsh laws of Hywel Dda in the tenth century (*Leges Wallicae*), but Giraldus Cambrensis, writing his *Itinerary through Wales* in 1188, noted that the 'hills are full of small ponies'. They were certainly there in the sixteenth century and in sufficient numbers to persuade Henry VIII to pronounce a law of annihilation upon these 'vermin' and 'nags of small stature' in which he could see no value and only a waste of fodder which could more profitably be given to animals capable of carrying his soldiers into battle.

In the nineteenth century, Sir Richard Green Price of Presteigne, Radnorshire wrote of the ponies on the Welsh hills:

> Persecuted by laws, by starvation, dog-driving, contaminated by gross carelessness in their mating, they survive where sheep and cattle only die and we may wonder indeed that these little animals thrive in such a perfect state as we find them today in their native pastures.

In those times it was 'survival of the fittest', with every instinct sharpened by self-preservation. To survive the ravages of the weather the ponies developed thick coats and plenty of mane, tail and feather; the most hardy being a 'cobby' type, with indigenous colours (black, brown and dark dun) with very little white marking on their legs or faces.

Some wealthy, well-meaning landowners tried to 'glamorise' the cobby hill ponies in the nineteenth century by turning out Arab or Thoroughbred stallions onto the Welsh hills, a practice decried by the Church Stretton hill pony breeders as producing 'pretty animals which are not capable of surviving on their native heath'. In South Wales, Mr Richard Crawshay Bailey, ironmaster of Merthyr Tydfil, turned out a grey Arab stallion (possibly an ancestor of Dyoll Starlight) on the Brecon Beacons, and Mr Williams of Aberpergwm turned out another grey Arab stallion onto his hills around 1840. In North Wales, Colonel Vaughan of Rug, near Corwen, ran a half-Arab stallion named Apricot on the Denbighshire hills, and Sir Watkin Williams Wynn turned out the English Thoroughbred Merlin (a direct descendant of the Byerly Turk, imported in 1689) onto the Ruabon hills. The ponies of this area are still referred to in the Welsh language as *'merlyn'* and *'merlynnod'* (plural).

BELOW *Dyoll Starlight in 1920, aged 26. Photo by Lady Wentworth.*

When the Welsh Pony and Cob Society (WPCS) was launched at Llandrindod Wells on

25 April 1901 and produced the first volume of the WSB in 1902, Dyoll Starlight (referred to above and foaled in 1894) was the only grey stallion to be included in the registration. There would probably have been 10,000 Mountain ponies in the principality around the 1900s. A photograph of the roundup of Church Stretton ponies moving through the main street of the town on 23 September 1892 was published in the local newspaper along with a report announcing the roundup of 1,250 ponies from this one hill alone. With the exception of Dyoll Starlight, who was of the 'improved grey' type, the majority of the remaining thousands of Mountain ponies were of the dark-coloured 'cobby' sort recorded in paintings. The advent of photography showed some of the earlier examples to be Matchless (foaled in 1890 and registered in the Polo Pony Stud Book, height 11 hands 3 in), Prince of Cardiff (foaled in 1895, height 12 hands 1 in) and the mares Titw

TOP LEFT *Matchless c.1895.*

TOP RIGHT *Prince of Cardiff c.1900.*

BOTTOM LEFT *Titw c.1904, WN champion 1904.*

BOTTOM RIGHT *Mountain Lass c.1908. Photo courtesy of Dai Davies.*

ABOVE LEFT *Coed Coch Glyndwr.*

ABOVE RIGHT *Emrys Griffiths with Clan Pip RW champion 1963, 1964*. Photo: Wynne Davies.*

(Denotes overall champion)*

(foaled in 1897), champion at the first Welsh National (WN) Show in 1904, and Mountain Lass (foaled in 1899), prizewinner at most of the WN Shows from 1904–10, owned locally by David Davies, Frondeg, Llanfarian, and fourth in 1911 (Welshpool), then owned by John Jones and Son, Dinarth Hall, Colwyn Bay.

Typical of a herd of ponies in a major breeding stud (the Llwyn Stud of Mr Marshall Dugdale of Llanfyllin, Montgomeryshire, who was Chairman of Council of the WPCS from 1901 until his death in 1918), was a photograph taken in 1900 of 14 mares, of which 13 were dark bays, one a chestnut and only two having narrow blazes on their faces.

The height limit for the Welsh Mountain pony, section A of the first volume of the Welsh Stud Book (published in 1902) was 12 hands 2 in. Animals of similar height and type, e.g. Klondyke, bred by my grandfather's uncle in 1894, but who might be just over 12 hands 2 in, were registered in section B (12 hands 2 in to 13 hands 2 in). These ponies of Cob-type crossed well with the more refined Dyoll Starlight type. The next most influential sire after Dyoll Starlight was Coed Coch Glyndwr (foaled in 1935) whose bloodlines were a mix of Dyoll Starlight, Klondyke and Prince of Cardiff.

Every so often in the history of any breed a great progenitor is produced; it may only happen once in every twenty years or perhaps

> forty years, but once it has happened the future of that breed is directed onto another course and will never be the same again. (*Welsh Ponies and Cobs*, p. 81)

It is hoped that readers of this book will appreciate the enormous contribution that these few influential sires have had on the Welsh Mountain pony (chapter 1), the Welsh pony (chapter 2) and the Welsh pony of Cob-type (chapter 3).

The four Welsh Mountain pony progenitor sires selected for this book to cover the century of the WPCS are:

First quartile: Dyoll Starlight (1894–1929);

Second quartile: Coed Coch Glyndwr (1935–59) and his grandson, Coed Coch Madog (1947–78);

Third quartile: Clan Pip (1959–81), another grandson of Coed Coch Glyndwr and top of the WPCS sire ratings for eight years between 1971 and 1981;

Fourth quartile: Revel Jeeves (1972– 2002, sire of the two top sires, Pendock Legend (1984–2003) and Penual Mark (foaled in 1977) and his son, Springbourne Caraway (foaled in 1986), these three having headed the WPCS sire ratings 16 times!

BELOW LEFT *Harold Zoet with Revel Jeeves*

BELOW RIGHT *Mrs Jenny Kilbey with Pendock Legend*

ABOVE LEFT *Mrs Corrine Mahoney with Penual Mark. Photo: Bleddyn Pugh.*

ABOVE RIGHT *Mark Northam and judge Mrs Mary Edwards with Springbourne Caraway, RW reserve champion 1989. Photo: Wynne Davies.*

FIRST QUARTILE: Dyoll Starlight (1894–1929)

It might be asked why so many thousands of ponies were bred annually around the beginning of the twentieth century (with fewer than 300 of them registered in the WSB) and what outlet there would be for them. Most of the 1,250 ponies rounded up at Church Stretton in 1892 would be destined for a life in the pits or pulling newspaper or milk carts or costers' barrows in the large English cities. The export trade gave an incentive for breeders to register their ponies within the WSB; 31 ponies from Church Stretton were exported to the USA in 1909 at an average price of £8 each; 61 in 1910 at £12; and 50 in 1911 at £14. This was considerable income for the breeders when one considers that the average annual wage of an agricultural worker at that time was £39. The Church Stretton ponies were very successful in the USA.

The next important milestone in the fortunes of the Welsh Mountain pony was the passing of the Commons Act (8 Ed 7.Ch. 44) in 1908 which empowered recognised pony breeding societies to remove unapproved stallions and colts over one year old (and also rams and ram lambs!) from the hills and commons. A society of pony breeders from the Longmynd hills area of Church Stretton had been set up in 1892. Meticulous records of their proceedings were kept and they instigated their own inspection procedure for approving stallions. Unfortunately, interest had waned by

1902 and individual breeders then 'did their own thing' until the 1908 Commons Act offered generous financial incentives from the National Exchequer and the Church Stretton Society was resurrected under the aegis of the Longmynd Commoners' Association.

The regulations laid down by the Board of Agriculture, Whitehall, London for Welsh Mountain ponies (which also applied to Dartmoor, Exmoor, Fell, Highland and New Forest ponies) were:

(i) the stallions must be registered in the WSB;

(ii) the stallions will be selected at a show for the Board of Agriculture premiums by a judge appointed by the Board (the first Inspection Show at Church Stretton took place in April 1911);

(iii) each premium stallion shall roam at large on the mountains from 1 May to 1 August and serve only mares which have been registered in the WSB;

(iv) to receive the premiums, the secretary of the local society must supply a certificate, signed and dated 2 August, stating that the above conditions have been complied with.

In 1912, four premiums of £5 each were awarded at Church Stretton to Survivor (bay, bred by Mr Marshall Dugdale), the Longmynd Society's Dyoll Dynamite (grey by Dyoll Starlight), Stretton Torchlight (grey by Dyoll Starlight) and the society's Little Jap (bay). The Board of Agriculture representative was so impressed with the organisation of the Church Stretton Society that, at the next show, held on 23 April 1913, he awarded six premiums of £5 each to Survivor, Dyoll Dynamite, Stretton Torchlight, Ragleth Rocket (grey by Stretton Torchlight), Stretton Sportsman (black whose sire, also black, had been exported to New Zealand) and Longmynd Emperor (grey by Stretton Torchlight) who was owned by local school-master Mr W. J. Roberts who had been the secretary and treasurer of the society since its inception, a post continued by his son, Mr Tommy Roberts, until his death at 90 years old in 1979.

The reserve stallions that day were Grove Stalactite (grey by Grove Ballistite by Dyoll Starlight), the Society's Dyoll Radium (grey by Dyoll Starlight), Lamanite (grey by Dyoll Dynamite) and the Society's Dyoll Lightning (black by Dyoll Starlight). Again on the recommendation of their representative, the Board of Agriculture promised to increase their grants to eight for 1914.

One problem which began to emerge in the Welsh Mountain pony breeding circles at this time was the dominance of the Dyoll Starlight bloodlines over all others and the danger of inducing lack of stamina through in-breeding. Dyoll Starlight held his own in everyone's affections as the 'high priest' of Mountain ponydom. The mark of the incomparable old warrior was ever plainly to be seen and so it remained until 1919 when the health of Starlight's owner/breeder Mr Meuric Lloyd (Dyoll is Lloyd spelled backwards) began to fail and Starlight was sold, at 25 years of age, to Lady Wentworth who sold him on to Spain, at 28 years old in 1922, for £800 (equivalent to about £40,000 today) and he died there in 1929, aged 35.

Apart from several mares bought in by Mr Lloyd to capitalise on his good fortune in having bred such a prepotent sire, visiting mares travelled

RIGHT *Bleddfa Shooting Star.*

from far and wide to Llanwrda in Carmarthenshire and Starlight's progeny dominated the show rings and stallion premiums. His two most famous sons were Bleddfa Shooting Star who died at the Grove Stud in 1932 aged 31 years, and Greylight who was sold to Australia for the enormous sum of 1,000 guineas in 1911, and they reigned supreme in the show ring for the first ten years of the twentieth century. By 1912, 65 Starlight progeny were registered in the WSB: 27 stallions (19 greys, one roan, five bays and two blacks) and 38 mares (22 greys, five roans, four bays, three browns, two blacks and two chestnuts). At the 1912 Royal Agricultural Society of England (RASE) Show at Norwich, all five stallions were his sons and he was also sire of the champion female, Lady Starlight. At the Church Stretton Agricultural Show that same year all 11 entries in the stallion class (seven of them greys) were either his sons or grandsons!

Encouraged by the success of the Board of Agriculture premium allocations, other area associations applied for recognition and, in 1913, in

LEFT *Greylight, WN champion 1904, 1905, 1906, 1907, 1909, 1910.*

addition to the eight premiums of £5 at Church Stretton, nine premiums of £5 were allocated to the Eppynt Forest, three of £5 to the Gower Common and three of £5 to Penybont Common in Radnorshire. The driving forces behind these successful applications were Mr J. L. Davies of Yscirfechan, Merthyr Cynog, Brecon (Eppynt), the Hon. Odo Vivian (who became Lord Swansea in 1923 and was Chairman of the WPCS from 1927 until his sudden death in 1932) (Gower) and Mr Charles Coltman Rogers (Vice-Chairman of the WPCS) of Stanage Park, Radnorshire (Penybont). (Gower Common comprises Fairwood, some 3.2 km [2 miles] square, and Pengwern, which is approximately 2.4 km by 1.6 km [1.5 miles by 1 mile].)

The judging of the Eppynt stallions was conducted at Cwmowen Inn on 14 May 1913 when the inspection was interrupted from time to time by squadrons of mounted yeomanry from the Eppynt camps. Eppynt was home for the Army in 1913 and 94 farms, covering 14,160 hectares (35,000 acres), were commandeered in 1938 for military practice, so that the long-established families (many of whom were prominent Welsh pony breeders) were dispersed all over Britain and overseas. In order to cover the whole of the 80 km (50 miles) length and 32 km (20 miles) breadth of the Eppynt, the premium selections were alternated every three years between the Drovers Arms, Merthyr Cynog, and Cwmowen Inn (which became the site of an annual sale from *circa* 1950 until it was moved to Brecon Market in 1990). Present at Cwmowen in May 1913 were the WPCS judges Mr Coltman Rogers and Mr J. R. Bache (WPCS secretary) and Captain Hamilton Pryce and Mr McCall from the Board of Agriculture. A photograph, taken at the Cwmowen Inspection on 5 May 1917 (above right), shows Mr Coltman Rogers (owner of the car), Mr Bache, Mr F. Carter from the Board of Agriculture and the local secretary, Mr J. L. Davies, whose grandson, Mr Elwyn Davies, was WPCS President in the year 2000. The top premium was awarded to the dark pony (next to the car), Duhonw Prince, owned by Mr E. P. Williams of Dollynwydd Farm, Builth Wells. Standing in front of him (bending down) is Mr Jack Roberts, stud groom to Lord Swansea (who then lived at Caer Beris, Builth Wells). This stallion was present for exhibition purposes only, not to compete for a premium.

LEFT *Judging the premium stallions at Cwmowen, 5 May 1917.*

On Eppynt a 5-shilling reward was offered to any shepherd who reported the presence of any unapproved stallions or mares upon the hills. This money was raised by inflicting a monetary penalty on the owner of any such animal, or, if the owner could not be traced, the animal was sold to defray expenses under powers given in the Commons Act.

An interesting report by Mr J. F. Rees, MRCVS (who accompanied the premium judges and Board of Agriculture representatives for the first 20 years) was that, after having subjected every stallion to a minute and exhaustive examination, and despite their often poor condition and their wild lives on high ground, never once did he find a stallion which had to be rejected on veterinary grounds. Defective genital organs (Ministry of Agriculture figures for 1973 show that out of 443 stallions inspected, 33 were found defective) is a fault which must have been introduced into the Mountain pony stock at a later date because there is no suggestion of it earlier.

Some societies (e.g. Church Stretton) bought their own stallions for about £20 to £30, recouping this sum by charging every member half a crown for every mare running on the moorland, with an excess of £8 being paid to members to keep the nine Church Stretton stallions over the winter. One such stallion, bought by the Church Stretton Society for £20, was Dyoll Sirocco by Dyoll Starlight. Unfortunately, he got out one night among some large, shod horses and suffered a badly shattered hind leg, so he had to be put down. His purchase price had been paid for with a loan from the Longmynd Commoners' Association who, upon hearing of the sad fate of Sirocco, voted £9 as a 'donation' towards this loss.

A newly participating society in 1914 was the Carmarthenshire Society which was subdivided into two areas: Brynamman and Gwynfe, two hills each of some 1.6 km (10 miles) length and 11 km (7 miles width, benefiting from an underlying limestone formation which was regarded as the best geological prescription for the development of bone in equines. During the first inspection at Gwynfe, over 100 mares were inspected and registered in the WSB. However, following the outbreak of the First World War, when their enthusiastic convenor (Mr Edgar Herbert, 1950 WPCS President) was called up into the Army, the allocation of premiums to the Gwynfe and Brynamman Societies was short-lived until Mr Herbert returned from the war and carried on the work from 1920.

During the war years (1914–18) the judges remarked on the impoverished and bare-boned condition of the animals presented in some centres. Many were in 'ribs of wreck' condition, never having been the recipient of so much as a kindly thought, let alone a chance wisp of hay.

For the 1916 inspections, owing to the dearth of stallions and of menfolk to organise the scheme, Mrs Greene of the famous Grove Stud lent four valuable and fashionably bred stallions: two to Eppynt and one each to Penybont and Church Stretton. The cost of travelling would have absorbed most of the premium grant and the WPCS was very grateful to Mrs Greene for sending some of her best stallions to a rather problematic destiny in strange lands. It was also in 1916 that graduated premium awards were implemented, at £7, £5 and £3, rather than the previous £5 'all round'.

The Church Stretton inspection on 11 April 1918 was a day full of surprises. Three of the stallions entered in the programme failed to put in an appearance when two of them, Stretton Klondyke and Stretton Sweep, avoided the many attempts made to catch them on the hills! The other absentee, Gwyndy Prizeman, was described as 'about done in'. The ravages of time and the wear and tear of a long life upon the hilltops had obviously brought his career to an end. The judges awarded a premium to Mr Beddoe's stallion by Bleddfa Shooting Star but the Commoners refused to accept him, preferring Mr Fred Hills's piebald stallion! By 1919, however, Stretton Klondyke had at last allowed himself to be caught and was awarded a premium. Stretton Sweep and Gwyndy Prizeman were never heard of again.

A praiseworthy innovation in 1919 was the purchase of a stallion who had proved his worth in one area to spend a further three years in another area, and Captain Christy of Llyswen was thanked by the Eppynt Society for purchasing Ragleth Rocket from Mrs Gibbon of Little Stretton and allowing him to spend the summer with the mares on Eppynt hills.

The scheme operated successfully throughout the 1920s, with the stallion inspection day becoming an important event in the calendar of many rural areas. Many new societies were set up to benefit from the Board of Agriculture grants. For example, in 1928 eight premiums were awarded at Radnorshire Beacon Hill; two at Rhos Fallog Hill; five at the Great Forest of Brecon (Van); three at Mynydd Bwlch-y-Groes; four at Fairwood; three at Cefn Bryn (Gower); two at nearby Llanrhidian; nine at Church Stretton; 13 at Eppynt; four at Black Mountains (Eastern at Talgarth); and six at Black Mountains (Carmarthenshire at Gwynfe) – in all, a grand total of 59 premiums.

In the early 1930s, Britain experienced a period of unparalleled economic depression. In 1932, the Treasury withdrew the stallion grant to the War Office and in 1932 and 1933 no grants were made available for the ponies to run on their native heath or for Welsh Cobs to travel the Welsh counties. By 1934, the situation had improved marginally and the Treasury voted a reduced sum to the War Office for stallion grants. This money was boosted by an additional grant from the Racecourse Betting Control Board, which continued until 1999 when it was stopped, only to be reintroduced in 2002 when the WPCS was able to prove that the numbers of feral Welsh Mountain ponies on the hills had been reduced so drastically as to cause them to be regarded as an endangered species.

Stallion premiums were awarded during the war years at Church Stretton, Eppynt, Gower and the Black Mountains, sponsored by the RBCB. In 1946, premiums were also awarded at Vaynor and Pontsarn, near Merthyr Tydfil, and, for the first time ever, in a North Wales area at Aber Hills, Bangor, the hills where the ponies of the Snowdon herd of the University College of North Wales, Bangor had roamed since the stud was established in 1919. The judging of the stallions during the 1950s took almost a week. There were two judges who started at Aber Hills, then crossed the border to Church Stretton, then travelled back to mid-Wales at Elan Valley, Beggins Hill (Radnorshire), Llanafan, Eppynt, Black Mountains, Brecon Beacons, before ending up in South Wales at Gower, Penderyn, Dowlais, Vaynor and, finally, at Ebbw Vale where a photograph of the judges, Miss Brodrick and Mr Douglas Meredith, with the stallion Clan Gille was taken in 1958.

BELOW *Judging the premium stallions at Ebbw Vale, 1958. Trevor Morgan with Clan Gille. Photo: Wynne Davies.*

In 1960, to save the judges from having to travel around Wales for so many days, some of the area associations were invited to bring their stallions to Glanusk Park, Crickhowell on the day of the Glanusk One-day Horse Trials. This arrangement proved so successful that, for the next ten years, all the premiums were judged at Glanusk on the one day, along with an Open Show for section A, B, C, D and WPB stallions and youngstock. By 1970, the sheer volume of competition had outgrown the facilities available at the picturesque Glanusk Park and the show and premium judging were moved to the Royal Welsh Showground where they have gone from strength to strength, resulting in 553 showing entries in 34 classes and 39 stallions competing for premiums in 17 areas in 2003.

Running parallel to the premium stallions, the Welsh Mountain ponies provided a substantial proportion of the competition at agricultural shows. The Welsh National Agricultural Society was inaugurated in 1904, with a council selected from all the counties in the principality. It held its first show at Aberystwyth, attracting Shire Horse and Hackney entries from all over Britain. The Welsh breeds were also well represented: Mr Evan Jones's Greylight won the Welsh Mountain pony championship, with Dinarth Hall's Titw winning the brood mare class. The judge for the Welsh breeds was Mr R. Brydon, The Dean, Seaham Harbour, who was not a member of the WPCS Panel of Judges, nor even a member of the WPCS, but who bred eight to ten Hackneys annually. Mr Rees from Tylerstown in the Rhondda Valley judged the Mountain ponies in 1905, with Greylight winning the second of his six Welsh National victories and Marshall Dugdale winning the mare class with the chestnut Llwyn Nell, sired by the noted Cob Eiddwen Flyer. Three of the stallions (out of five) were sired by Dyoll Starlight. They were the winner, Greylight, Brigand (who was offered in the catalogue as 'for sale £40' and was bought by Mr Evan Jones, the owner of Greylight, who later sold him as a premium stallion to Church Stretton from where he was sold to the USA) and Sirocco who also went as a premium stallion to Church Stretton but, as already mentioned, was soon lost as a result of being kicked.

The judge at the 1906 WN Show was Mr W. S. Miller of Forest Lodge, Brecon, who had bought Klondyke at the 1905 show. He again placed Greylight to win the stallion class, with Brigand fourth and Mr Meuric Lloyd's own Dyoll Ballistite fifth. Ballistite, who was three years old, was catalogued as 'for sale £100' which was a very substantial figure in those days. He was bought by Mrs Greene of the Grove Stud where he became a leading winner throughout Britain under the name of Grove Ballistite, winning at the WN Show in 1908 in the absence of Greylight. Mr Marshall Dugdale won the mare class with Kerry Lassie of unregistered parentage.

The most exciting stallion competition of 1906 was at Knighton Show on 31 August, with a 'dual of the giants' between Greylight and Bleddfa Shooting Star who had returned to his native Radnorshire in the ownership of Sir Walter Gilbey of Elsenham Hall, Essex. Greylight carried the day at Knighton and these placings were repeated at the 1907 WN Show under judge Mr J. R Bache. (WPCS Secretary 1909–28). The mare class was won by Lady Starlight (foaled in 1903, by Dyoll Starlight), owned by Mr J. Lloyd Morgan, Abergwili, Carmarthen. This little mare was to become very important in the history of the Welsh Mountain pony. She was also champion at the 1911 and 1912 RASE Shows for Lloyd Morgan, and she later appeared at the 1914 WN Show in the ownership of Miss E. C. V. Hughes, Bryn Hawddgar, Llanarthney, where she won again. By 1914 her name had been changed to Hawddgar Lady Starlight and she was then sold, along with Hawddgar Dewdrop, to Lady Wentworth.

While with Lloyd Morgan in 1910, Lady Starlight was put back to her sire, Dyoll Starlight, and produced Towy Lady Moonlight who was sold to Mrs Greene who changed the mare's name to Grove Star of Hope. At Grove, Star of Hope was many times a member of the winning group at the NPS Show at Islington, e.g. in 1921 with Bleddfa Shooting Star, Grove King Cole II and Grove Lightheart. From Grove, Star of Hope was sold to Lady Wentworth who then sold her to the Arab breeder William Hay of Winestead Hall, Patrington, Yorkshire, who bred Welsh ponies from *circa* 1932 to 1945 using the stallions Winestead Don Juan and Cwm Cream of Eppynt. For William Hay, Star of Hope produced Winestead

Larina in 1932 and when Mr Hay decided to give up his Welsh ponies in 1945, Larina, Winestead Teresa, Winestead Zenia and a few more of uncertain parentage (which were registered as FS although they probably should have been fully registered) were all bought by Mr Emrys Griffiths. One FS mare was Revel Fair Lady, bred by William Hay out of Revel Mysteria, whose 1952 daughter by Ceulan Revolt was Revel Fair Maid FS2, the foundation of the Weston section A 'Fair' family, which included the RW winners Weston Mink Muff and Weston Song. Weston Mink Muff topped the 1974 Weston Sale, selling to Australia for 2,300 guineas. Larina was dam of the 1959 RW champion Revel Rosette (foaled in 1948), Revel Light (foaled in 1950), Revel Lady (1951) and so on, and every current section A at Fayre Stud traces back to her. In the 1950s I spent my summer holidays at the Revel Stud, and Winestead Larina died while I was there, on 2 July 1952. Winestead Zenia (also foaled in 1932) was a daughter of Ness Thistle (1913 WN Show) and she was the dam of Revel Playtime, grand-dam of Brierwood Blue Boy and Revel Pye (also at Brierwood).

To get to the earlier shows, the animals and people travelled by rail, often walking long distances at both ends. On their way home from the 1907 show, the North Wales train became derailed at Abermule and three persons and several horses and ponies were killed but there is no record of any Welsh ponies or their owners or grooms being involved in this terrible accident.

The noted Hackney judge Mr William Foster, Mel Valley judged at the 1908 WN Show where Grove Stud won both classes: the stallion class with Grove Ballistite and the mare class with Mrs Greene's favourite, Bleddfa Tell Tale, who had been bred by Mr Roberts, the Church Stretton schoolmaster. Mr Evan Jones did not enter Greylight for the 1908 show, and stood second and third to Ballistite with Cymru Fydd (by Eiddwen Flyer III) and Sparklight (son of Greylight who was described in the programme as 'for sale by auction').

The 1909 WN judge was Mr John Hill of Church Stretton who wrote many articles on Welsh ponies in the early stud books. Greylight won the stallion class for the fourth time, beating Grove Ballistite. Bleddfa Tell Tale was beaten into second place by Mr Lloyd Morgan's Lady Greylight (he was also fifth with her half-sister, the one-year-older Lady Starlight who had won in 1907), with Dyoll Dazzle third and Llwyn Flyaway (later to produce Revolt, the sire of Coed Coch Glyndwr) fourth. In 1908, for Lloyd Morgan, Lady Greylight bred Emlyn Grey Star (winner at the 1912 WN Show as Grove Limelight) and, in 1910, Towy Model Starlight, winner of many championships for Mrs Nell Pennell when known as Bwlch Quicksilver. She was then sold to Mr Evan Jones (owner/breeder of her sire, Greylight) for whom she won the championship medal at the 1913 National Pony Show. Evan Jones sold her to Lady Wentworth in 1917 and she then produced Lady Wentworth's favourite, Wentworth Springlight, a son of Dyoll Starlight, foaled just after Starlight arrived at Wentworth Stud, aged 25 years. Previously, in 1918, Lady Greylight had produced Grey Princess, sired by Wentworth Windfall. Grey Princess is important in section A history as the dam of Tanybwlch Prancio (foaled in 1932), grand-dam of the 1964 and 1965 RW champion, Coed Coch Pelydrog, and great-grand-dam of the 1954 champion, Coed Coch Planed. A surprising

RIGHT *Tanybwlch Prancio.*

fact to learn about Tanybwlch Prancio is that, after winning the section B mare class (class 60) for Miss Brodrick at the 1938 RASE Show at Cardiff, she went on to win the ridden class (class 67), with John Jones holding her colt foal (born 4 May) at the side of the ring! In 1946, Prancio was exported by Lady Wentworth to Miss Violet Nicholls of the Kuriheka Stud, Otago, New Zealand, with her colt foal Wentworth Southern Cross (by Coed Coch Glyndwr) at foot and, shortly after arriving, she produced a filly, Kuriheka Venus, again by Glyndwr. Prancio continued breeding at Kuriheka until 1959 and died there that year.

At the 1909 RASE Show at Gloucester, Bleddfa Shooting Star won the male championship for Sir Walter Gilbey and Bleddfa Tell Tale was female champion for Mrs Greene, while at the Islington National Pony Show, Greylight was male champion with the roan Gwyndy Bessie female champion. Mr Bache judged at the WN Show again in 1910; Greylight made his last WN appearance before setting off for Botany Bay and Gwyndy Bessie won the female championship.

After six WN Shows at Aberystwyth it was decided that the show should travel the counties of Wales, alternating between north and south, and this was the case until the permanent site at Llanelwedd was purchased in 1963. The 1910 show was held at Llanelli. The 1911 WN Show, judged by Mr Tom James, Myrtle Hill, was held at Welshpool. Mrs Greene won the stallion class with Grove Ballistite. Evan Jones was second with the three-year-old bay My Brother, and won the mare class with the chestnut six-year-old Towyvale Myfy, full-brother and sister to the great Greylight. Myfy was later sold to Miss Beryl Chapman's Kilhendre Celtic Stud, producing influential stock such as Kilhendre Celtic Silversand, a top sire at the Revel.

Until 1908 the section A Welsh Mountain pony was allowed to be up to 12 hands 2 in (127 cm) but in WSB, volume 7 section A was sub-divided into Part I (up to 12 hands) and Part II (up to 12 hands 2 in), with similar descriptions, only that Part II 'had proportionately longer ears and had certain traits of the Cob character and type'. Part I and Part II animals were allowed to be hogged and/or docked.

Separate classes were offered for Parts I and II at the 1912 WN Show at Swansea where Evan Jones had the only two Part II stallions, both three year olds sired by Greylight and, in the absence of all the leading lights of the day, won with Dewi Stone of whom nothing further was ever heard. Both Part I stallions were disqualified for some unrecorded reason. Mrs Greene won the Part II mare class with the aforementioned Grove Limelight, by Dyoll Starlight, and the Part I class with Nantyrharn Starlight, also sired by Dyoll Starlight. Dyoll Starlight, who had 'retired' from the show ring in 1901, made a guest appearance for parading only and was awarded a WPCS special silver medal in honour of his great services to the breed.

The judges at the 1913 WN Show at Portmadoc were Evan Jones and the Reverend John Owen, Taihirion, Tregaron, who had owned the famous Cob stallion Ceffyl Pregethwr (the horse of the preacher). Only one stallion was entered in each of the Part I and Part II classes, Mrs Greene's Grove Ballistite in Part I and Miss Lort's four-year-old Revolt in Part II. Revolt did not attract much attention until he was 26 years old, when he sired the section A cornerstones, Coed Coch Glyndwr and Coed Coch Serliw. Mrs Greene also won the Part I mare class with Nantyrharn Starlight and Miss Lort the Part II class with Jenny Pembroke. With Greylight already in Australia, it was thought that nothing could worry the great Bleddfa Shooting Star with only Grove Ballistite coming within any distance of him. In the meantime, for 1912 and 1913, Shooting Star had been leased to Dafydd Evans and Sons of Llwyncadfor who prepared him for the 1913 shows. It was at this time that he sired the brilliant show mares Ness Sunflower and Ness Thistle for Evan Jones of Caerwedros, Blaentwrch Firefly (chapter 3) for Alfred Williams and the foundation mare of the Menai Stud, Menai Queen Bess, for William Jones, Pantydefaid.

Exhibitors arriving at the National Pony Show at Islington in 1913 were astonished to find Dyoll Starlight (reputedly retired in 1901) entered in the catalogue and even more surprised when the old patriarch appeared in the show ring and was placed first, with Bleddfa Shooting Star second. All the equine newspapers allocated their headlines to this sensational

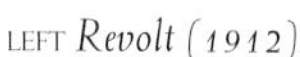

LEFT *Revolt* (1912).

result, *The Field* reporter agreeing with the decision but *The Livestock Journal* reporter violent in his disapproval! Two months later the same two stallions competed at the RASE Show at Bristol where Shooting Star gained the first prize, with his sire second. It was thought that *The Livestock Journal* reporter would have been jubilant but readers were disappointed when he remained silent and only the placings were reported.

The 1914 WN Show was held at Newport, with judges Mr Bennett Owen of Caersws and Mr Tom Jones Evans who was then still at Newcastle Emlyn before moving to Dinchope Farm on Mrs Greene's estate in 1921. Considering the generous prize money offered (£6: £4: £2), entries were still low, Mrs Greene winning the Part II class with Grove Arclight (although he was only 11 hands 3 in) and Mr Evan Jones the Part I class with Towyvale Freckles. Miss Hughes of Llanarthney won both mare classes with Hawddgar Spinaway (Part II), by Bleddfa Shooting Star, and Hawddgar Lady Starlight (Part I). Sir Walter Gilbey died in November 1914, his famous Elsenham Stud was dispersed by auction and, despite the country being at war, Mrs Greene paid the handsome sum of 280 guineas for Bleddfa Shooting Star.

Although many English shows had started up again after having been suspended during the war years, there was no indication of any attempt to resurrect the RW Show until Mr Tom Jones Evans 'went it alone', approached several influential former members and 'got the show on the road' again in 1922 at Wrexham with judge Mr J. R. Bache, secretary of the WPCS. The prize money was increased to £10: £5: £3 and £2, which resulted in ten stallion and 16 mare entries in the section A classes where Parts I and II had been combined into section A under 12 hands high. With her limitless finances and flair for correct conformation and presentation (her grooms were all immaculately dressed in red waistcoats and her ponies turned out to perfection), Mrs Greene was proving indefatigable. She won the stallion class with the magnificent Grove King Cole II, son of her favourite, Bleddfa Tell Tale, and the mare class with Grove Fairy Queen from another daughter of Shooting Star, Mr George Lyell's Ness Thistle. In an extra class for mares entered in the NPS Stud Book, Fairy Queen stood second to Mr Lyell's other entry, Ness Daisy.

Grove King Cole II was unbeatable during 1922, but then Major Dugdale of Llwyn bought Kilhendre Celtic Silverlight from his breeder, Miss Beryl Chapman, and at the first show of 1923 (Shropshire) Silverlight beat King Cole which did not please Mrs Greene! King Cole (although entered) was not shown at the 1923 RW Show at Welshpool for fear of being beaten again but, in fact, Silverlight was not entered either and Major Dugdale won with his 'second fiddle', Llwyn Mighty Atom, who also won in 1924 at Bridgend. Llwyn stallions also won in 1925 at Carmarthen and 1926 at Bangor, with the two full-brothers, Llwyn Temptation (foaled in 1922 and g-g-g-sire of Clan Pip) and Llwyn Satan (foaled in 1923, g-sire of Coed Coch Glyndwr and owned by Dinarth Hall), sired by Kilhendre Celtic Silverlight (who, to the relief of Mrs Greene, was sold to Lady Wentworth for £250 in 1923) out of Llwyn Tempter by the Cob-type Temptation which Major Dugdale bought from my grandfather's uncle after he won at the 1913 WN Show. The Starlight Supreme Challenge cup (which had to be won four times by the same pony to be won outright) was presented to Major Dugdale and Llwyn Temptation at Carmarthen by HRH Prince Henry, later to become the Duke of Gloucester. The winning mares in those years were Dawn of Bryntirion (bred by Mrs Greene and full-sister to Grove Will O'The Wisp, Grove Peep O'Day, etc.) in 1923, Ness Sunflower (also by Bleddfa Shooting Star) in 1924, Irfon Marvel (by Dyoll Starlight, g-dam of Coed Coch Glyndwr and g-g-dam of Coed Coch Berwynfa) in 1925 and Ness Daisy (the 1922 extra class winner, sired by Wentworth Windfall) in 1926.

In 1927 Mrs Greene decided that she had achieved all possible pinnacles (she had won the group class at the NPS Show at Islington against all native breeds every year from 1920 to 1927) and the Grove Stud (with the exception of the 'pensioner' Bleddfa Shooting Star) was dispersed on 29 June, with Lady Wentworth buying all the top lots, including the mare Grove Moonstone (full-sister to Dawn of Bryntirion etc.) at 141 guineas, the stallion Grove King Cole II for 130 guineas and the stallion Grove Sprightly (bought jointly with Mr Tom Jones Evans) for 126 guineas. There were excellent classes at the 1927 RW Show at Swansea, with Major Dugdale judging. Grove King Cole II won the 12-strong stallion class from Llwyn Satan, with Grove Sprightly fifth, and Dinarth Hall's Kittiwake (sired by Revolt) won the 15-strong mare class where Grove Moonstone (top-priced mare at the sale) could only achieve seventh place. Kittiwake was bred by Miss Lort in 1916, her dam being Jenny Pembroke (foaled in 1905, sired by Greylight and bred in Pembrokeshire). Kittiwake's photograph appeared on page 30 of the RWAS *Journal*, held by my father, and she will be met later in chapter 4 as the dam of the Frongoy 'flapping' mare, Lucy Grey. (A 'flapping' race is a pony galloping race not held under Jockey Club rules or, indeed, any other rules.)

Mr Tom Jones Evans had not exhibited any Mountain ponies while his landlord (Mrs Greene of Grove) was exhibiting but at the 1928 and 1929 RW Shows he won the stallion class with the chestnut Craven Master Shot (foaled in 1924 and sired by Craven Star Shot who beat all the American Hackneys in harness) and he was exported to the USA after the 1929 show.

Lord Swansea's Caerberis Dazzle was the winning mare in 1928 and Dawn of Bryntirion (now in the ownership of Mr Tom Jones Evans) won in 1929. She was also sold to the USA after the show.

By 1930 Mr Tom Jones Evans had bought out Lady Wentworth's share in Grove Sprightly and then won every RW Show championship up to the outbreak of war in 1939, with the exception of 1937 when Mr Evans was

RIGHT *Tom Jones Evans with Grove Sprightly, RW champion 1930*, 1931*, 1932*, 1933*, 1934*, 1935*, 1936*, 1939*.*

appointed judge to give other exhibitors a chance! Sprightly won the Starlight cup outright for the first time in 1933 and for the second time in 1936. Most years Mr Evans's Grove Will O'The Wisp was second, until he was sold to Dinarth Hall in 1936 and then won the 1937 championship after which he was sold to the Italian Count Idefonso Stanga. At the 1933 show, Bowdler Brightlight (leased by Ceulan Stud) was second and Will O'The Wisp was third. Dinarth Hall's Faraam Mercury was reserve champion in 1930 and 1932, after which he was sold to Australia. Mercury's son, Dinarth What Ho, was reserve champion in 1939 and we showed him to win further RW championships in 1947 and 1952.

The winning mares at the pre-war shows were Misses May and

Summers's Clumber Miss Mary (1930), Miss Mathieson's Dunchurch Venus (g-g-g-g-dam of the 1974 champion Bengad Love in the Mist), (1931 with Caerberis Dazzle second), Mr Tom Jones Evans's Grove Ladybird (1932, 1933 and 1934), Miss Mathieson's Craven Jean (1935) and Miss Mathieson's Craven Shot Star, by Craven Star Shot, (1936) beating Grove Ladybird, now in the ownership of Lord Mostyn. The blood of Grove Ladybird permeates

BELOW LEFT *Tom Thomas with Grove Will O'The Wisp, RW champion 1937*. Photo: G. H. Parsons.*

BELOW RIGHT *(from left) Grove Will O'The Wisp, Grove Sprightly and Bowdler Brightlight at 1933 RW.*

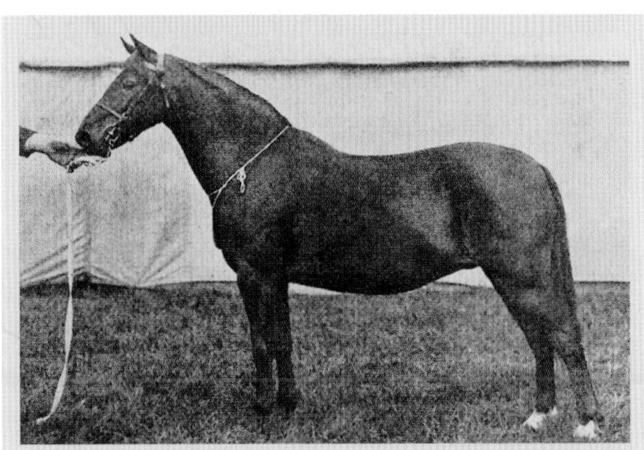

to the present day via her daughter, Mostyn Partridge (foaled in 1939), and Partridge's daughters, Kirby Cane Pheasant (foaled in 1956), Kirby Cane Prattle (foaled in 1958) and Twyford Plover (foaled in 1964).

Mr Tom Lewis's Grove Peep O'Day was placed first in 1937 but disqualified owing to the weight of her shoes, with the first prize then going to Dinarth Hall's Criban Socks. There was no RW Show in 1938, with the

ABOVE LEFT *Wynne Davies with Dinarth What Ho, RW champion 1947*, 1952, reserve champion 1939.*

ABOVE RIGHT *Grove Ladybird, RW champion 1932, 1933, 1934.*

RIGHT *Criban Socks, RW champion 1937. Photo: Rouch.*

RASE Show being held in Cardiff, and Mr Matthew Williams, Vardra Stud judged the 1939 show at Caernarfon. In those days judges were allowed to judge animals which they had bred or owned and Vardra Sunflower, by Craven Master Shot, won her class, with Grove Sprightly, making his last show ring appearance, winning the championship. Sprightly died at the Craven Stud at the age of 31 in 1949. Of all the hundreds of ponies and Cobs owned by Mr Tom Jones Evans, Sprightly was his favourite and he was buried alongside his stable at Dinchope Farm, Craven Arms.

SECOND QUARTILE: the Coed Coch Glyndwr era

Coed Coch Glyndwr was foaled in 1935. His 26-year-old sire, Revolt, was a son of Llwyn Tyrant, by Prince of Cardiff by the Hackney Hamlet Prince of Denmark, and Tyrant's dam, Florence (bought at the 1905 WN Show), was by the 12 hands 2 in Eiddwen Flyer III (stud card in chapter 3) by Eiddwen Flyer II (13 hands) by Eiddwen Flyer (14 hands 2 in), foaled in 1877. Revolt's dam, Flyaway, was by the same 14 hands 2 in Eiddwen Flyer and yet Revolt measured only 12 hands 1 in. Glyndwr's dam, Dinarth Henol, was sired by the 1926 champion Llwyn Satan whose sire, Kilhendre Celtic Silverlight, was Mountain pony bred (by Bleddfa Shooting Star) but his dam, Llwyn Tempter, was by the Cob-type Temptation. Dinarth Henols's dam, Irfon Marvel, was a Mountain pony bred at Henallt, Builth Wells and sired by Dyoll Starlight; she appears in chapter 2 as g-g-g-dam of Coed Coch Berwynfa.

Glyndwr was bought for 45 guineas at the extraordinary Coed Coch Sale of 28 August 1937 where a Mr Walton (who had never previously owned any ponies and did not have any land on which to keep them) bought 35 of the 38 ponies on offer for a total cost of £1,099 (including Glyndwr and, top of the sale at 63 guineas, his half-sister Coed Coch Serliw). The ponies (along with cattle, sheep and implements which Mr Walton had also bought) remained at Coed Coch another until another sale could be arranged on behalf of Mr Walton. At the second sale two weeks later, my father bought Serliw and was under-bidder on Glyndwr whom Miss Brodrick of Coed Coch bought back for 30 guineas. Glyndwr sired some exceptional stock at Coed Coch and neighbouring studs for another six years until he was sold to Lady Wentworth (while Miss Brodrick was away on war effort) for 400 guineas in 1943. Glyndwr stayed at Crabbet Park, Sussex until he went to Mr McNaught at Clan Stud in 1949. In 1953 Glyndwr was given to Miss Marguerite de Beaumont of the Shalbourne Stud where many mares from all over Britain visited him until his death in 1959.

At the first few shows after the war, it was the pre-war 'carry overs' who reigned supreme; the 1947 champions being Dinarth What Ho and Vardra Charm, followed by Tregoyd Starlight and Coed Coch Serliw (for Ceulan) in 1949. There was no show in 1948 due to petrol rationing. Tregoyd Starlight was awarded the male championship again in 1950 but was disqualified on veterinary grounds and the award went to his son, the two-year-old Coed Coch Meilyr. Meilyr was a grandson of Glyndwr on his dam's side and the female and overall champion was a Glyndwr daughter, the exquisite Coed Coch Siaradus. This was the start of the Coed Coch

ABOVE LEFT *Vardra Charm, RW champion 1947.*

ABOVE RIGHT *E.S. Davies and judge Captain T.A. Howson with Coed Coch Serliw, RW champion 1949. Photo: Wynne Davies.*

Glyndwr dominance in the show ring, with Siaradus winning five overall RW championships and Coed Coch Madog (same dam as Meilyr, Coed Coch Mefusen, but sired by the Glyndwr son, Seryddwr) winning nine male championships (but not once overall!) every year from 1951 to 1962 with the exception of 1952 when, to my great surprise and delight, I beat him with Dinarth What Ho, 1954 when he was beaten by his son, the two-year-old Coed Coch Planed and 1961 when he was beaten by Bowdler Brewer who won the stallion class.

Though carrying the 'Coed Coch' prefix, Siaradus was not actually bred at Coed Coch but at the Rhydyfelin Stud of Mr Cyril Lewis at Trawsfynydd in 1942. In those days, if the animals had not been registered by their breeders, the owners could register them with their own prefix. Siaradus really deserved a 'Coed Coch' prefix as her dam was Coed Coch Sirius, another of the animals bought (as a foal) by Mr Walton at the first 1937 Coed Coch Sale.

In total, five Coed Coch Glyndwr grandsons claimed 16 RW championships and four great-grandsons another six championships. His female descendants were even more successful, two daughters receiving six overall championships, five grand-daughters seven championships and five great-grand-daughters five championships.

Looking at Glyndwr grandsons, we have already met the 1950 champion, the two-year-old Coed Coch Meilyr who became champion by

LEFT *Coed Coch Siaradus, RW champion 1950*, 1951*, 1952*, 1953*, 1955*.*

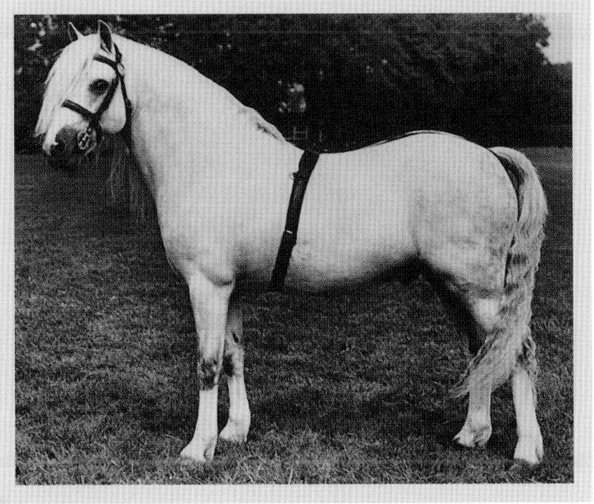

BELOW LEFT *Coed Coch Madog, RW champion 1951, 1953, 1955, 1956, 1957, 1958, 1959, 1960, 1962.*

BELOW RIGHT *Coed Coch Planed, RW champion 1954. Photo: Wynne Davies.*

default of his sire, Tregoyd Starlight, and who was descended from Glyndwr via his dam, the Glyndwr daughter Coed Coch Mefusen (foaled in 1943) whose grand-dam, Grove Lightheart (foaled in 1914), was a daughter of the 1908 champion Bleddfa Tell Tale. Mefusen was also dam of Madog (foaled in 1947) who had been sold as a foal to Mr Owen Ellis of the Hendre Stud and then bought back in 1951 to fill an export order for southern Rhodesia (now Zimbabwe). Luckily for Coed Coch and for

Britain, his potential was realised just in time, Coed Coch Moelwyn was exported to Rhodesia in November 1951 and on 24 May, two months after Madog returned to Coed Coch, he was placed second at the Shropshire Show to the seven-years-older Eryri Gwyndaf whom we had at Ceulan in 1947. Madog was then RW male champion nine times between 1951 and 1962, beating the eight-times record of Grove Sprightly in the 1930s. Having spent 29 years at Coed Coch, Madog would not have been happy to be moved and he was put down just before the dispersal sale at the age of 31.

It was in 1965 that the WPCS initiated a 'sire ratings scheme', allocating 5:3:1 points to the top three in-hand winners at seven major shows. By 1965, Madog had become the most sought-after section-A sire, with 51 prize-winning progeny contributing to his winning total of 93 points. No doubt Madog would have headed the sire ratings prior to 1965 had the scheme been in existence then. The 1965 total cannot be compared points-wise with the 2003 figure of 143 points obtained by Pendock Legend with 20 progeny, as the results from 44 shows are now collated. Madog topped the sire ratings every year between 1965 and 1974, with the exception of 1971 and 1973 (Clan Pip). Clan Pip (Glyndwr grandson on his sire's side and great-grandson on his dam's) was also twice RW champion but warrants his own third quartile category.

Two other Glyndwr grandsons dominated the RW scene from 1967 to 1970; Treharne Tomboy was champion three times but did not compete in 1969 when the champion was Coed Coch Pryd. Tomboy, always produced by David Reynolds of Springbourne for his owner, Lt.Col. Clement Rosser-John, was sired by Treharne Reuben who was by Glyndwr out of a Glyndwr daughter, Stoatley Bright Dawn. After winning his third RW championship, Tomboy was exported to Lady Diana Isaac, New Zealand, where he was very successful, especially as a sire of performance ponies. Tomboy's dam, Coed Coch Blodyn, was a granddaughter of Rhydd FS1 (foaled in 1934) who with her full-sister Taran (foaled in 1936), and along with Coed Coch Glyndwr and Coed Coch Serliw, were the only progeny of Revolt in his old age when owned by

Mrs Chadwick of the Bryntirion Stud, Bryngwyn Hall on Anglesey. Taran was the foundation mare of the Glascoed and Eryl Studs, Glascoed Tesni being one of the top lots (sold to Adele Rockwell, Canada) of the 1959 Coed Coch Sale, and Glascoed Tryfan, Eryl Marog and Eryl Alis were valued brood mares at Ceulan. The Taran daughter Glascoed Trysor was dam of Eryl Timothy, sired by the Glyndwr son Shalbourne Prince Daybreak. Eryl Timothy was the sire of the 1980 and 1982 champion Crossways Merle whose dam, the 1968 champion Ready Token Glen Bride, was by Coed Coch Bugail out of Ready Token Hyacinth, half-brother and -sister, both out of Whitehall Bluebell.

Coed Coch Pryd was a grandson of Glyndwr through his dam, Coed Coch Prydferth (daughter of Tanybwlch Prancio who was also exported to New Zealand), and great-grandson through his sire, Coed Coch Madog, and he is therefore full-brother to the magnificent Coed Coch Pelydrog RW female champion in 1964 and overall and HOYS qualifier in 1965. Altogether, Pelydrog won 65 first prizes and 30 championships, including the Lord Arthur Cecil supreme at the NPS Show. The current families representing Pryd are via his son Betws Serenllys (foaled in 1968, out of the Criban Golden Spray daughter, Betws Seren) and via his daughter Coed Coch Lili (foaled in 1975), the pony selected by Wyn Jones as a gift when the Coed Coch Stud was dispersed in 1978. Her son, Nerwyn Cadno, was RW champion in 1987.

The Glyndwr third generation RW male champions start with Coed Coch Planed (foaled in 1952) who has Glyndwr as three of his four great-grandsires, two from his sire, Coed Coch Madog, and the other as sire to his grand-dam, Coed Coch Pioden. Planed was male champion, beating his sire, when he was only two years old, a feat which he never repeated despite coming very close several times. Planed was a 'round', fiery little stallion with breathtaking movement, sire of many beautiful daughters, but he did not leave much in the way of sons. He went to Gredington Stud as a yearling, where he stayed for the rest of his life.

The other Glyndwr third-generation RW male champion at Gredington was the home-bred Gredington Simwnt (foaled in 1961), sired

ABOVE LEFT *Lord Kenyon with Gredington Simwnt, RW champion 1972*, 1973*. Photo: Wynne Davies.*

ABOVE RIGHT *Lacy Justyn, RW champion 2000. Photo: Carol Jones.*

by Coed Coch Madog out of Coed Coch Symwl who was the record-priced top (1,150 guineas) of the 1959 Coed Coch Sale and RW overall champion the following year. Simwnt was twice RW overall champion (1972 and 1973) and is the sire of the sire (Saltersford Justin) and dam (Morwyn Nicandra) of the 2000 RW male champion, Lacy Justyn.

Also in the 1959 Coed Coch Sale was the two-year-old colt Coed Coch Siglen Las (700 guineas), a double Glyndwr third-generation descendant through his sire, Madog, and dam, Coed Coch Sws (sold to Twyford Stud for 900 guineas at the same sale), daughter of the great Siaradus. Siglen Las was of a type reminscent of Planed, small and deep with spectacular action. Siglen Las was bought by Lord Swansea at the Coed Coch Sale, then, at the dispersal of his Caerberis Stud at the 1964 Fayre Oaks Sale, he became the property of Miss Rosemary Russell-Allen for whom in the years to follow, he won the male championships at the 1965 and 1966 RW Shows.

Coed Coch Norman (foaled in 1968) (Coed Coch Shon x Coed Coch Pibwydd) had Coed Coch Madog as three of his four grandsires. The first time I saw him I placed him as youngstock champion as a yearling at the Ponies of Britain Show and he was also youngstock champion at the RW in 1970 and 1971. It was a very close decision when I placed him male champion at the 1971 RW Show above the senior winner, Gredington Simwnt. Coed Coch Norman was sire of Cledwyn Seren Goch (foaled in 1977), female champion in 1983 and overall in 1987. Seren Goch's dam, Chieveley Silver (foaled in 1967), was by Coed Coch Planed and her grand-dam, Reddicap Bella Donna, was by Glyndwr. Chieveley Silver was also dam of Cledwyn Seren Wen (foaled in 1976), reserve female champion in 1983, and Cledwyn Seren Aur (foaled in 1973), reserve male champion for Persie Stud in 1976. The other grandsire of Coed Coch Norman was Llanerch Titmouse and Norman was used extensively by Llanerch Stud to reintroduce the Titmouse bloodlines. Norman was sire of Llanerch Destiny whose daughter, Llanerch Decima (foaled in 1977, sired by Twyford Gendarme), was RW female champion in 1984. Norman qualified for the Lloyds Bank In-hand championship of the HOYS in 1973 at the Bath and West Show.

TOP *Coed Coch Symwl, RW champion 1960 at the 1959 Coed Coch Sale.*

ABOVE *Coed Coch Norman, RW champion 1971. Painting by Lionel Hamilton Renwick.*

The two RW champion daughters of Glyndwr were Coed Coch Siaradus (one of the first, foaled in 1942) and Coed Coch Swyn (one of the last, foaled in 1958 and champion in 1969), daughter of Coed Coch Siwan, grand-daughter of Coed Coch Serliw. In addition to her five RW championships, Siaradus won another 51 first prizes, 36 championships and the Lord Arthur Cecil supreme championship trophy at the NPS Show no fewer than five times. Siaradus's son, Coed Coch Salsbri (foaled in 1957, by Coed Coch Madog), was almost as successful, with 42 first prizes and 12 championships without ever actually being RW champion. Salsbri was offered for sale (lot 69) on 23 September 1961 at Gredington and Coed

RIGHT *(from left) Coed Coch Salsbri, Clan Pip, Coed Coch Brenin Arthur. Photo: Wynne Davies*

Coch Sale with the very modest reserve of 300 guineas. The two-year-old filly Coed Coch Sucr (Coed Coch Proffwyd x Coed Coch Siwan) sold to the USA for 800 guineas. Another two-year-old filly, Gredington Pefren (Coed Coch Madog x Coed Coch Sidan), also went to the USA at 760 guineas. However, luckily for the WPCS and for the Coed Coch Stud, there was no bid over 275 guineas for Salsbri and he remained at Coed Coch where his stock commanded enormous prices. Salsbri spent his last years at Sunwillow Stud with the Siaradus daughter Coed Coch Seren Wen and her illustrious daughter Sunwillow Bernina, RW progeny group winner in 1988.

Salsbri's greatest claim to fame was as sire of Coed Coch Bari (foaled in 1971) and Coed Coch Saled (foaled in 1963), both sons of Coed Coch Swyn. Bari was reserve male champion at the 1973 RW Show, overall champion and reserve HOYS qualifier in 1974, HOYS qualifier at the Bath and West in 1976 and sold for the world record price of 21,000 guineas to Australia at the Coed Coch dispersal sale in 1978. His full-brother, Coed Coch Saled, eight years older, sold at the sale to Bengad Stud for 14,000 guineas, and he was the sire of the palomino 1980 RW male champion, Revel Saled, the first non-grey RW male champion in 50 years since Craven Master Shot in 1929. Swyn was also dam of the dun Coed Coch Marli, sire of the dark brown 1979 RW female champion, Coed Coch Ateb, who was sold for 1,100 guineas to Sunwillow Stud in the Coed Coch dispersal sale.

ABOVE *Coed Coch Bari, RW champion 1974*, sold for 21,000 guineas. Photo: Wynne Davies.*

Siaradus must be one of the greatest mares ever of any section within the WSB. She had a long lean front, nice clean limbs and a happy free walk. As soon as she started to walk her tail would be carried gaily and she always had that 'look at me' expression. The RW champion who followed her in 1956 was Brierwood Honey, foaled in 1947. Every one of her great-grand-dams was the same Mathrafal Mistress, with four different great-grand-sires. Honey was of a completely different type to Siaradus, with enormous eyes, minute ears, an upright shoulder, abundant bone and feather, rounded quarters and laboured movement. These two consecutive RW champions represent the two extremes within the breed standard.

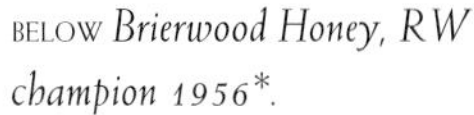

BELOW *Brierwood Honey, RW champion 1956*.*

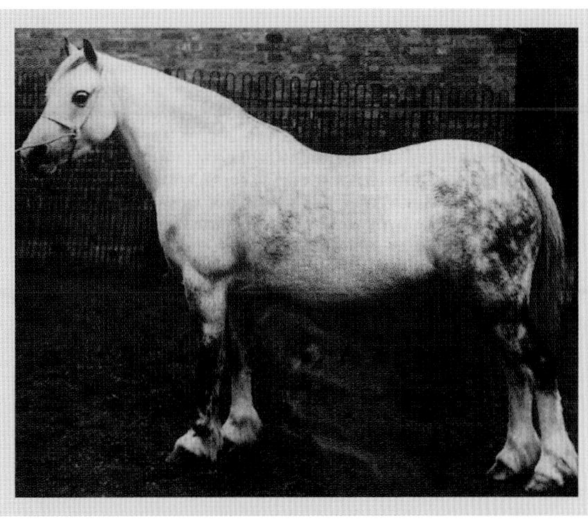

In addition to Coed Coch Symwl (1960 champion) and Coed Coch Pelydrog (1964 and 1965 champion) already dealt with, the other second-generation Glyndwr RW champions were Ankerwycke Clan Snowdon (foaled in 1952, champion in 1954 and sired by the Glyndwr son, Clan Dana), Clan Peggy (champion in 1966 and 1967) full-sister to Clan Pip, the subject of the third quartile, and Revel Jewel, foaled in1954 and champion in 1962. Revel Jewel is one of the few Glyndwr descendants to be bred at the Revel but she is enormously important as the dam (in 1972) of Revel Jeeves, the subject of the fourth quartile. Revel Jewel was sired by Revel Hailstone who was bred by Mrs Armstrong Jones (mother of Lord Snowdon) in 1946, sired by Glyndwr out of Touchstone of Sansaw who later became the property of Twyford Stud and was dam of Dinas Moonstone (full-sister to Hailstone) one of the two foundation mares of the Twyford Stud whose influence has been far-reaching all over the world. In September 1953, after siring Jewel, Hailstone was exported to Rupert Richardson's Bereen Stud in New South Wales, Australia where he was widely used by other breeders.

BELOW *Emrys Griffiths with Revel Jewel, RW champion 1962*. Photo: Wynne Davies.*

Next in the Glyndwr chapter are three more third-generation RW female champions, Coed Coch Glenda (1973), Rowfant Prima Ballerina (1970) and Springbourne Hyfryd (1975). The Coed Coch Stud won both brood mare classes at the 1973 RW Show, the novice class with Coed Coch Glenda from Fayre Zany and Revel Venetia, and the open class with Coed Coch Mari from Pendock Pansy and Chieveley Silver, and Glenda went on to be female champion from the winning yearling, Twyford Minorca. Glenda was sold for 1,400 guineas in the 1978 Coed Coch dispersal sale. Her bay yearling son, Coed Coch Gwyndaf, was one of the best males in the sale and he went, at 2,100 guineas, to join the Twyford Sprig daughter, Penllyn Carina, at Ann Coxon's Stud in Victoria, Australia.

Rowfant Prima Ballerina was owned by Foxhunter Stud when she was RW female champion in 1970. She was sired by Coed Coch Madog out of the 1959 RW youngstock champion, Dovey Prima Donna, whose dam, Gwen Tafarn Jem, was also dam of Ceulan Calypso and Ceulan Madam Butterfly, one of the foundation mares in Sweden. Foxhunter Stud held annual collective sales at Llanvair Grange, and Prima Ballerina topped the 1974 sale when she was sold to Wright Stephenson of Victoria, Australia.

BELOW *David Reynolds with Springbourne Hyfryd, RW champion 1975*. Photo: John Keene.*

Springbourne Hyfryd was descended from Glyndwr through her sire, Revel Carefree, whose sire was the Glyndwr son, Rhydyfelin Syndod (full brother to Siaradus), who was purchased by Mr Griffiths of the Revel for 250 guineas in the 1959 Coed Coch Sale. Carefree was a son of the 1963 RW champion Revel Caress and Hyfryd's dam, Cwmgarn Heidi (RW champion in 1977), hailed from a long line of Dowlais Improvement Society premium stallions – Shimdda Hir Stardust (grandson of the 1939 RW champion, Vardra Sunflower), Criban Silver Sand and Criban Grey Grit from the original FS mare, Vaynor Linda. The Springbourne Hyfryd grandson, Springbourne Halwyn (foaled in 1975 and by the 1975 RW male champion, Holland-bred Rondeels Pengwyn), still has important descendants at Springbourne/Blanche, such as his 1984 daughter, Blanche Minuet, dam of the 1993 RW champion, the two-year-old filly Blanche Mimic. Other RW champions with Springbourne Hyfryd bloodlines at other studs are the daughter Churchwood Promise (foaled in 1982, champion in 1988), out of Springbourne Pioden, daughter of the start of the Springbourne 'P' line, Revel Peaches Too by Twyford Sprig, and the Halwyn grand-daughter Fouroaks Reanne (foaled in 1991, champion in 2002), who was a daughter of Springbourne Caress whose dam, Springbourne Cariadus, was sired by Halwyn.

Rondeels Pengwyn was bred by Mrs Anne Peletier in Holland in 1955, sired by Twyford Thunder, by Twyford Grenadier by Coed Coch Madog,

out of Coed Coch Pwffiad, also by Madog. Pengwyn, who was also grandsire of Churchwood Promise and the 1996 male champion, Revel Paul Jones, was RW champion in 1975 when owned by Springbourne Stud and is the sire of Breachwood Marwyn who, prior to being champion in 1989 was second in 1984 and 1986, third in 1987 and fourth in 1988! Marwyn's dam was Bartletts Maria (foaled in 1973) sired by the 1976 and 1977 champion, Revel Cassino, a member of the third quartile family. Maria's dam was Bartletts Millie by Revel Carefree (the sire of Springbourne Hyfryd) and Millie's dam was Bryniau Misty Morn, another product of the Dowlais premium stallions, who, after being bought as the third-highest priced foal at the 1957 Fayre Oaks Sale, went on to win at the RASE Show. After her stint at Bartletts Stud, Misty Morn became the foundation of the 'M' family for Springbourne/Blanche. Misty Morn's dam, Bryniau Greylight, was the foundation mare of the Trefaes section As and the dam of Trefaes Grey Lady (foaled in 1968 by Belvoir Sundowner) dam of the 1999 male champion, Trefaes Guardsman. Grey Lady was also the grand-dam of Trefaes Taran (foaled in 1986 by Wynswood Little Acorn) whose RW Show record was third in 1991, second in 1993 and fourth in both 1998 and 1999, as well as being four times champion at the RASE

ABOVE *Breachwood Marwyn, RW champion 1989*. Photo: Remco Dobber.*

BELOW LEFT *Dee Lloyd with Trefaes Guardsman, RW champion 1999. Photo: Eberhard Holin.*

BELOW RIGHT *David Davies with Trefaes Taran, RASE champion 1994, 1997*, 1998, 1999.*

before being exported to the USA. Taran was the HOYS Templeton qualifier at the 1997 Royal Bath and West Show and ended up reserve pony champion at Wembley. Trefaes Guardsman was sired by Skellorn Daylight (foaled in 1980, a grandson of the 1972 and 1973 champion, Gredington Simwnt) who was also sire of the 1991 champion, Silvester out of Maesglas Heather, whose sire, Gredington Balch, and grandsire, Persie Big Ben, both spent periods running out as premium stallions.

One of the most successful families originating in the second quartile came from Dyfrdwy Midnight Moon (foaled in 1961), sired by Coed Coch Planed out of Betws Arian who was bred by William Pryce of Castell Caereinon, near Mathrafal where her sire and dam, Mathrafal Finalist and Mathrafal Silver, were bred. Mathrafal Finalist (foaled in 1938) was so named because he was the last pony to be bred by Mr Meyrick Jones of Mathrafal, thus bringing a chapter of 60 years of pony and Cob breeding to an end at this famous stud. Finalist's dam, Llwyn Silver, bred at the close of Major Dugdale's Llwyn Stud at Llanfyllin, represented another previous important stage in WPCS history, Llwyn Silver's dam, Llwyn Coralie, having won her class at the 1922 RW Show and representing 50 years of Llwyn breeding. Midnight Moon's 1972 son, Aston Superstar, was sired by Whatton Pennaeth who was by Dovey Dynamite (Grove Sprightly breeding on both sides) out of Melai Priscilla by Coed Coch Madog. Superstar was RW overall champion in 1978, 1979 and 1983 and qualified for the HOYS Show in 1983. With Grove Sprightly having been RW overall champion eight times, Aston Superstar is the stallion with the next best record, having been champion three times.

BELOW *Aston Superstar, RW champion 1978*, 1979*, 1983*.*

An inspired purchase by the Dyfrdwy Stud in 1960 was of Highfields Delight (foaled in 1957, Coed Coch Planed x Gwyndy Penarth Relight) at the same time as I bought her year-younger sister, Highfields Highlight. This was another very old strain; the Gwyndy Stud going back to the start of the WPCS, with Gwyndy Penarth Relight being a g-g-g- daughter of Llwyn Nell who won at the second WN Show in 1905. The progeny of Aston

ABOVE *Miss Russell-Allen with Dyfrdwy Seren Arian, RW champion 1991*, 1994*. Photo: Carol Jones.*

Superstar x Highfields Delight (of which there were ten full brothers and sisters) include the 1991 and 1994 RW champion, Dyfrdwy Seren Arian (foaled in 1984), (who also qualified for the HOYS both times), Dyfrdwy Starlight who won the RW harness class seven times, Dyfrdwy Seren Fwyn who was RW champion in 2000 and Dyfrdwy Seren-Y-Gogledd who was male champion in 2004. Altogether, at the RW Shows, this family has won a fantastic total of six overall championships, six male championships, four female championships, three HOYS qualifiers, the progeny competition in 1991 and reserve in 2000!

The five champion Revel mares, Springsong (1957), Rosette (1959), Choice (1961), her daughter, Caress, (1963) and Jewel (1962) certainly left their mark on the breed. The beautiful palomino Springsong (foaled in

1950, Pendock Playboy x Revel Serenade) is great-grand-dam of the 1992 champion Winneydene Satellite (foaled in 1974, sired by Revel Sabu, son of Revel South Wind, daughter of Springsong). Satellite qualified for the HOYS in 1983 and went on to win the championship; he is one of only three section As to have captured this prestigious award, along with Treharne Tomboy (1968,1969) and Glenfield Chocolate Soldier (1977) who appears in the third quartile family. Springsong is also dam of Twyford Sprig who has an unsurpassed RW progeny group record, winning in 1982, 1983, 1984, 1985, 1990 and 1994 and grandsire of the 1993, 1998 and 2004 (Ty'rcapel Sprig) winners. His grandson, Penual Mark, is the subject of the fourth quartile. When one considers that Sprig was only at the Revel for one year as a two year old (1967) and sired four Revel colts (including the Australian champion, Revel Playsome) and two Revel fillies, his influence

BELOW *David Davies with Twyford Sprig, RW progeny winner 1982, 1983, 1984, 1985, 1990, 1994. Photo: Wynne Davies.*

BELOW *Darrell Owen with Revel Playsome in Australia, 1984 with judge Dr Wynne Davies.*

ABOVE *Lewis Edwards with Neuaddfach Skylark, RW champion 1998. Photo: Wynne Davies.*

has been way above expectations. Revel Playsome is grandsire of Dukeshill Magnum who was reserve male champion at the 2002 RW Show and HOYS Breeders Challenge qualifier at the Three Counties Show. The 1998 RW female champion was Neuaddfach Skylark (foaled in 1986). Her sire, Revel Coco, is by Revel Carlo by Sprig, Coco's dam, Revel Choosey, is by Sprig and Skylark's dam, Neuaddfach Solitaire, is by Revel South Drift by Sprig! The other Sprig daughter was Revel Cayenne, dam of Revel Carreg, grandsire of Springbourne Caraway.

Revel Rosette (foaled in 1948, Revel Revolt x Winestead Larina) was a big mare with an impressive head and long neck, powerful rounded quarters and plenty of bone. She was the dam of Revel Rex, sire of Eppynt Rosemary, the dam of the 1990 champion, Waitwith Romance. It has already been shown how Rosette was descended from the 1907 champion, Lady Starlight, via Winestead Larina.

Revel Choice (foaled in 1949, Vardra Sunstar x Vardra Charm) was a son x mother product, bred at Vardra and bought by Mr Emrys Griffiths of the Revel at the Vardra dispersal sale on 16 April 1951 following the death of Mr Matthew Williams. No one is quite certain how much Mr Griffiths paid for Choice (whether she was 32 or 10 guineas!). The three two-year-old fillies in the sale catalogue, lots 7, 8 and 9, sold for 32, 10 and 20 guineas, lots 7 and 8 to Mr Griffiths and lot 9 to Miss Brodrick. None of them had been registered so the purchasers could register them under their own prefixes. Lot 7 was the largest and her pedigree was given as 'sire: Vardra Sunstar; dam Vardra Nance'. She was registered as Revel Nance and, three months later, was section B champion at the RW Show. Lot 8 was the smallest and described as 'sire: Vardra Sunstar; dam Brown Sugar by Royal Pom which could not have been correct for such a small filly who was registered as Revel Choice. Lot 9 was 'sire: Vardra Sunstar; dam: Vardra Moonshine FS' who was registered as Coed Coch Nans and produced Coed Coch Nest (sold to Twyford at the 1963 FO Sale and then went to Scrafton Stud), Coed Coch Nerys (South Africa), Coed Coch Neli (Canada), Coed Coch Nill (Glenfield Stud, dam of Glenfield Playmate, Guardsman, etc.).

Choice was a very small mare with huge eyes, minute ears and heavy bone, very different from the big 'reachy' mares Rosette and Springsong who were bred at the Revel. Revel Caress, her 1957 daughter by Revel Springlight (a son of Winestead Larina), was RW champion in 1963 and Caress's son, Revel Carefree, was sire of the 1975 champion, Springbourne Hyfryd. Choice's other progeny were mainly by Clan Pip and will be the subject of the third quartile.

Revel Jewel (foaled 1954 by Revel Hailstone), hails from a very old Revel strain. Her dam, Revel Jean, was foaled in 1949, sired by Bolgoed Squire whose sire, the eight-times RW champion, Grove Sprightly, was also grandsire of Revel Hailstone. The rest of her female line is: g-dam: Revel Judy (foaled in 1934), g-g-dam: Revel Bay Leaf (foaled in 1931), g-g-g-dam: Forest Black Style (foaled in 1922), g-g-g-g-dam: Forest Bright Style (foaled in 1915), g-g-g-g-g-dam: Forest Style (foaled in 1905), g-g-g-g-g-g-dam: Forest Extra Style (foaled in 1900), i.e. back to the start of the WSB. Being the dam of Revel Jeeves, Revel Jewel is the subject of the fourth quartile.

THIRD QUARTILE: the Clan Pip era

Clan Pip was foaled in 1959, the product of two 'Clan' parents, Clan Tony and Clan Prue. Clan Tony (foaled in 1954) was sired by Coed Coch Glyndwr during the last year that Glyndwr lived at Clan Stud before his owner, Lady Wentworth, gave him to Miss Marguerite de Beaumont of the

Shalbourne Stud where he died in 1959. Tony's dam was Llwyn Tinwen (foaled in 1938) who was descended on both sides from the Cob-type Temptation who Major Dugdale of Llwyn bought from my grandfather's uncle after he had won at the 1913 RW Show. Clan Prue was FS2, sired by Clan Dana (foaled in 1946) a son of Glyndwr out of Wentworth Grey Dapples by Craven Cyrus by the Arab King Cyrus. Prue's dam was Tanybwlch Penllyn by Tanybwlch Berwyn by the Barb Sahara out of Tanybwlch Penwen by the Arab Cairo. Some breeders avoided using Clan Pip due to the preponderance of Arab, Barb and ponies of Cob-type in his background, but his emergence on the Welsh scene was a much needed outcross that did a power of good for the breed. Clan Pip was a big, powerful stallion with enormous length of rein, tail well up, powerful hindquarters and excellent limbs and a very successful sire to use on small, 'stuffy' mares. On the death of his breeder, Mr Arthur McNaught, in 1961, Clan Pip was sold (along with another seven males and two females, including Clan Peggy) to Mr Emrys Griffiths of the Revel. Peggy was a full sister to Pip, one year younger, and both won two RW championships for

RIGHT *Flydon Henri ap Pip.*

the Revel, Pip male champion in 1963 and overall in 1964 and Peggy twice overall in 1966 and 1967. In 1968, Pip was leased to a syndicate comprising Sir Harry Llewellyn (Foxhunter), Mrs Robina Mills (Rookery), Mrs Serena Homfray (Penllyn) and Mrs Claire Hunter (Escley). He was sold to Flydon Stud in 1977 and died there in 1981, his last foal, Flydon Henri ap Pip, being born one week before Clan Pip died. Over 400 Clan Pip progeny are registered in the WSB.

The small and 'dumpy' 1961 RW champion, Revel Choice, was an ideal type of mare to put to Pip and this mating produced the colts Chip (1963), Cello (1964) and Cassino (1966) and the fillies Chase (1965) and Chelsea (1967). Revel Cassino took the show ring by storm in the 1970s, winning over 200 first prizes and championships, including the male championship at the 1976 RW Show and overall in 1977. In his earlier years he was shown by David Reynolds of Springbourne for Revel Stud. This was the period when he sired Bartletts Maria, dam of 1989 RW champion Breachwood Marwyn. Later, in the ownership of Mr Robert Thomas of the Hollybush Stud, he was produced by Mr Frank Pearce. For many years

LEFT *Peter Jones with Revel Japhet, RW champion 1982, 1984*, 1986*.* *Photo:* Horse and Hound.

Revel Chip was a premium stallion on the Breconshire Black Mountains. His best known son was Revel Japhet, three times RW champion in 1982, 1984 and 1986, the last time also being the HOYS qualifier. Japhet's dam, Clan Jill, was also bred at Clan Stud and was one of the total consignment bought by Mr Emrys Griffiths following the death of Mr McNaught. Some of the most successful matings with Chip were to the Revel 'H' family, originating from Rhydyfelin Seren Heulyn, who was purchased by the Revel in 1961. The 1968-foaled Revel Hetty was the result of mating Revel Chip to Revel Hipip (Clan Pip x Seren Heulyn) and Hetty became a noted broodmare at Waxwing Stud. In 1982 (by Cantref Glory) Hetty produced Waxwing Herod, the youngest ever Welsh pony to qualify for the HOYS Show (in 1983), after which he was sold to Australia where he has been leading sire for many years. Cello was the smallest of the three brothers and Mrs Gadsden of the Bengad Stud was allowed to lease him a few times before Mr Griffiths finally gave in and sold Cello to her. The first Cello offspring to be RW champion (1974) for Bengad Stud was Bengad Love in the

RIGHT *Waxwing Herod, RASE champion 1983*. Photo: Leslie Lane.*

Mist (foaled in 1968), daughter of Melai Melody by Coed Coch Madog out of Penarth Music of a very old strain going back to the 1920 premium stallions on Penybont Common and descended from the 1931 RW champion, Dunchurch Venus. The second Bengad champion was the exceptionally beautiful Bengad Day Lily (1978, 1981 and 1985) whose dam was a Madog daughter, Glenfield Dawn (foaled in 1962) out of Arenig Enwyn, one of only two ponies registered by Mrs Pam Ridgeway with the Arenig (the brook near her holiday cottage in the North Wales hills) prefix before she changed her prefix to Sunrising. Enwyn was bought by Coed Coch as a yearling, then, the following year, she was offered (lot 89) in the September Gredington and Coed Coch Sale where Glenfield Stud bought her for the unbelievably low price of 100 guineas, especially in that she was in foal to Madog and produced Glenfield Dawn the following year. Enwyn was sired by Rhydyfelin Syndod before being bought by the Revel Stud. Day Lily qualified for the HOYS in 1979 at the East of England and in 1981 at the RW Show; her son Bengad Dogberry (foaled in 1987 by Bengad Cockscomb) qualified in 1996 at the Royal Highland.

ABOVE *Colin Tibbey and judge Robert Owens with Bengad Dogberry. Photo: Wynne Davies.*

The 1981 champion, Clan Pip son Glenfield Chocolate Soldier (foaled in 1971), was also out of a 'Glenfield' daughter of Coed Coch Madog, this time Glenfield Giselle, daughter of the consistently successful show mare Gredington Oriana, daughter of Coed Coch Seirian, daughter of the 1949 champion, Coed Coch Serliw. Chocolate Soldier was champion of the pony section at the 1977 HOYS Show, with another Clan Pip son, Revel Cassino, standing second and the section B Lydstep Ladies Slipper third; the best HOYS ever for the Welsh! Chocolate Soldier also qualified for the HOYS at the South of England Show in 1978 and again in 1979 when he ended up reserve champion to the Welsh Cob Llanarth Flying Comet.

ABOVE *Colin Tibbey with Gredington Calon Lan, RW champion 1993*, 1994.*

The other Clan Pip sons to sire RW champions were Revel Janus (foaled in 1970 out of Revel Jade by Owain Glyndwr) and Revel Pye (foaled in 1968 out of Revel Pinup by Revel Light). Revel Janus spent all his stud life at Baledon Stud and his two RW champion daughters were Baledon Jubilation (1986) out of Coed Coch Dunos whose g-g-dam was Coed Coch Sensigl, dam of the 1960 champion Coed Coch Symwl, and Baledon Verity (1989) whose dam, Revel Venetia, was also by Clan Pip. Revel Janus was also sire of Gredington Calon Lan (foaled in 1985), first-prize winner in 1988, overall champion in 1993 and male champion in 1994. In 1993, Calon Lan narrowly missed qualifying for the HOYS at both the Three Counties and Great Yorkshire, but finally made it at the Royal Welsh and all the hopes of Wales were pinned on him and his 80-year-old owner, Gordon Jones, the former Gredington Stud groom. Calon Lan's dam was the beautiful, many-times champion Gredington Judith, sired by the 1972 and 1973 champion, Gredington Simwnt, out of Gredington Dugesau by the 1954 champion, Coed Coch Planed, out of Twyford Musette who Lord Kenyon bought from Twyford Stud at the 1962 FO Sale for 135 guineas. Musette was sired by Coed Coch Socyn (the main sire at Stoatley Stud for many years) out of the original Clan Music by Coed Coch Glyndwr.

Revel Pye lost his nearside eye as a foal but this did not prevent him making an indelible mark on the breed, both in the UK and in many countries overseas. Pye had the main characteristics which Captain Brierley looked for in a Mountain pony, with emphasis on bone, head and ears, and Pye went to the Brierwood Stud where he remained until the dispersal sale on 10 September 1977 when he was bought for 1,100 guineas by Mr Jack Edwards of the Weston Stud, who had previously used him extensively. Top of the sale that day, at 2,000 guineas, was Pye's four-year-old daughter, Brierwood Victoria, and she went to Australia (Mrs Lewis, Fairway Stud, Victoria) following the previous Brierwood exports, Rosebud and Fumble (also to Mrs Lewis), Crumpet (Mrs Richmond, NSW) and Fusilier (Mrs Soster, NSW). Pye followed them to Australia (Mark Bullen, NSW) in August 1978.

A very shrewd purchase at the 1977 Brierwood Sale, at 320 guineas, was lot 18, the yearling colt Brierwood Rocket II. Described in the catalogue as 'A very nice colt, rather out of the ordinary', he was bought by Cerdin and Doreen Jones of Synod Stud. Rocket II was a double Clan Pip, being sired by the Clan Pip grandson Revel Pye out of Brierwood Rosemarie (foaled in 1967) by Revel Pip (foaled in 1964) who was a brother x sister product, Clan Pip x Clan Peggy. Revel Pye's dam, Revel Pin Up (foaled in 1953), was champion at the 1955 Brecknockshire Bi-cente-

ABOVE *Brierwood Rocket II, RW champion 1985*, 1988*.*

nary Show when the award was presented by Her Majesty the Queen to Mrs Dinah Griffiths and Pin Up. During the presentation, the Revel other entry, the stallion Owain Glyndwr with Mr Emrys Griffiths, took a liking to Her Majesty's bouquet! Revel Pin Up was a double grand-daughter of Pendock Playboy, a very influential little colt who died at two years old at the Revel in 1949. Playboy left only four foals, two of whom, Revel Light and Revel Playtime, were parents of Pin Up, another daughter being the 1957 RW champion, Revel Springsong. Revel Playtime was also grand-dam of Brierwood Rosemary, dam of the 1971 RW overall champion, Brierwood Rosebud, whose daughter, Brierwood Rosemarie, was dam of Rocket II. The dam of Revel Light was Winestead Larina who has already been met as grand-daughter of the 1907 champion, Lady Starlight. Playtime's dam, Winestead Zenia, was a daughter of Ness Thistle who was second to Grove Fairy Queen at the 1922 RW Show and she was also dam of the 1936 female champion, Craven Shot Star.

Only three favourite mares were retained at Brierwood Stud in 1977, Brierwood Fussy, Brierwood Rosemarie (dam of Rocket II) and her grand-dam, Brierwood Rosemary. Rosemary was sold for 65 guineas to Nantfechan Stud at the 1963 Fayre Oaks Sale (her filly foal, later RW champion, Rosebud, was retained that year) where she bred section Cs. One section C daughter who came to Ceulan was Nantfechan Seren, prizewinner at the RW in 1973 and 1976. She was dam of Ceulan Nesta, dam of Sackville Nicky who was WPCS Performance Competition champion in 1997, 1998 and 1999. Rosemary was then bought back by Captain Brierley and retained in 1977. Then, in 1978, Captain Brierley went into hospital and Fussy, Rosemarie and Rosemary were sold to Synod Stud where Rosemary produced Synod Captain in 1981.

Brierwood Rocket II was second for Synod Stud at the 1978 RW Show behind the year-older Saltersford Justin, and he then ran out with his mares until he was RW champion and HOYS qualifier in 1985. Rocket II was also champion at the RW Show in 1988, followed by winning the supreme championship at the International Show at Groenendaal, Belgium that year, beating another UK entry, the section D Llanarth Sally.

Rocket II's grand-dam, Brierwood Rosebud, was RW champion when I judged in 1971, and at the 1997 RW Show, with judge David Davies, the male champion and reserve were Rocket II's sons, Synod The Colonel and Betws Fflach. The female (and overall) champion and reserve were Rocket II's grand-daughters, Fronbach Crystal (daughter of Synod Captain), and Yaverland Delight (daughter of Scrafton Halley).

Fronbach Crystal's sire, Synod Captain, is in-bred to Rocket II, sired by Rocket II out of Brierwood Rosemary (foaled in 1960), dam of Rosebud,

ABOVE LEFT *Cerdin Jones with Synod The Colonel, RW champion 1997. Photo: Janneke de Rade.*

ABOVE RIGHT *Fronbach Crystal, RW champion 1997*. Photo:* Eventer.

grand-dam of Rocket II. Crystal's dam was Cennen Cadi, the foundation mare of Fronbach Stud. She was sired by Sinton Solomon (sire of Cui Mi'Lord and Bengad Nepeta) out of Cennen Cariad, daughter of the Cennen foundation mare Revel Curly. Cennen Cadi was sold by her breeder, Mrs Mary Bowen, as a foal at Hay-on-Wye in 1975 and died at Fronbach Stud in 2003, having produced, in addition to Crystal, Fronbach Carys who sold at the 2000 Fayre Oaks Sale for £2,800 at fifteen years old, the 1996 RW winner, Fronbach Confetti, and Fronbach Hello Charlie, stud stallion at Forlan. Yaverland Delight's sire, Scrafton Halley (foaled in 1986), is by Rocket II out of Persie Heidi by Brierwood Fusilier and her dam, Lippens Dolly (by Springbourne Herian), broke the Fayre Oaks section A record at the 1991 sale (with Yaverland Delight at foot) when she sold for 3,600 guineas. Synod The Colonel, who was reserve champion at the 1993 RW Show, was another Fayre Oaks Sale record breaker when he sold for £7,000 in 2003. His dam, Synod Isabella, must have been the bargain of the 1977 Brierwood Sale when she sold for only 250 guineas! Betws Fflach was nine years old when he won the senior stallion class and reserve male championship. His dam was Betws Sandra, a prolific producer who died in 1997 aged 23 years, while her dam, Betws Glenys (daughter of the famous Criban Golden Spray), was still alive and going strong at 30 years. Mr John Berry, who bought Golden Spray at the 1946 Criban Sale for the

ABOVE *Barry Shepherd with Yaverland Delight, RW reserve champion 1997. Photo: Wynne Davies.*

then-record foal auction price of 20 guineas, had stayed with us at Ceulan and we travelled together to Brecon Market where we bought Criban Rally (daughter of the 1937 RW champion Criban Socks) for 33 guineas, the second-highest section-A adult price.

Sadly for the breed, Betws Fflach died shortly after the show but his blood came to the fore at the 2003 show when the male champion was Gartconnel Shooting Star, sired by the Fflach son, Betws Llew. The parents of Shooting Star's dam, Gartconnel Seirian, were Gartconnel Salad and

ABOVE *Gartconnel Shooting Star, RW champion* 2003.

Gartconnel Springtime, both of whom are out of Betws Ser-y-Bore (who died in February 2004, aged 35), a daughter of Criban Golden Spray. Another daughter of Criban Golden Spray was Betws Glenys (foaled in 1967 by Coed Coch Pela) and she was dam of Betws Emrys (foaled in 1978 by Coed Coch Bari) sire of the 1999 overall champion, Betws Gwenno.

The Eppynt Stud often leased two-year-old colts from the Revel to try them out, therefore it is understandable that the two 'Eppynt' champions, the mare Victoria in 1996 and the stallion Skyline in 1998, are full of Clan Pip blood from many channels. Revel Jiro (foaled in 1975), sire of Victoria, was sired by Revel Chelsea Fan (full brother x sister cross, Revel Cello x Chelsea) out of Revel Junipa by Clan Pip. Victoria's dam was Eppynt Vanilla, sired by Revel Chip (full brother to Cello and Chelsea), with grand-dam Eppynt Vanessa (winner of many championships in the 1960s)

ABOVE LEFT *Betws Gweno, RW champion 1999*. Photo: Eberhard Holin.*

ABOVE RIGHT *Kevin Davies with Eppynt Skyline, RW champion 1998*. Photo: Carol Jones.*

and great-grand-dam Cilrhedyn Vanessa (foaled in 1957) by Ceulan Revelry (foaled in 1943). Cilrhedyn Vanessa was bought by Eppynt Stud with the intention of exporting her to Holland, but when the time came she failed the veterinary inspection and so could not travel. What a stroke of luck for Eppynt Stud! She quickly recovered and both Victoria and Skyline are descended from her. Vanilla was 17 years old when she produced Victoria and when she was 20 she produced Skyline's sire, Valderama, sired by Revel Humming Top by Revel Centre, another full brother x sister cross, this time Revel Chip x Chelsea. Skyline's dam was Eppynt Snapshot by Revel Jiro and Skyline's pedigree contains nine strains of Clan Pip. After weaning, Skyline was turned back out on the Eppynt mountains where all attempts to catch him failed for four years! After he had been entered for the Royal Welsh Show, a determined effort was staged and when he was eventually captured the family had only six weeks to get him to lead and put him in good shape, so his magnificent success was all the more creditable.

THE FOURTH QUARTILE: the Revel Jeeves era

Finally we come to the top sires of the last quartile, Revel Jeeves and his sons, Pendock Legend and Penual Mark, and Mark's son, Springbourne Caraway. Revel Jeeves (foaled in 1972) was a son of the 1962 RW champion Revel Jewel and we have already seen how Jewel's pedigree can be traced back through seven generations, all in Breconshire, to the beginning of the WPCS, to Forest Extra Style, foaled in 1900. Jeeves's little-known sire, Bengad Parrotia (foaled in 1969) was all 'Coed Coch' breeding, by Coed Coch Salsbri out of Coed Coch Perot, a daughter of Coed Coch Pibwydd who was also dam of the 1971 champion, Coed Coch Norman. Perot was purchased by Bengad Stud at the 1968 Fayre Oaks Sale when the three top lots were Coed Coch Pert (950 guineas), Twyford Matador (925 guineas) and Coed Coch Perot (900 guineas).

The 1995 RW Show was the highlight of Penual Mark's show ring career, his son, Criccieth Arwr (foaled in 1990), was male champion, and Arwr's three-year-old full-brother, Criccieth Carreg, was reserve male champion. Their dam was Eden Willow (foaled in 1987), sired by Hisland Hyderus (foaled in 1979) whose sire, Carnalw Hyderus, went out to Australia with the Weston Stud when they emigrated in 1979. Arwr's son, Criccieth Simba, was RW youngtsock champion as a yearling in 1998. The palomino Penual Mark daughter, Tiffwyl Melodi (foaled in 1986), who had been RW champion in 1992, was again champion in 1995, HOYS qualifier both times and RASE champion in 1988, 1994 and 1995. Her dam, Tiffwyl Majic, was by Twyford Juggler, her grand-dam, Tiffwyl Myfi,was by Clan Pip, the third and fourth generation by Fayre Whoopee and Revel Liberty (descendants of Winestead Larina) back to the g-g-g-g-g-dam, Fayre Rosamund, the favourite foundation mare of the Fayre Stud, foaled in 1952.

BELOW *Tiffwyl Melodi, RW champion 1992*, 1995*. Photo: Ann Tilley.*

The second generation Penual Mark RW champions are Friars Bonheddwr (first-prize winner in 1997 and male champion in 2002) and Fouroaks Reanne (overall champion the same year). The sire of Friars Bonheddwr was a Penual Mark son, Pontgam Supreme, who, when he was bought as a foal by Friars Stud in 1989, was reintroducing Friars breeding back into the stud as his dam, the many-times champion, Pontgam

Sorceress, was sired by Friars Commander. The dam of Friars Bonheddwr, who had also won at the RW as a two year old in 1997, was Friars Ave Maria by Cefnfedw Golden Glory from Friars Lowland Flower by Friars Happy Boy.

The Friars Stud was established in 1958 and, with many 'near misses', it took them until 2004 for Friars Goldilocks to win the Captain Howson RW supreme section A trophy. Goldilocks was a wedding gift in 1997, from Sian Owens's parents on her marriage to Dafydd Morris of Neuaddparc. Goldilocks (foaled in 1992) began her show ring career at Lampeter in 1994 when she won, followed by the reserve female championship at the 1995 RASE. She is sired by Cefnfedw Golden Glory out of Friars Golden Charm whose other progeny include the 1989 RASE champion, Friars Flo Jo, the 1993 RW reserve female champion, Friars Dreams of Glory, and the 1996 RASE winner, Friars Chanel.

BELOW *Mrs Sian Morris with Friars Goldilocks, RW champion 2004. Photo: Janneke de Rade.*

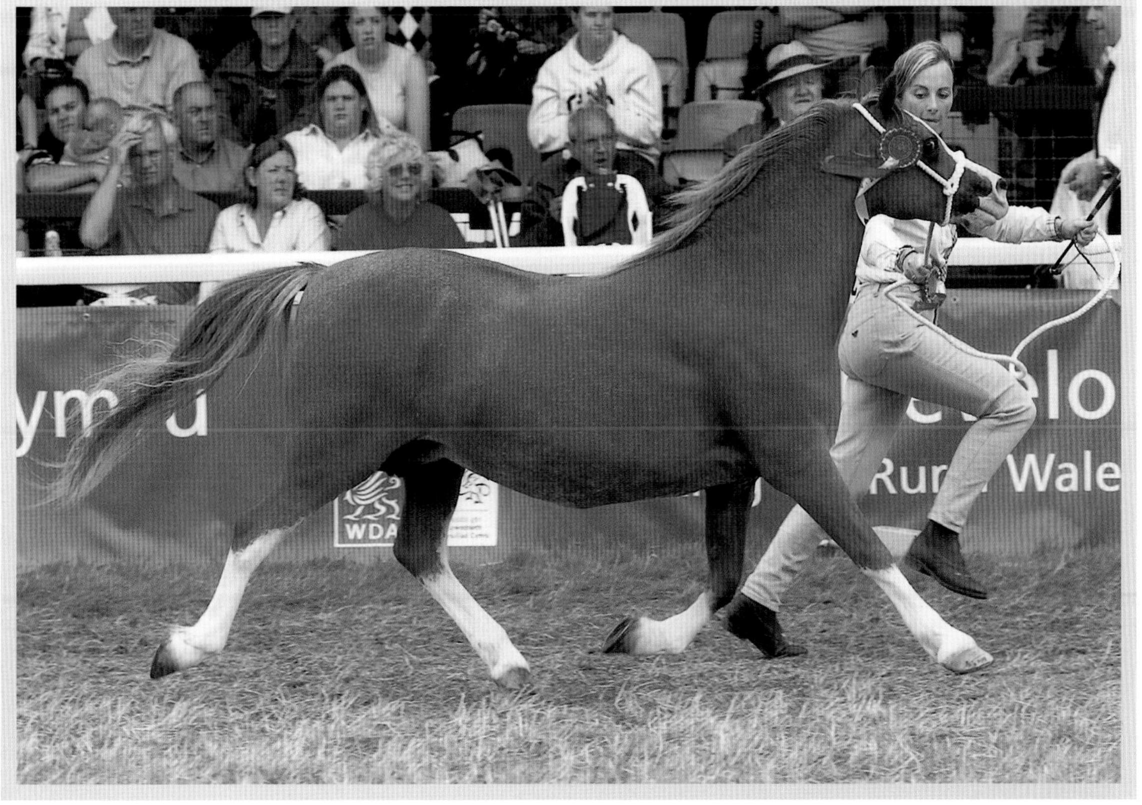

Fouroaks Reanne is sired by Gwynrhosyn Frenin (Coch Rhion x Twyford Mama by Twyford Gamecock) out of the Penual Mark daughter Springbourne Caress who is grand-daughter of the original 'C' mare Belvoir Columbine by Coed Coch Asa (sire also of Twyford Sprig).

We have already met the two Springbourne Caraway daughters, Blanche Mimic (female champion in 1993) and Springbourne Elly (overall champion in 2003), Mimic being descended from Bryniau Misty Morn and Elly being a daughter of Springbourne Eirian of the 'E' family originating with Dundon Elf. Springbourne Elly was the second-highest-priced female when sold by her breeders to Scotland as a yearling at the 1993 Fayre Oaks Sale and had not long since been bought by the Perrins family of Wakefield. Elly was expertly shown by twelve-year-old William Perrins who also won the prize for the best young handler.

Pendock Legend was reserve youngstock champion to Friars Sarah at the RW in 1986 as a two year old and already in the ownership of the Idyllic Stud where he died in 2003. Legend's dam was Pendock Lilactime (foaled in 1972), sired by Twyford Juggler out of Cui Flora (foaled in 1953) who was top-priced youngster when bought at the 1954 Cui Sale. Legend won the progeny competition at the 2000 RW Show with Idyllic Tosca, Colne Tatiana and Betws Mari Lwyd, a feat which he repeated in 2002 with Colne Hightop, Idyllic Fonteyn and Brynodyn Scarlet. In

BELOW *Pendock Legend, RW 2000 progeny winners. From left: Idyllic Tosca, Colne Tatiana, Betws Mari Llwyd. Photo: Wynne Davies.*

LEFT *Brynodyn Scarlet, champion WPCS Centenary Show 2002, with (from left) Mark Bullen (Australia), Richard Miller (producer) and Keith Hughes (owner). Photo: Wynne Davies.*

2003 the RW progeny competition was reorganised, the result being calculated on a points basis throughout the section, and Pendock Legend won again with first-prize yearling filly (and reserve youngstock champion) Thistledown Xtravaganza (from 97 entries), first-prize three-year-old colt with Idyllic Entrepreneur who was youngstock champion, second-prize barren mare with Idyllic Privalova, fourth-prize junior brood mare with Idyllic Lady in Red and first- and second-prize senior brood mare with Idyllic Tosca and Maestir Miss Pepsi. The first championship win for Pendock Legend progeny was in 1990, with Idyllic Pavlova (foaled in 1987) whose dam was Knodishall Pandora (foaled in 1978) by Georgian Shandy by Twyford Gamecock. Pavlova was sold at the 1996 Fayre Oaks Sale where she was the joint second-highest section-A adult at 2,000 guineas. The most prolific winner of all the Pendock Legend progeny was Brynodyn Scarlet (foaled in 1993), daughter of Dryfe Sheer Heaven. Scarlet commenced on her RW success as a foal when she won the filly foal class, the winning colt foal that day being a Pendock Legend son, Maestir Odyssey. Scarlet was twice Breeders Youngstock champion over all breeds at the RASE in 1995 and

1996, twice RASE section A champion as an adult, HOYS qualifier at the Royal Bath and West in 1996 and at the NPS Show in 1999 and champion at the WPCS Centenary Show in 2002.

To summarise a century of the history of the Welsh Mountain pony, it is astounding that, with 47,000 males and almost 100,000 females registered, the ones which achieved most success belong to just four main families. Their relationships are sometimes many generations away, yet still important: e.g., the g-g-dam of the 1967 RW champion, Treharne Tomboy (Rhydd), is a sister to the g-g-dam of the 1980 champion, Crossways Merle (Taran). Bryniau Greylight, dam of Bryniau Misty Morn the g-g-dam of the 1993 champion Blanche Mimic, is g-dam of the 1999 champion, Trefaes Guardsman. Our forefathers laid solid foundation stones on which we could build. The 1991 champion, Dyfrdwy Seren Arian, traces back to the 1905 champion, Llwyn Nell, the 1990 champion, Waithwith Romance, is descended from the 1907 champion, Lady Starlight, Coed Coch Planed and Coed Coch Pelydrog bloodlines come from the 1909 champion, Lady Greylight, and the pedigree of the multi champion, Coed Coch Madog, goes back in only four generations to the 1908 champion, Bleddfa Tell Tale.

CHAPTER TWO

The Welsh Pony, the Present-day Section B

FROM 1901 to 1930, section B of the WSB was occupied, in the main, by Welsh ponies of Cob-type from 12 hands to 13 hands 2 in, which were allowed to be docked and hogged and their Stud Book description was the same as that for section A Part II. The rare pony of Riding-type (e.g. with an 'Oriental' sire, such as Tanybwlch Berwyn, foaled in 1924 and sired by the Barb Sahara, or Craven Cyrus, foaled in 1927 and sired by the Crabbet Arabian King Cyrus) which was bred during this period could also be registered in this section. The Cob-type ponies and the ponies of Riding-type competed against one another in the same classes at shows.

BELOW *Tanybwlch Berwyn aged 24 (1948) at the International Horse Show.*

Major Dugdale of the Llwyn Stud wrote in the 1920s that: 'it is not possible to produce the average Welsh pony at the price that can be obtained for it'. Major Dugdale concluded, therefore, that if the Welsh pony breeder was to obtain a commensurate price for his product,

RIGHT *Miss Bobbie Dugdale (left) riding Llwyn Snowstorm and Miss Eldrydd Dugdale riding Llwyn Bridget in the early 1920s.*

that pony would attract a better financial return if it was broken for children to ride and offered for sale in an area where allowing children to ride their own ponies was very much the 'in thing'. Major Dugdale was fortunate in having two daughters, Bobbie and Eldrydd, who were very competent child riders and soon well-broken consignments of five or six Llwyn ponies were loaded up annually at the railway sidings at Llanfyllin and transported to London where they were offered for sale by auction at the Tattersall's Annual Sale in Knightsbridge. Typical of the ponies sold at Knightsbridge (1925) were Llwyn Snowstorm and Llwyn Bridget who fetched the very remunerative prices of 71 guineas each.

Tanybwlch Berwyn was registered as one of only six stallions entered in section B of the WSB volume 26 (1927), along with his half-brother (also by Sahara), Tanybwlch Rhaiadr Ddu, three docked Cob-type stallions and Manomet Greylight, owned and bred in the USA. The female section Bs in the same volume of the WSB numbered nine, including two other Tanybwlch daughters of Sahara and seven Cob-type mares, two of which were daughters of Seren Ceulan bred by my father, Ceulan Aven Bun and Ceulan Kitty, and Myrtle Rosina the 1929 RW champion Cob-type pony. Craven Cyrus (mentioned above), who was foaled in 1927, was originally registered in section A Part I but eventually grew to 13 hands and was transferred to section B.

The section B situation, which was bad in 1927, became desperate over the next three years, with only one stallion and no mares entered in the WSB volume 27 (1928); three stallions sired by a Cob, one sired by a Hackney and one Cob-type mare in volume 28 (1929); and two stallions (again both bred by my father, sons of Seren Ceulan, Ceulan Comet and Brenin Cymru) and three Cob-type mares in volume 29 (1930). Registration numbers in subsequent years did not warrant annual stud books and volume 30 contained all the registrations for 1931–34.

It was in volume 30 that section B was allocated to Welsh ponies of Riding-type which relieved some confusion on this front but created more confusion on the 'Cob' front as section C now contained Welsh ponies of Cob-type and Welsh Cobs from 12 hands to 16 hands all together in the same section.

It was at the WPCS Council Meeting in January 1932 that the decision was taken to allocate section B to 'ponies of riding-type having low, straight action'. In a letter dated 12 January 1932, Miss Brodrick made the suggestion, which was accepted by the Chairman of Council, Lord Swansea, that the proposal to Council should be that section B would be for ponies 'from 12 hands 3 in to 13 hands 3 in'. Council amended the description to 'between 12 hands and 13 hands 2 in' and this new regulation came into operation in volume 30, with four section B stallions (one already in the USA) and 24 mares, along with 19 foundation stock (FS) mares. Of the 24 fully registered mares, ten were of Cob-type who should have been in section C (including Hafan Polly, grand-dam of the famous Mathrafal), six of the remaining 14 were bred at Tanybwlch, and four were under 12 hands and should therefore have been in section A but presumably were 'of riding type' rather than 'mountain type'. Fifteen of the 19 section B foundation stock mares were bred by Lord Howard de Walden of Chirk Castle and sired by the Arab-bred Gray Cross. When Lord Howard de Walden offered these ponies for sale at his regular auctions, they were often described as having been lent out to children of the estate tenants to ride. Ponies of Cob-type were still incorrectly registered within section B of volume 31 (1935–38) which consisted of five stallions, 12 registered mares (six of which were of Cob breeding) and 24 FS mares (four of Cob and Hackney breeding).

When the FS scheme was introduced in 1930 for females on inspection, the WSB was closed to males with non-registered sires (such as Tanybwlch Berwyn and Craven Cyrus). Females such as Tanybwlch Penwen (foaled 1930, Cairo x Grey Princess) were registered as section B FS, whereas the progeny of Grey Princess by Berwyn (e.g. Tanybwlch Prancio, foaled in 1932) were eligible for full registration. The female progeny of FS mares by a registered Welsh sire were eligible for registration as FS1 on inspection by a WPCS panel judge. The progeny of FS1 mares by a registered Welsh sire were then eligible for registration as FS2 after inspection and both male and female progeny of FS2 mares by a registered Welsh sire were eligible for registration within the Welsh Stud Book proper (without inspection).

By 1960 it was agreed that sections A, B, C and D within the WSB were 'safe' numerically and that no more FS animals were to be accepted. This decision was prompted by animals of unknown parentage being frowned upon in some overseas countries. Also, in some overseas countries stallions were accepted as 'fully registered' when their dams were only FS or FS1, such as Horshaga Cyrano out of Downland Wildflower FS1 and Stoatley Pride out of Revel Colleen FS in Sweden. Understandably, owing to its later start, there are more foundation stock RW champions within section B than within sections A and C, even up to 1985 (e.g. Millcroft Suzuya, daughter of Briery Starlet FS1) or with FS2 dams up to 1996 (e.g. Rotherwood Lorrikeet, daughter of Weston Lark FS2).

The progeny of Craven Cyrus and Tanybwlch Berwyn were very successful as children's riding ponies. For example, a photograph taken at the 1937 RW Show (see above right) depicts (left) Craven Bess (grand-daughter of Craven Cyrus), (right) Tanybwlch Rhos (daughter of Tanybwlch Berwyn) and (centre) Pixie (section A: Bowdler Baron II x Bowdler Betty).

ABOVE *(from left) Craven Bess, Pixie and Tanybwlch Rhos at the 1937 RW Show. Photo: E. H. du Haume.*

Mrs Inge of Plas Tanybwlch, Merionethshire was a staunch supporter of the Welsh pony of Riding-type and used Sahara and Cairo extensively. Sahara (a Barb from Morocco) was owned by the renowned animal painter Denis Aldridge (whose studios were in Leicestershire) and the stud fees and railway transport charges were considerable. Cairo was bred at Tanybwlch in 1927, sired by Crosbie out of Jordania who was given as a gift to Mrs Inge by the Emir Abdullah of Transjordan. Sadly, Cairo was killed by lightning in 1935. After the outbreak of war in 1939, Mrs Inge gave Tanybwlch Berwyn and Tanybwlch Penwen to Miss Brodrick of Coed Coch. One of their earlier progeny had been Tanybwlch Penllyn (foaled 1937) who went on to Clan Stud and became grand-dam of the great Clan Pip. Three full sisters (Berwyn x Penwen) foaled at Coed Coch were Pilia (foaled 1945), Pendefiges (foaled1946) and Pluen (foaled1947). When there was a major

dispersal of section Bs at Coed Coch in 1959, Pilia went to Chirk, Pendefiges went to Brockwell and Pluen went to Kirby Cane. Unfortunately, Pendefiges was lost to the UK when Mrs Binnie of Brockwell sold her to Holland at the 1963 FO Sale.

Also in the 1959 Coed Coch Sale was Pilia's three-year-old daughter, Coed Coch Perfagl, sired by Coed Coch Blaen Lleuad. Perfagl was sold for 220 guineas to Lady Astor of Hever and Blaen Lleuad went to Elliott Bonnie of Ohio, USA for 320 guineas. The stallion at Hever at that time was Trefesgob Benedict and he sired Wickenden Pheasant out of Perfagl in 1961 (Wickenden being the original prefix for Hever Stud). The next stallion at Hever was Brockwell Berwyn (foaled 1960) and, by a coincidence, he was also a product of the 1959 Coed Coch Sale, being a son of Berwyn Beauty who Mrs Binnie purchased at the sale for 170 guineas. Berwyn Beauty was in foal to Rhydyfelin Selwyn (son of Coed Coch Blaen Lleuad) who was also sold at the sale for 320 guineas to Sweden. Selwyn, foaled in 1956, returned to the Twyford Stud in Sussex and, in 1971, sired Twyford Sparkle who was exported to Denmark where she produced the three-times RW champion, Mollegaards Spartacus. Selwyn died on the Isle of Wight aged 34.

ABOVE *Tanybwlch Penllyn.*

BELOW *Downland Mohawk, RW champion 1971*. Photo: Idris Aeron.*

OPPOSITE TOP *Keston Royal Occasion with owner Mrs Elizabeth Mansfield (left) and judge Miss Elspeth Ferguson.*

OPPOSITE BOTTOM *Shamrock Mr Oliver, RW champion 1995. Photo: Ellen van Leeuwen.*

Hever Grania, foaled in 1968, was sired by Brockwell Berwyn out of Wickenden Pheasant and became a very important brood mare at Boston Stud, Bilton in Ainsty, York. The 1991 RW overall champion, Boston Bodecia, foaled in 1984, was sired by Downland Mohawk (the 1971 RW champion) out of Hever Grania.

Pluen's 1960 daughter, Kirby Cane Plume, was g-dam of the famous Keston Royal Occasion and also g-dam of Keston Blue Chip who was g-sire of the 1995 Dutch-bred RW

champion, Shamrock Mr Oliver. Kirby Cane Plume then went to the Droskyn Stud from where, when Droskyn was dispersed, she joined the influential Tetworth Nijinski brood-mare band at Laithehill Stud. The Nijinski progeny groups were a major force to be reckoned with at the RW Shows in the 1980s, being very successful most years. In 1981, sired by Nijinski, Plume produced the beautiful chestnut Laithehill Pavlova. Laithehill Stud was now short of a second stallion to cross on the Nijinski daughters and, having failed to acquire Pennwood Eldorado (who went to Cottrell Stud), Laithehill bought another Pennwood Mujib son, Abercrychan Spectator (top of the WPCS sire ratings in 1990), from Sunbridge Stud. Pavlova's 1992 daughter, sired by Abercrychan Spectator,

RIGHT *Mark Tamplin with Griashall Kiwi, RW champion 1999*. Photo: Arthur Thomson BEM.*

was Laithehill Pirouette who has been one of the most successful recent winners on the South Wales circuit and is also the dam of Griashall Kiwi who was RW champion in 1999 when only two years old.

Tanybwlch Berwyn himself went on to sire over 300 progeny while at Coed Coch. He had an enormous influence on section Bs and also a considerable influence on section As through his daughters, such as Tanybwlch Prancio (g-g-dam of Coed Coch Planed), Tanybwlch Penllyn (g-dam of Clan Pip) and Coed Coch Sensigl (dam of Coed Coch Symwl).

The progeny of Tanybwlch Berwyn dominated the section B scene in the immediate post-war Royal Welsh Shows, with Coed Coch Siabod winning every male championship between 1950 and 1953 and overall in 1952. He was exported to Australia in 1954. Coed Coch Siabod (foaled 1945) was bred by Mr Cyril Lewis of Rhydyfelin, sired by Tanybwlch Berwyn out of Coed Coch Sirius from whom Mr Lewis had previously bred section As, such as the magnificent Coed Coch Siaradus (foaled 1942) and her full-sister, Coed Coch Serog (foaled 1941), who was exported to the USA in 1948. Mr Lewis also bred Coed Coch Seron (foaled 1947) by

Tanybwlch Berwyn out of Serog, and she was the foundation of the Kirby Cane Stud. These ponies, Siabod, Seron, Serog and Siaradus, all with the Coed Coch prefix, were bred by Mr Cyril Lewis of the Rhydyfelin Stud but in those days purchasers of animals which had not already been registered were allowed to register them under their own prefixes. At Kirby Cane, Seron produced, among others, the 1969 RW champion, Kirby Cane Scholar (foaled 1965), the last Welsh pony to be exported to New Zealand by sea, and Kirby Cane Shuttlecock (foaled 1954), sire of the 1969 RW champion, Revel Glimpse, and 1973 RW champion, Reeves Fairy Lustre (foaled1961). Fairy Lustre was responsible for the continuation of the 'Lustre' dynasty started by her dam, Ceulan Silver Lustre (foaled 1938), most recently through her daughter, Paddock Fairy Lustre (foaled1981) who was champion at Northleach in 1989 and reserve champion at the 1991 RASE for Millcroft Stud. Paddock Fairy Lustre was sired by Keston Royal Occasion just before he left for Australia. The line is continued through her sons, the two-year-old 1987 RW champion, Millcroft Copper Lustre, and Millcroft Royal Lustre (foaled

ABOVE LEFT *Coed Coch Siabod, RW champion 1550, 1951, 1952*, 1953.*
Photo: Rouch.

ABOVE RIGHT *Kirby Cane Shuttlecock.*
Photo: Wynne Davies.

BELOW *Reeves Fairy Lustre, RW champion 1973*.*

ABOVE *John Carter with Paddock Fairy Lustre. Photo: Wynne Davies.*

1991), winner of the stallion class at the 1986 RW Show and reserve for the Creber HOYS qualifier at the 1993 Royal Cornwall Show. The strain continues at Paddock Stud through Reeves Fairy Lustre's last foal, Paddock Silver Lustre (foaled1987, by Watermans Mandolin), who is the dam of Paddock Northern Lustre (foaled1995, by Paddock Camargue), champion at the first WPCS National Show in 2003.

Revel Glimpse ended her days at Cottrell Stud where her daughter, Weston Glimpse (foaled 1971, by Chirk Crogan), had gone for 3,000 guineas at the 1978 Weston Sale. Also in the sale, and sold for the same figure, was Weston Glimpse's full-brother, Weston Gigli (foaled 1969), who was bought by Miss Jannys Macdonald of the Glenmore Stud in New South Wales, Australia. Weston Glimpse was overall champion at the 1980 RW Show for Cottrell Stud, also female champion in 1982 and produced two other RW champions by Rotherwood State Occasion, the 1992 champion, Cottrell Charm, and later on the 2000 champion, Cottrell Royal Glance.

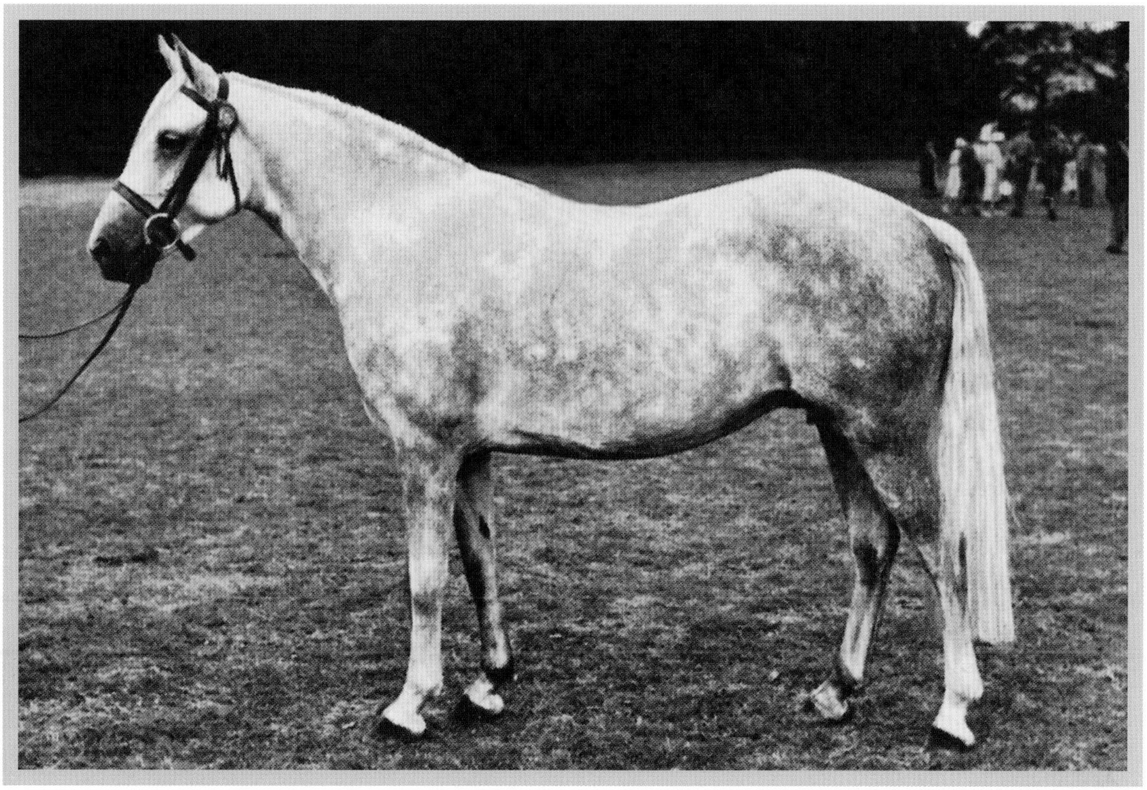

Another Tanybwlch Berwyn daughter to become RW champion was Coed Coch Silian (foaled 1947), her dam being Coed Coch Seirian who was the foal left behind at Coed Coch when her dam, Coed Coch Serliw, came to Ceulan in 1937. Silian was RW champion in 1952 and 1955 in the ownership of Mrs E.G. E. Griffith of Plasnewydd. Silian's 1952 foal, Verity, by Criban Victor was RW champion in 1953 and 1954 and her son, Valiant (foaled 1953), also by Criban Victor, was RW champion in 1955 before he was exported to Miss Ida Illingworth of South Africa. To this day, countless riding ponies in South Africa carry the 'Valiant' name, all tracing back to Valiant and his son, Foresyte Valiant's Image.

TOP *Coed Coch Silian. Photo: Miles Bros.*

ABOVE *Sandy Anderson with Paddock Northern Lustre. Photo: Cherry Ann Wilde*

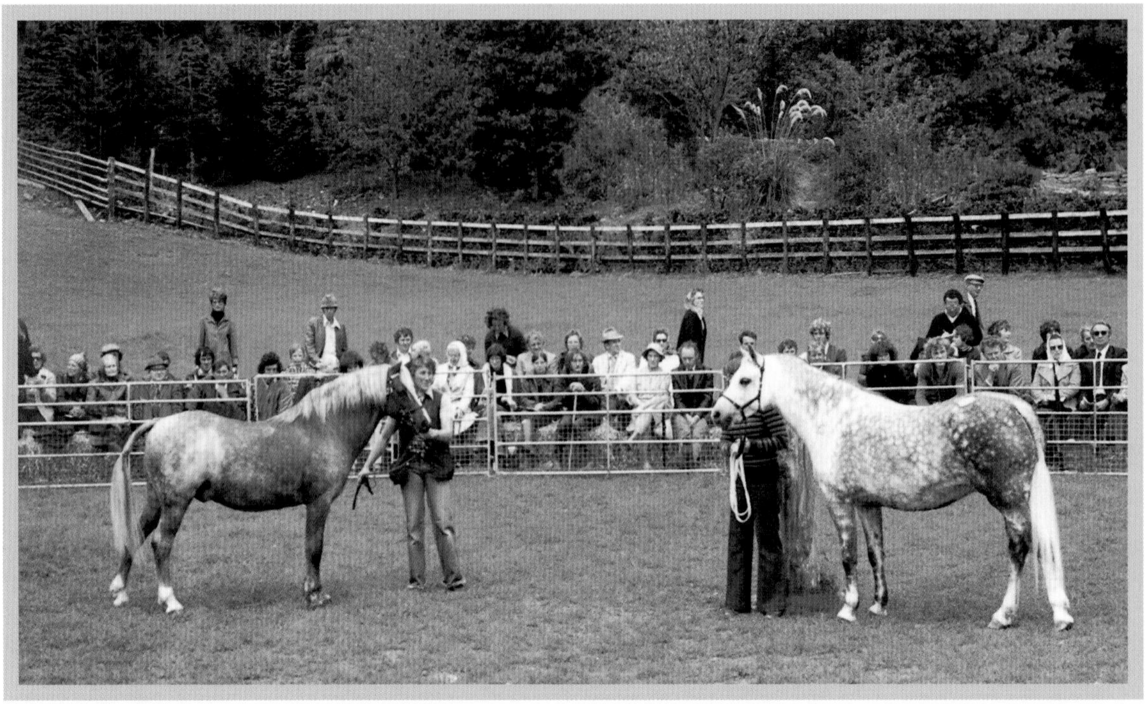

ABOVE *Weston Glimpse (right), RW champion 1980*, 1982 and her full-brother Weston Gigli at the 1978 Weston Sale.*

RIGHT *Valiant, RW champion 1955, photographed in South Africa.*

ABOVE *Coed Coch Berwynfa at Coed Coch with Miss Margaret Brodrick MBE. Photo: Wynne Davies.*

The most influential of the Tanybwlch Berwyn sons was Coed Coch Berwynfa (foaled 1951), sired when Tanybwlch Berwyn was 28 years old. His dam was Berwyn's daughter, Berwyn Beauty (foaled 1942), daughter of Dinarth Wonderlight whose dam, Irfon Marvel, was the 1925 RW section A champion. When Coed Coch held a reduction sale in 1952 (when many of the top-priced ponies were sold to go overseas), it was fortunate for the breed, and for Coed Coch Stud in particular, that Berwynfa did not reach his modest reserve of 50 guineas and stayed on at Coed Coch until his death in 1978. At the Coed Coch final dispersal sale that year, several Berwynfa progeny sold for between 3,000 and 4,000 guineas, including the top-priced Coed Coch Gala (foaled 1964), dam of the 1991 RW champion, Paddock Camargue, whose daughter, Paddock Picture, was RW champion in 1998. Paddock Camargue, who was the 1990 Creber HOYS qualifier at the Great Yorkshire Show, is the subject of the WPCS section B bronze model and is now a very successful sire in Sweden. His dam, Coed

Coch Gala, had previously been sold to Lord Bruntisfield for whom she bred some good 'Hillbarn' ponies such as Hillbarn Garland (Carolinas Stud) before being bought back by Coed Coch in 1972. Coed Coch Gala (foaled 1964) was sired by Berwynfa out of Coed Coch Peioni by Coed Coch Blaen Lleuad (1957 RW champion), both Berwynfa and Blaen Lleuad being sons of Berwyn Beauty. The dam of Peioni was Coed Coch Penllwyd (foaled 1953), one of only three section B females retained at Coed Coch after the 1959 sale when Blaen Lleuad was sold to the USA. Fortunately, Chirk Heather had produced the two Blaen Lleuad sons, the yearling colt Chirk Caradoc and the colt foal Chirk Crogan, just before he was exported. Penllwyd was RW female champion to her sire, Criban Victor, in 1964 and her daughter, the bay Coed Coch Priciau (foaled 1960), by Coed Coch Berwynfa, was overall champion in 1966. Another daughter, the grey Coed Coch Dawn (foaled 1966), was RW champion in 1974 and was sold for 1,300 guineas at the 1978 Coed Coch dispersal sale to Mrs Olive Weston of the Seaholm Stud. The 17-year-old Seaholm Dawn (Seaholm Fritz x Coed Coch Dawn) was one of the top mares (sold for £1,300 to Farchynys Stud) when the Polaris Stud of the late Countess of Dysart was dispersed on 26 September 2004.

The dam of Paddock Picture was Paddock Princess Charming, daughter of Coed Coch Penwn, a full-sister (one year older) to Gala. Both Penwn and Gala were bought by Paddock Stud at the 1978 Coed Coch dispersal sale. Bernard and Maureen Butterworth of the Paddock Stud had gone to the Coed Coch Sale intending to buy Gala (which they did at 3,800 guineas) but also bought Penwn, the previous lot (at 1,400 guineas), in case they did not get Gala! Both Gala and Penwn repaid Paddock Stud for their faith several times over, producing their last foals at 26 and 27 years old. Penwn's 1981 son by Coed Coch Lygon was Paddock Mystral whose daughter, Polaris Elsie (foaled1986), is the dam of the 2004 RW champion, Polaris Elmer (foaled 1994). Polaris Elsie sold for £1,400 to Mrs Lane of Lyndhurst at 18 years old at the September 2004 Polaris dispersal sale.

Coed Coch Endor (foaled 1970) was the progeny of a Berwynfa son (Coed Coch Derwas) by a Berwynfa daughter (Coed Coch Llawrig). He

LEFT *John Kristensen with Coed Coch Endor (right) with his progeny group at Mollegaard Stud in Denmark. Photo: Wynne Davies.*

ABOVE LEFT *Mark Northam with Twyford Signal. Photo: Wynne Davies.*

ABOVE RIGHT *Mollegaards Spartacus, RW champion 1992*, 1993*, 1994*.*

was exported to Denmark where, in 1986, he sired Mollegaards Spartacus, RW champion in 1992*, 1993* and 1994*. Spartacus has the enviable record of qualifying for the HOYS Creber championship in four successive years: 1991 (Devon County), 1992 (Royal Bath and West), 1993 (Herts County) and 1994 (South of England), as well as qualifying twice for Olympia under saddle. Spartacus's half-brother (both out of Twyford Sparkle), Twyford Signal (foaled in 1976 and died in 2004), shared the record of four HOYS tickets: 1987 (Royal Norfolk), 1988 (Royal Bath and West), 1989 (RASE) and 1990 (Royal Highland), and he also went to Olympia under saddle twice. There is more Tanybwlch Berwyn influence in Spartacus and Signal through their dam, Twyford Sparkle, who was

(= overall champion)*

RIGHT *Len Bigley with Douthwaite Signwriter. Photo: A. Reynolds LBIPP, LMPA.*

sired by Rhydyfelin Selwyn, a son of Coed Coch Blaen Lleuad out of Rhydyfelin Seren Wyb, a daughter of Tanybwlch Berwyn. Signal's progeny have been very successful at the RW Shows. His son, Douthwaite Signwriter, was first-prize stallion and reserve male champion in 2003, and his daughter, Brenob Finch, was female champion in 1999.

A Berwynfa daughter, Coed Coch Aden (foaled 1972) is responsible for two RW champions, Lemonshill Alarch (female champion in 1997 as a three year old) and Lemonshill Top Note (male champion in 2003 when a yearling). Alarch was sired by the Lemonshill senior sire, Cottrell Artiste (foaled 1986, sired by Rotherwood State Occasion out of Downland Almond by the 1971 RW champion, Downland Mohawk, out of Lechlade Angelica by Downland Chevalier), who was top of the WPCS sire ratings in 1995 and 1999 after his sire had been top for nine years. Artiste, who won at the RW as a three year old in 1989, is a full-brother to Cottrell Amethyst (foaled 1987) who was reserve female champion at the RW as a yearling and champion at the RASE. Amethyst's progeny include Cottrell Aurora, RW champion as a two year old in 1995 and exported to Australia, Cottrell Aur, who was reserve youngstock champion at the 1993 RW

LEFT *Mrs Karen Cheetham with Lemonshill Alarch, RW champion 1997. Photo: Roy Parker.*

BELOW LEFT *Edwin Prosser with Cottrell Ambassador Photo: Wynne Davies.*

Show, and Cottrell Ambassador, who was overall supreme champion at Glanusk. What a family!

Alarch's dam, Baughurst Aderyn, was also bred by Mrs Gilchrist-Fisher (but before the Lemonshill prefix was registered with the WPCS) and was sired by Downland Mohawk out of Coed Coch Aden. Lemonshill Angelica (foaled 1993), dam of Lemonshill Top Note, was sired by Artiste so Angelica and Aderyn are three-quarter siblings. Soudley Taliesin, sire of Top Note, was an interesting outcross. Surprisingly for a stallion born in 1996, he has absolutely no 'Downland' blood and was conveniently close to Lemonshill Stud in 2001, the year when movement of animals in a foot and mouth disease 'hot spot' was strictly restricted. What a bargain Taliesin was when bought at the 1998 FO Sale for 400 guineas despite having won a WPCS medal. He has regal bloodlines: sired by Eyarth Rio out of Rotherwood Primrose, daughter of Rotherwood Red Rose by Brockwell Cobweb out of the original 'fountain', Gredington Tiwlip.

After Tanybwlch Berwyn and Craven Cyrus, the next milestone in the history of section B occurred in 1944 with the birth of Criban Victor, sired

BELOW *Criban Victor, RW champion 1947*, 1954, 1956*, 1958*, 1959*, 1960*, 1964*, with Lord Kenyon. Photo: John Slater.*

by the section A Criban Winston (son of Coed Coch Glyndwr) out of the Cob-type Criban Whalebone by the Cob sire Mathrafal Broadcast. Had Victor been foaled three years later, new WPCS regulations would have required him to be registered as a Welsh pony of Cob-type section C, and his progeny, including the RW champions Valiant (1955), Verity (1953, 1954), Gredington Daliad (1956, 1957*) and Gredington Milfyd (1958, 1962, 1963, would not have been allowed into section B.

Criban Victor was sold at the 1946 Criban Sale for 40 guineas to Mrs Cuff of the Downland Stud and he was the only male section B competing at the 1947 RW Show where he was sold to Lord Kenyon of Gredington where he stayed until he died in 1973. At the 1949 RW Show, Lord Kenyon showed Victor in class 35 for 'Welsh Ponies of Cob-type' and he stood third to Welsh Echo. Criban Victor was RW champion in 1947*, 1954, 1956*, 1958*, 1959*, 1960* and 1964* and was also the subject of the 11p postage stamp issued in 1978.

The three bloodlines of Tanybwlch Berwyn, Craven Cyrus and Criban Victor were not sufficient by themselves as a foundation on which to build a new breed and therefore breeders had to resort to 'in-breeding' and 'line-breeding' which requires great expertise as otherwise the results can be disastrous. An example of an 'in-bred' RW champion (1971) is Gredington Blodyn (foaled1965), sired by Coed Coch Berwynfa (Tanybwlch Berwyn x Berwyn's daughter, Berwyn Beauty) out of Gredington Saffrwm (Criban Victor x Victor's daughter, Gredington Milfyd).

In 1959, a 'short cut' experiment was tried to introduce some new male lines into section B by allowing the progeny of registered sires out of FS and FS1 mares into the Stud Book, thus saving the necessity of having the intermediate FS2 stage which would involve at least another five years. Two stallions accepted under this route were Coed Coch Pawl (foaled 1958, Coed Coch Blaen Lleuad x Coed Coch Pluen FS1) and Reeves Golden Lustre (foaled 1945, Ceulan Revoke x Ceulan Silver Lustre FS, daughter of the fully registered Ceulan Silverleaf). These two stallions did their bit and sired some RW champions. Reeves Golden Lustre was the sire of the 1968 RW champion, Springbourne Golden Flute. Coed Coch Pawl

RIGHT *Vivian Eckley with Cusop Banknote, RW champion 1974, 1975, 1976*, 1979*. Photo:* Horse and Hound.

was the sire of the 1965 RW champion, Cusop Hoity Toity and g-sire of four-times RW champion, Cusop Banknote. Banknote is g-sire of the 1999 RW female champion, Brenob Finch, while Hoity Toity is g-sire of the 1981 and 1985 RW champion, Downland Goldleaf. Mrs Cuff of Downland bought Mere Fire Myth (FS2), the dam of Goldleaf, at the 1974 Hay-on-Wye Sale at the same time as I bought Fire Myth's colt foal, Twylands Firecracker. Mere Fire Myth was sired by Cusop Hoity Toity out of the former champion riding pony Bwlch Firebird whose dam, Bwlch Goldflake, was also dam of the immortal Bwlch Valentino. Downland Goldleaf's son, Cusop Steward (foaled 1982), was the sire of Linksbury Celebration who was the 1989 RW male champion when only a yearling. Cusop Steward's dam was Cusop Sunshade, daughter of Monkham Snow Bunting. Interestingly, Snow Bunting's 1977 daughter by Twylands Firecracker, born at Ceulan but named Tricula Jenny Wren, was the champion ridden Welsh Pony at the 1981 RW Show.

Hoity Toity is one of the few section Bs to have won at the RW Show in hand and under saddle and he also sired two HOYS ridden show pony champions, Cusop Sequence and Cusop Escalade.

LEFT *Downland Goldleaf, RW champion 1981*, 1985*. Photo:* WPCS Journal.

Cusop Bumble (foaled 1962, daughter of Coed Coch Pawl) is responsible for the two RW champions, Bunbury Mahogany (male champion 1986) and Downland Edelweiss (overall champion in 1988). Bumble is the dam of Downland Beechwood (foaled 1969), the sire of Bunbury Mahogany, and she is also dam of Carnalw Evergreen (by Downland Romance) whom Downland Stud bought to produce Downland Eglantine, the dam of Edelweiss. Carnalw Evergreen is also the dam of Downland Gondolier, sire of Lydstep Praire Flower, dam of Douthwaite Signwriter.

However, two swallows do not make a summer, and the major breakthrough in section B breeding, which also occurred in 1959, was the birth of four stallions who altered the course of section B history. These four stallions (along with one full-brother foaled in 1958) were the result of three generations of 'top-side', fully registered sires mated to FS, FS1 and FS2 mares, and they are listed below.

SOLWAY MASTER BRONZE

Although his dam, Criban Biddy Bronze, had the 'Criban' prefix, she was actually bred in 1950 by Mr Llewellyn Richards's neighbour, Mr William Thomas

MAIN SIRES FOALED IN 1958 AND 1959 FROM FS2 DAMS

(i)
Solway Master Bronze
(foaled 1959)
(Coed Coch Glyndwr x Criban Biddy Bronze FS2

(ii)
Brockwell Cobweb
(foaled 1959)
(Harford Starlight x Fayre Ladybird FS2);

(iii)
Downland Dauphin
(foaled 1959)
(Criban Pebble x Downland Dragonfly FS2);

(iv)
Chirk Crogan
(foaled1959)
(Coed Coch Blaen Lleuad x Chirk Heather FS2) and his full-brother

(v)
Chirk Caradoc
(foaled1958)

LEFT *Solway Master Bronze, RW champion 1961*, 1962*, 1963*.*

OPPOSITE TOP LEFT *Criban Biddy Bronze (dam of Solway Master Bronze), ridden by Jabeena Maslin, receiving her award from HM Queen Elizabeth.*

OPPOSITE BOTTOM LEFT *Brockwell Cobweb, RW champion 1966. Photo: Wynne Davies.*

OPPOSITE TOP RIGHT *Downland Dauphin. Photo: Les Mayall.*

OPPOSITE MIDDLE RIGHT *Chirk Crogan. Photo: Kevin Townsend.*

OPPOSITE BOTTOM RIGHT *Chirk Caradoc.*

WEEKLY

(Wil Coity Bach), who had been given her dam, Criban Belle, for retirement. Biddy Bronze produced a daughter, Strawberry Queen by Gaerstone Beacon, for Mr Thomas as a two year old but, being so young, was not covered again and was bought by Mr Richards in 1953. Strawberry Queen stayed on at Coity Bach. One of her daughters, Ceulan Strawberry Princess by Ceulan Revolt, came to Ceulan as a foal in 1957. Biddy Bronze probably suffered in her development through having the foal at such a tender age and was placed only fourth out of four for Mr Richards at the 1953 RW Show. However, her potential was recognised by Miss Elspeth Ferguson, and Biddy Bronze then went to Rosevean where she did not stay long before being spotted by Lady Reiss of the Solway Stud and she was soon winning ridden championships against all heights at all the major UK shows. Biddy Bronze retired from ridden showing in 1958, was mated to the 23-year-old Coed Coch Glyndwr (who died the following year) and Solway Master Bronze was the result. Although Biddy Bronze was hardly over 12 hands in height, Master Bronze got his section B height from Biddy Bronze's grand-dam, Criban Bowbell (foaled 1939), whose sire was the Polo pony Silverdale Bowtint.

Solway Master Bronze was bought as a foal by Miss Miriam Reader of the Elphicks Stud and was RW champion in 1961, 1962 and 1963. Between 1962 and 1975, still in the ownership of Miss Reader, he sired an average of 42 foals a year (a total of 541). He was then sold to the Hon. Mrs Ponsonby of the Lechlade Stud where he continued siring some outstanding ponies. He died at Lechlade in 1983. Master Bronze was top of the WPCS sire ratings in 1969 and 1970. Solway Master Bronze bloodlines are most influential today through his daughter, Clyphada Periwinkle (foaled 1964 out of Kirby Cane Plume), who was dam of Keston Royal Occasion and Keston Bluechip. His daughter Keston Fantasia (foaled 1969 out of Twyford Silk) is dam of the 1994 RW female champion, Talhaearn Eirlys-y-Pasg, who herself was dam of the 1996 RW overall champion, Cwrtycadno Cadfridog, and he was the sire of the 2005 overall champion and HOYS qualifier, Mintfield Songthrush.

A North Wales influential sire was the Master Bronze son Georgian Red Pepper, sire of Carwed Petra (foaled 1971), dam of the 1997, 2000 and

TOP LEFT *Edwin Prosser and judges Mrs Yvonne Abrey and John Hendy with Cwrtycadno Cadfridog, RW champion 1996*. Photo: Wynne Davies.*

TOP RIGHT *Edwin Prosser with Mintfield Songthrush, RW champion 2004*. Photo: Theo ten Brinke.*

BOTTOM LEFT *Dewi Evans with Carwed Charmer, RW champion 1997*, 2000*, 2002. Photo: Eberhard Holin.*

2002 RW champion, Carwed Charmer. One son produced at Lechlade was Lechlade Scarlet Pimpernel who, before he went to New South Wales, sired Chamberlayne Don Juan (foaled 1975), sire of Thornwood Royalist (foaled 1981), a successful sire at Waxwing and Pennwood Studs. A major female influence was via Carolinas China Rose (daughter of Downland Dresden), dam of many champions at Cottrell Stud, such as Cottrell Fabergé (foaled 1991, by Rotherwood State Occasion) who was HOYS Creber qualifier at the 1994 RASE Show. Of all the Master Bronze progeny, probably Carolinas Purple Emperor (foaled 1980) was the one who most resembled his sire. Purple Emperor's dam was Eden Blue Bunting (foaled 1966) who was the start of Mrs Carolyn Bachman's Carolinas Stud. Mrs Bachman went to the 1977 Fayre Oaks Sale intending to buy the section A mare Sunwillow Chamonix but she was sold for 800 guineas to Australia and, instead, Mrs Bachman bought a wild 11-year-old section B mare, Eden Blue Bunting, sired by Gorsty Dark Shadow out of Talfan Snow Bunting by Ceulan Gondolier. Blue Bunting's breeder, Mr John Owen of Trawsfynydd, had bought the dam, Talfan Snow Bunting, for 40 guineas at the 1963 FO Sale. Blue Bunting died at Carolinas Stud in 1990, having produced the 1983 Essex County HOYS qualifier, Purple Emperor, the RW winner, Carolinas Swallowtail, the RASE winner, Carolinas Hollyblue, and the Lampeter winner, Carolinas Queen of Spain.

BROCKWELL COBWEB

Brockwell Cobweb lived all his life with his breeder, Mrs Barbara Binnie of Minehead, Somerset and died in 1981. Mrs Binnie bought his dam, Fayre Ladybird, for 85 guineas at the 1957 FO Sale when she was the top section B. She found his sire, Harford Starlight, in a poor state in a pigsty in the Elan Valley and bought him for £25 with 10 shillings back for luck! Cobweb's breeding on his sire's side is all the best 'Wentworth' section A bloodlines purchased for the top prices at the 1927 Grove dispersal sale. Fayre Ladybird was also of Wentworth section A breeding but her grand-dam was the large FS mare Geisha whose dam was bred in the New Forest. Cobweb was RW male champion in 1966 and his grandson, Brockwell Chuckle, was overall champion in 1972 in the ownership of Mrs Margaret Williams of the Nefydd Stud.

BELOW *David Jones with Eyarth Rio (right) and his son Telynau Royal Charter with Geraint Thomas. Photo: Wynne Davies.*

The 1994 RW champion, Talhaearn Eirlys-y-Pasg, was sired by Nefydd Autumn's Chuckle (a son of Brockwell Chuckle) who is also g-sire of the four-times sire ratings topper Eyarth Rio, a very valuable sire who handsomely repaid the efforts of Eyarth Stud in rearing him when he was rejected by his dam. Brockwell Cobweb was top of the WPCS sire ratings

ABOVE *Four full-brothers and sisters at HOYS 2001 (Ernford Benjamin x Desarbe Polyanthus). From left: Wortley The Duchess (8 years), Wortley Cavalier (10 years), Wortley Wizard (6 years), Wortley Wild Jasmin (7 years). Photo: Real Time Imaging.*

in 1972. Brockwell Cobweb bloodlines were greatly appreciated at Weston Stud who acquired three of his daughters: Brockwell Japonica (sold at the 1974 Weston Sale), Brockwell Penelope (dam of the multi-champion Weston Vogue) and Brockwell Flirt, g-g-dam of Weston Rosebud who was RW champion in 1976 as a yearling and also g-g-dam of Weston Picture who was also RW champion as a yearling in 1979. Brockwell Cobweb was also g-sire of Tetworth Nijinski who sired Desarbre Polyanthus, dam of the four Wortley ponies, Wortley Cavalier, Wizard, The Duchess and Wild Jasmin, all of which qualified for the HOYS in 2001, and also sire of the two-year-old Desarbre Folksong, overall champion of the 1984 RW Show. Folksong's dam was Penyfan Rhapsody, one of the very few ponies bred by RWAS publicity chairman Mr John Kendall. Rhapsody was sired by Downland Romance out of Teybrook Piccolo by Kirby Cane Shuttlecock.

Other descendants to claim RW championship status were the 1986 male champion Bunbury Mahogany, whose dam was the Cobweb daughter Brockwell Muslin, and the 1985 female champion, Millcroft Suzuya whose dam was another Cobweb daughter, Briery Starlet, who was purchased by Millcroft Stud from Mrs Binnie in 1966.

Mrs Binnie had bought Starlet's dam, Criban Ester, at the 1957 Fayre Oaks Sale for 80 guineas (at the same time as Fayre Ladybird) and then sold her, in foal to Cobweb, to Major Hedley of the Briery Stud for 420 guineas at the 1961 FO Sale, but she then bought the foal, Starlet, back the following year.

DOWNLAND DAUPHIN

Downland Dauphin was a son of the liver chestnut mare Downland Dragonfly (foaled 1955) who had a broad blaze inherited from her grand-dam, Criban Sweetly, who Mrs Cuff had bought, unbroken and very wild, from Mr Moses Griffith in 1949 and produced to win the ridden class at the RW Show the following year. In 1958 we were looking for section A ponies for the USA (in volume 40 WSB it is recorded that we exported 28 stallions and 161 mares to the USA). We went to see Dragonfly at Llanddeusant and were offered her at a very reasonable price. I see from my notes at that time that there was a problem in that Dragonfly was registered in section B and her transfer to section A had not come through in time (she was transferred to section A in volume 41), otherwise Downland Dauphin would have been foaled in the USA and the course of section B history in the UK would have been very different.

Dauphin died in 1965 when he was only six years old but left behind a legacy of winners, mainly through his son Downland Chevalier (foaled 1962) who had Craven Cyrus breeding on his dam's side. The 1970 RW male champion, Bowdell Quiver (foaled 1966), owned by Lord Kenyon, was another Dauphin son. His dam, Kirby Cane Goosefeather, was descended from the section A Downland Grasshopper (foaled 1949) who died at Ceulan in 1974. Downland Grasshopper was the foundation of the

RIGHT *Downland Chevalier.*

Kirby Cane 'G' family, Golden Rod (Vardra Stud), Gauntlet (Pendock Stud) and Greensleeves who was HRH Princess Anne's riding pony in 1954 (see below). Bowdell Quiver was the sire of Gredington Lily, a noted in-hand and ridden winner who topped the section Bs at 1,200 guineas at the 1985 FO Sale when the Gredington Stud was dispersed. Lily's dam, Gredington Beryn, was sired by Coed Coch Berwynfa out of Gredington Milfyd and so was a full-sister to Gredington Tiwlip (Rotherwood Stud).

Evidence of the esteem in which Downland Chevalier was regarded by section B breeders is gleaned from the fact that when stallion services were offered at the 1973 Fayre Oaks Sale for charity, the service to Chevalier realised 740 guineas compared with services to most other stallions selling for between 20 and 60 guineas. His RW champion progeny include Downland Goldleaf, Lydstep Ladies Slipper (1977 RW champion and HOYS qualifier), and Glansevin Melick (1980 RW male champion) out of the section A Meadow Flower of Maen Gwynedd.

The original influence of Downland Chevalier outside the Downland Stud was on Coed Coch Berwynfa daughters, producing the son Baledon Squire and the full-sisters Rotherwood Lilactime and Rotherwood Honeysuckle. Honeysuckle's daughter, Rotherwood Penny Royale (foaled 1978), sired by Keston Royal Occasion, was RW champion in 1983. Her full-brother, one year younger, was Rotherwood State Occasion, nine times top of the WPCS sire ratings.

ABOVE *Kirby Cane Greensleeves with HM Queen Elizabeth and HRH Princess Anne in 1954. Photo: Valentine's Postcards.*

The 1977 and 1982* RW champion Rosedale Mohican (foaled 1973) has interesting breeding as he was sired by the 1971 RW champion Downland Mohawk (whose sire, Downland Romance, and dam, Downland Water Gypsy, were both out of Downland Love-in-the-Mist) and his dam, Downland Flair (bought for 200 guineas at the 1970 FO Sale), was sired by Downland Chevalier who was another son of Downland Love-in-the-Mist. Mohican's son, Orielton Aristocrat (foaled 1977), was the most successful

RIGHT *Rotherwood State Occasion. Photo: Trevor Newbrook.*

sire of riding ponies in the last quarter of the twentieth century. Aristocrat's dam, Hollytree Bettryn, was sired by Kirby Cane Guardsman (whom I sold to Bertil Bengtsson, Sweden in 1968) out of Blossom Bach by Ceulan Revelry. Hollytree Bettryn was purchased from her breeders as a yearling for 200 guineas at the 1970 FO Sale by Mr Elwyn Davies of the Sunbridge Stud.

Downland Chevalier was top of the WPCS sire ratings ten times between 1968 and 1981 with his son, Downland Mandarin, top in 1979 and Mandarin's son, Keston Royal Occasion (foaled 1972 out of a daughter of Solway Master Bronze), top four times from 1980 to 1984. They are followed by Royal Occasion's son, Rotherwood State Occasion (foaled 1979, out of the Chevalier daughter Rotherwood Honeysuckle), nine times top of the sire ratings from 1985 to 1994 and he was then followed by his son, Cottrell Artiste (foaled 1968, out of Downland Almond), who was top in 1995 and 1999. Another of the rare occasions when a yearling became RW champion was in 1990 when the dun yearling son of Artiste, Lemonshill Limelight, was champion for his owner/breeder Mrs Gilchrist-Fisher, and another son, the three-year-old Wortley Fisher King, was male champion in 1998. The 1999 RW overall champion was the two-year-old colt Griashall Kiwi, sired by the Artiste son Lemonshill Great Occasion who very sadly died at Griashall Stud when still only six years old.

ABOVE *Rosedale Mohican, RW champion 1977, 1982*. *Photo: Carol Gilson.*

The grey mare Downland Misty Morning was a full-sister to Chevalier but a year younger, foaled in 1963. Misty Morning was RASE champion in 1968 and 1972. Downland Romance was another foal out of Downland Love-in-the-Mist but sired by Downland Roundelay and foaled in 1961. The progeny of half-brother x half-sister, Romance x Misty Morning, foaled in 1974, was Downland Manchino who spent most of his life as senior sire at Sunbridge Stud. Manchino's son, Sunbridge Aristocrat (foaled 1980), was sold for 1,000 guineas at the 1981 FO Sale and sired Wynswood Zara who was RW champion in 1990 as a two year old. Zara's dam, Wynswood Zandra (foaled 1981), was also of Downland bloodlines, being sired by Downland Sheridan out of Wynswood Zarina who was by the palomino son of Downland Chevalier, Belvoir Zoroaster.

Downland Mandarin (mentioned above) was also sire of the 1983 RW male champion, Tetworth Mikado (foaled 1977, out of Tetworth Czarina by Downland Chevalier), and of Varndell Right Royal who sired the 1988 RW male champion, Broadlands Coronet. It is seen, therefore, that, with four exceptions, this family has captured the WPCS sire ratings every year from 1971 to 1999, with Abercrychan Spectator (grandson of Downland Chevalier) being top in 1990, and Eyarth Rio (whose dam, Eyarth Zsa Zsa, is grand-daughter of Keston Royal Occasion) top in 1996, 1997, 1998 and 2002. Eyarth Rio has been extremely successful in the show ring, twice qualifying for the HOYS Show, for the Templeton In-hand in 1995 at Notts County and for the Breeders challenge in 2000 at the Great Yorkshire.

CHIRK CROGAN

Chirk Crogan spent most of his life at the Weston Stud where he was very influential as a sire with such progeny as Weston Glimpse (foaled 1971,

RW champion in 1980* and 1982), his grand-daughter Weston Rosebud (foaled 1975 and RW champion in 1976) and two great-grand-daughters, Weston Mary Ann (foaled 1974, RW champion in 1975*) and Weston Picture (foaled 1978, RW champion in 1979). These RW successes with three yearling fillies is a record which will probably never be broken. Another Crogan daughter, Weston Teresa, went to the Moorfields Stud on the Isle of Wight and her 1972 son, Moorfields Tarragon, by Solway Master Bronze, was RW champion in 1973 after which he was sold at the 1975 Hever Castle Sale. Crogan was sold at the 1970 Fayre Oaks Sale for 850 guineas to Mrs Olive Weston of the Seaholm Stud where he continued to produce many chestnut roans, similar to himself and his sire Coed Coch

BELOW *Weston Mary Ann, RW champion 1975**. *Photo: Helen Sloane.*

Blaen Lleuad; his g-sire on both sides, Criban Victor, was a red roan. Crogan's dam, Chirk Heather, died in 1960 and Crogan was her last foal.

Chirk Caradoc stayed on at Chirk Castle all his life and won championships all over the country but the RW championship always eluded him. His stock were also successful in hand and under saddle. One daughter, Firby Fleur de Lis (foaled 1968 out of Sinton Perl, daughter of Coed Coch Pefr by Coed Coch Blaen Lleuad), won the 127 cm class at the 1973 HOYS, ridden by Ruth Illsley. Chirk Caradoc was the sire of the two full-sisters Nantcol Arbenning (foaled 1971) and Nantcol Cariadus (foaled 1973) out of Llechwedd Annwyl by Kirby Cane Gauntlet. Cariadus was top of the 1982 Chirk Castle Sale when she was sold to the Twylands Stud for 1,100 guineas and Arbennig was dam of the 1986 RW overall champion, Nantcol Katrin. The 1996 HOYS mini-champion, having also won the first-ridden class in 1995, was Nantcol Lady Julia (foaled 1988), another Arbennig daughter but sired by Orielton Aristocrat. Lady Julia then retired from ridden competition but continued her winning ways as a brood mare and was champion at the 1998 P (UK) Show. Caradoc was also sire of Desarbre Hollyhock, g-dam of the four Wortley ponies who all qualified for Wembley under saddle in 2001. Caradoc also stamped his authority on the riding pony world through the part-breds Chirk Cattleya, Catmint and Caviar from the Thoroughbred mare Kitty's Fancy.

The original FS mare of this family was Silver, of unknown parentage, foaled in 1938, who was bought by Lord Kenyon from Mr Cheetham of Whitchurch in 1946 with her foal, Gredington Bronwen (dam of Chirk Heather), at foot. In 1948, for the first time classes were offered at the Shropshire Show for 'Welsh Ponies of Riding Type' and Silver was placed fifth out of ten mares; the comment that I wrote in the catalogue that day for Silver being 'very big'! Despite her unknown ancestry, Silver certainly had a lasting influence on the section B breed. Apart from being g-g-dam of Chirk Caradoc and Crogan, Silver was also dam of Gredington Milfyd who was dam of Gredington Tiwlip (Rotherwood) and Gredington Saffrwm, dam of Gredington Blodyn (Baledon). Gredington Daliad (foaled 1949, sired by Criban Victor), who was RW champion in 1956 and 1957* in the

ABOVE *Cwmwyre Samantha, RW champion 1987*. Photo: Fiona Leadbitter.*

ownership of Miss Marguerite de Beaumont, was another of Silver's daughters; she was full-sister to Milfyd, both being sired by Criban Victor but Daliad was bay and Milfyd was grey although she produced plenty of colour. At Chirk, in addition to producing Chirk Heather, Silver's daughter, Gredington Bronwen also produced Chirk Deborah (foaled 1951, by Craven Debo) who was sold to Ardgrange Stud where she produced Ardgrange Dihafel (sire of 1987 RW champion, Cwmwyre Samantha, and 1996 female champion, Rotherwood Lorrikeet) and Ardgrange Debonair, g-sire of Bayford Just Flea, dam of Cwmwyre Samantha.

Cwmwyre Samantha is a story in herself. She was bought as a yearling in 1979 by Miss Fiona Leadbitter (who had never previously owned a Welsh pony), as the result of an advertisement in *Horse and Hound*, to keep company

ABOVE *John Carter with Thornberry Royal Gem, RW champion 1993. Photo: Wynne Davies.*

to a retired dressage horse. Samantha ended up as the foundation of the Thornberry Stud and overall RW champion in 1987. One daughter, Thornberry Demelza (foaled 1986, sired by Abercrychan Spectator), was overall RW champion in 1989; another daughter, Thornberry Royal Gem (foaled 1982, sired by Keston Royal Occasion), was RW female champion in 1993 and reserve for the HOYS Creber qualifier at the Royal Cornwall. A son, Thornberry Gamekeeper (foaled 1985, sired by Rotherwood State Occasion), was RW reserve male champion in 1986 and 1989 and his full-brother, Thornberry Royal Diplomat (foaled 1987 and exported to Holland in 1996), was 1990 HOYS Creber qualifier at Devon County in 1990 and his son, Millcroft Royal Lustre (foaled1991, out of Paddock Fairy Lustre), was 1993 reserve for the HOYS Creber qualifier at Royal Cornwall.

Finally, to bring this chapter up to date, the overall champion in 2002 and 2003 and reserve in 2004 was Eyarth Windflower (foaled 1997), sired by the veteran Eyarth Celebration out of Eyarth Cordelia by Hilin Caradus who is descended on both sire and dam side from Tetworth Nijinsky. The

LEFT *Richard Miller with Eyarth Windflower. Photo: Eberhard Holin.*

Eyarth Stud was started in 1968 with the purchase of Tanlan Swynol at the Bangor-on-Dee Sale but these bloodlines are no longer at the stud. The next influential purchase was of the filly foal Leighon Glamour at the 1970 FO Sale. Glamour was sired by the very correct little Downland Dandini (sired by Downland Chevalier out of his grand-dam Downland Dragonfly) out of Leighon Butterfly by the good producer Sinton Gyration (sire of Ceulan Largo, a top mare in New Zealand). The next 'cornerstone' in the history of the Eyarth Stud was the purchase of the blue-eyed cream Weston Twiggy (foaled 1976, Weston Chilo x Llysun Blue Mist) who died in 2000 having produced six colts and ten fillies. Windflower therefore has Celebration on both sides as her grand-dam, Eyarth Arabella (foaled 1982), was sired by Celebration out of Weston Twiggy. Windflower also won first prizes at the RW as a two year old and, as a three year old, was reserve youngstock champion to the three-year-old Eyarth Beau Geste whose dam, Eyarth Zsa Zsa, is another daughter of Weston Twiggy.

To summarise the RW section B champions, one notices so many champions from within the youngstock section. Compared with the section A champions, where there were three males and two females, within section B there are 31! These are the yearlings: Verity* (1953), Belvoir Tosca* (1965), Moorfields Tarragon (1973), Cusop Banknote (1974), Weston Mary Ann* (1975), Weston Rosebud (1976), Weston Picture (1979), Linksbury Celebration (1989), Lemonshill Limelight* (1990) and Lemonshill Top Note (2003). The two-year-old champions are Gem (1950), Revel Nance* (1951), Valiant (1955), Gredington Milfyd (1958), Solway Master Bronze* (1961), Cusop Hoity Toity (1965), Springbourne Golden Flute* (1968), Rotherwood Honeysuckle* (1970), Downland Mohawk* (1971), Desarbre Folk Song* (1984), Millcroft Copper Lustre (1987), Wynswood Zara (1990), Cottrell Aurora* (1995) and Griashall Kiwi* (1999). Finally, the three-year-old champions are Criban Victor* (1947), Lydstep Rosetta* (1967), Weston Choice (1972), Rotherwood Royalist (1984), Thornberry Demelza* (1989), Lemonshill Alarch (1997) and Wortley Fisher King (1998).

CHAPTER THREE

The Welsh Pony of Cob-type

PREVIOUSLY regarded as the 'Cinderella' section of the Welsh Stud Book in terms of numbers and popularity, the Welsh pony of Cob-type, the current section C, now enjoys pride of place, having the fastest growth of all sections, and can justifiably claim the greatest improvement in quality within the WSB. RW Show in-hand entries reflect this growth, increasing from one in 1952 to three in 1960, eight in 1965, 31 in 1970, 112 in 1980, 226 in 1990, 287 in 2000 and 334 in 2004 (see p. 215).

The true Welsh pony of Cob-type, ranging from 12 hands to 13 hands 2 in, had been bred in its hundreds within the principality for many centuries and found a ready market for light farm work or harness work throughout Wales, England and even Scotland. From around 1910, wagonloads of Cob-type three-year-old geldings were sent from W. S. Miller's Forest Stud in Brecon to be sold at Lanark Sales in Scotland where they found a ready market for many decades. The frontispiece photograph of the 1969 WPCS *Journal*, taken in 1911, features 27 Cob-type ponies in their light traps, ready to distribute the *Manchester Evening News*. That was 27 for just *one* newspaper in *one* city, a number that could be multiplied five hundred-fold to cover every newspaper in every British city.

Butchers, greengrocers, fishmongers, milk producers and retailers all required these economical and hard-wearing ponies and there was great rivalry between them in terms of smartness of turnout and speed of delivery. Stud cards would boast achievements of speed, with races often held on the public highway.

With the advent of showing, such as the Welsh National Show in 1904, WPCS rules allowed 'alien' animals owned by wealthy aristocrats to be registered within the WSB and thus be eligible to compete under the 'Welsh' banner and win many WPCS silver medals. Just as Hackney horses, such as Viscount Tredegar's Melton Cadet, scooped up WPCS Cob medals at the 1907, 1908 and 1910 WN Shows, Hackney ponies without a jot or a tittle of evidence that a single teaspoonful of Welsh blood flowed in their veins were being awarded the pony medals in the presence of true-type Welsh ponies, often by judges who were the pillars of the WPCS. This unhappy state of affairs within the Cobs was somewhat remedied when, in 1908, HRH George, Prince of Wales offered a trophy for the 'best Welsh Cobs of true **Welsh** type'. In fact, the only winning Cob stallion who could claim the title of 'Welsh' at WN Shows between 1904 and 1911 was High Stepping Gambler II (1909). Similarly, the London Hackney Show champion ponies Tissington Goss, Southworth Swell and Tanrallt Paula spoke for five WPCS pony medals.

Financially, the genuine Welsh pony breeder could not compete against the wealthy invaders and in too many cases it was a case of 'if you can't beat them, join them' so that many germane, valuable bloodlines were lost forever. The stud card for Total (1910) proudly claims that his true-type sire, Klondyke, was sold at the 1905 WN Show for £100, a big sum compared with the annual agricultural wage of £39. The same stud card says that his Hackney ancestors, Ganymede and his sire Danegelt, were sold to T. Mitchell and Sir Walter Gilbey for 2,000 guineas and 5,000 guineas, respectively. Other stud cards implored breeders to safeguard the true Welsh type, e.g. the 1908 stud card of Llew Llwyd read, *'Cedwch I fyny*

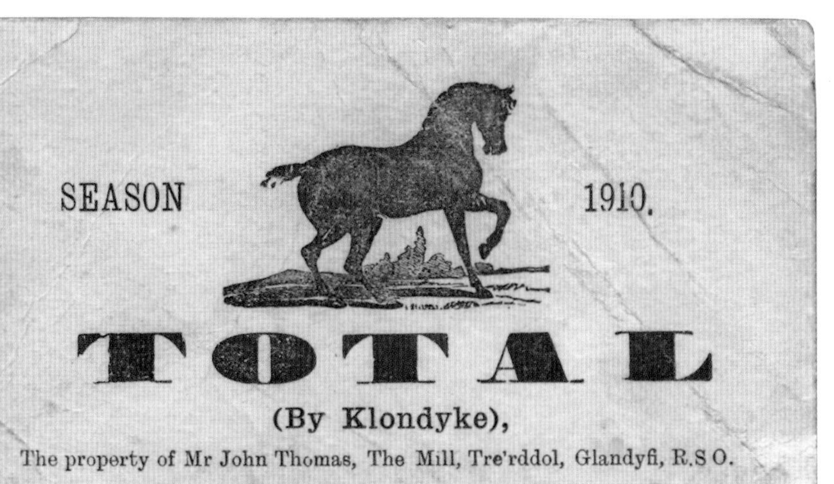

SEASON 1910.

TOTAL

(By Klondyke),

The property of Mr John Thomas, The Mill, Tre'rddol, Glandyfi, R.S O.

Will Serve Mares this Season,

At £1 1s. each Mare, and 2s. 6d the Groom The Groom's Fee to be paid at the first time of Serving.

TOTAL, No. 320 Vol. VIII. W.S B., Reserve at the Aberystwyth Cob Society's Shows 1908-1909, also Highly Commended at the Welsh National Show at Aberystwyth. Foaled in 1904, stands 13-1 h.h., a dark chestnut, free mover, fine action, a model in figure, and proves a good stock getter, on account of the blood and quality he possesses.

Sire—the celebrated and well-known KLONDYKE, No. 12 Vol. 1, W.S.B., the winner of numerous first prizes, including the first in his class at the National Show at Aberystwyth 1905. Afterwards sold to W. S. Miller, Esq., of Forest Lodge, Brecon, for £100.

Dam—A fine Chestnut Pony, winner of several prizes; last heard of was sold for £55 when only 3 years old. Her sire, Lord Ventry, 4386 H.S.B., a good cob, winner of many first prizes; also the Aberystwyth Cob Society's prize.

G. Dam—A very good action pony by Eiddwen Flyer I., No. 2053 H.S.B.

Lord Ventry, by Ganymede, 2076 H.S.B, which was sold to T. Mitchell, Esq., for 2 000 guineas. Ganymede, by Danegelt 176, was sold to Sir Walter Gilbey for 5,000 guineas. Danegelt, by Old Denmark 177, Old Denmark by Sir Charles 768.

Lord Ventry's Dam, Water Rose 4874 H.S.B., by Callis World 1483.

All Mares at owner's risk. All Mares tried by this Horse and afterwards put to another will be charged for.

WILL ATTEND ABERYSTWYTH AND MACHYNLLETH.

LEFT *Total: stud card for 1910.*

yr Hen Ach Gymreig' which translates as 'Keep up the Old Welsh Lineage'.

In 1904, the first WN Show at Aberystwyth got off to a good start with Klondyke winning the Welsh Cob-type stallion class and Llwyn Snowdrop heading the females and winning the WPCS medal. Klondyke

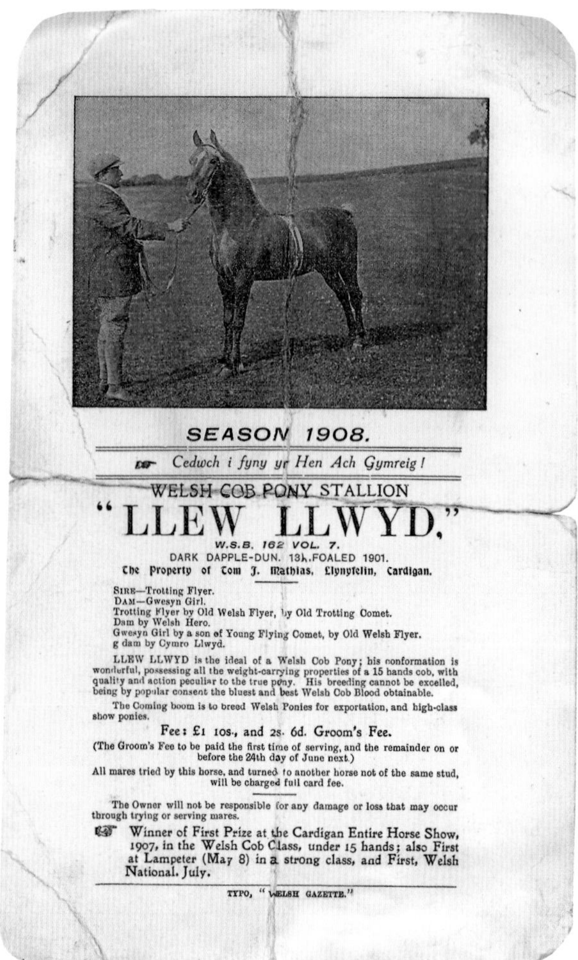

SEASON 1908.

Cedwch i fyny yr Hen Ach Gymreig!

WELSH COB PONY STALLION

"LLEW LLWYD,"

W.S.B. 162 VOL. 7.

DARK DAPPLE-DUN. 13h. FOALED 1901.

The Property of Tom J. Mathias, Llynyfelin, Cardigan.

SIRE—Trotting Flyer.
DAM—Gwesyn Girl.
Trotting Flyer by Old Welsh Flyer, by Old Trotting Comet.
Dam by Welsh Hero.
Gwesyn Girl by a son of Young Flying Comet, by Old Welsh Flyer.
g dam by Cymro Llwyd.

LLEW LLWYD is the ideal of a Welsh Cob Pony; his conformation is wonderful, possessing all the weight-carrying properties of a 15 hands cob, with quality and action peculiar to the true pony. His breeding cannot be excelled, being by popular consent the bluest and best Welsh Cob Blood obtainable.

The Coming boom is to breed Welsh Ponies for exportation, and high-class show ponies.

Fee: £1 10s., and 2s. 6d. Groom's Fee.

(The Groom's Fee to be paid the first time of serving, and the remainder on or before the 24th day of June next.)

All mares tried by this horse, and turned to another horse not of the same stud, will be charged full card fee.

The Owner will not be responsible for any damage or loss that may occur through trying or serving mares.

Winner of First Prize at the Cardigan Entire Horse Show, 1907, in the Welsh Cob Class, under 15 hands; also First at Lampeter (May 8) in a strong class, and First, Welsh National. July.

TYPO, "WELSH GAZETTE."

ABOVE *Llew Llwyd: stud card for 1908. Courtesy of D. Rowlands Harris.*

ABOVE RIGHT *Klondyke, foaled in 1894.*

BOTTOM RIGHT *Llwyn Snowdrop, winning mare WN shows 1904*, 1905 and 1907*.*

(registered in WSB volume 1) was chestnut with a star and off-hind white fetlock, 13 hands in height, foaled in 1894 and bred by John Thomas, Tre'rddol, whose sister, Jane Williams of Clettwr Hall, was the mother of my grandfather, L. O. Williams, one of the founder members of the WPCS and exhibitor of several Cobs, Hackneys and Shires at the 1904 show. It will be seen from his pedigree that Klondyke was 'Welsh through and through', with many avenues going back to Eiddwen Flyer (foaled 1877), Old Welsh Flyer (foaled 1861), Old Trotting Comet (foaled 1836) and Cymro Llwyd (foaled around 1850). The fact that these ancestors bear

<table>
<tr><td rowspan="16">(a) Winner of Trotting prizes :
1st, Talybont, 1895
2nd in 1896 & 1897,
1st in 1898, &c.,
1st Towyn, 1903
1st Dolgelly, 1904,
1st Machynlleth 1904.

(b) v. vol. ii., ped. v., p. lvi.

(c) Property of Morgan Davies, Gors., Aberystwith

W.S.B. 12
ch. 13.0
KLONDYKE
f. 1894.
Owner, Mr. John Thomas, Tre'rddol, Glandovey, Cardiganshire.
Prizes :
1st, Talybont, 1896
1st, " 1897
1st Machynlleth (1897)
2nd, Machynlleth 1898-99, 1900-01</td><td rowspan="8">YOUNG MESSENGER</td><td rowspan="4">W.S.B. 10
(b) EIDDWEN FLYER II.
ch. 13.0
f. 1888</td><td rowspan="2">H.S.B. 2053
EIDDWEN FLYER I. (b)
f.1877</td><td>H.S.B. 856
OLD WELSH FLYER
by OLD TROTTING COMET 834 f.1836</td></tr>
<tr><td>d. by WELSH JACK, by CYMRO LLWYD.</td></tr>
<tr><td rowspan="2">BLACK BESS</td><td>H.S.B. 1022
KING JACK
by WONDERFUL COMET H.S.B. (1225)</td></tr>
<tr><td>—d—</td></tr>
<tr><td rowspan="4"></td><td rowspan="2">H.S.B. 1022
(c) KING JACK</td><td>WONDERFUL COMET H.S.B. (1225) by OLD COMET H.S.B. (931) f.1845</td></tr>
<tr><td>d. by EXFRESS H.S.B. (964)</td></tr>
<tr><td rowspan="2"></td><td></td></tr>
<tr><td></td></tr>
<tr><td rowspan="8">W.S.B 128
LADY EIDDWEN (a)</td><td rowspan="4">H.S.B. 2053
ch. 14.1
(b) EIDDWEN FLYER I.
f. 1880</td><td rowspan="2">H.S.B. 856
OLD WELSH FLYER
br. 14.3.
f. 1861</td><td>OLD TROTTING COMET H.S.B. (834)</td></tr>
<tr><td>TROTTING NANCY, by CYMRO LLWYD</td></tr>
<tr><td rowspan="2">—d—</td><td>WELSH JACK, by CYMRO LLWYD</td></tr>
<tr><td></td></tr>
<tr><td rowspan="4">LIONESS
—d—</td><td rowspan="2">DANDYLION</td><td>TOM THUMB</td></tr>
<tr><td>d. A Champion Trotting Pony</td></tr>
<tr><td rowspan="2"></td><td></td></tr>
<tr><td></td></tr>
</table>

ABOVE *Klondyke: pedigree.*

registration numbers within the Hackney Stud Book does not infer that they were Hackneys, they were merely registered in the HSB (volume 1 of which appeared in 1884) until the WSB came into being in 1901. In 1905 there were two classes for Welsh stallions of this height, class 21 for stallions from 12 to 13 hands and class 22 (with prize money given by the WPCS) for stallions between 12 hands 2 in and 13 hands 2 in. Klondyke won class 21 and was bought by W. S. Miller, Forest Lodge for £100 and re-registered as Forest Klondyke in volume 8 of the WSB. Klondyke sired dozens of good strong Forest ponies and was eventually sold back to

ABOVE *Eiddwen Flyer II, foaled in 1888.*

Cardiganshire, to the Meiarth Stud of David Lloyd. Marshall Dugdale won class 22 with Llwyn True Blue, a bay stallion, foaled in 1900, sired by the Hackney Cassius. The Llwyn Stud also won the mare class in 1904, 1905 and 1907 with Llwyn Snowdrop.

Klondyke was sired by Young Messenger (known locally as 'Cardi Mawr') who, in turn, was sired by Eiddwen Flyer II, a 13 hand chestnut, foaled in 1888 and usually referred to as 'Tyreithin' (after his owner, Thomas Evans, Tyreithin, Bronant) who was himself a son of the original Eiddwen Flyer. In the 1963 WPCS *Journal* Mr Alfred Williams, Blaentwrch wrote in glowing terms of Eiddwen Flyer II: 'his influence on the breed must, indeed, have been unparalleled. His good progeny were very much in the forefront throughout his stud period and the fine qualities transmitted by him were much appreciated by breeders for decades to come'. Great praise indeed from someone who should know. Mr Williams bred leading ponies of Cob-type from the start of the WPCS until his dispersal sale in 1955, judged them at RW Shows in 1953, 1968 and 1973, and also won the championships in 1947 with Welsh Patriot and in 1949 with Welsh Echo. Eiddwen Flyer II ended his days amongst all the famous champions at Dinarth Hall where the photograph was taken.

Possibly the most influential of the progeny of Eiddwen Flyer II was Eiddwen Flyer III, foaled in 1895 and owned by Tom Parry, Cross Inn, Llandysul, Professor of Agriculture at the University College of Wales, Aberystwyth. Not only did Eiddwen Flyer III do a great job for the Cob-type ponies, he was also g-sire of the section A trump cards Ness Thistle and Ness Sunflower.

Llwyn Snowdrop was light grey, foaled in 1898, sired by the Hackney Winnal George out of a Welsh mare by Eiddwen Flyer. It was at the1905 WN Show that Marshall Dugdale bought the strawberry roan mare Florence by Eiddwen Flyer III and her colt foal by Prince of Cardiff quoted

WELSH MOUNTAIN PONY STALLION

(Winner of Second Prize Royal Show. Cardiff, 1901).

Eiddwen Flyer III.

(W.P.C S. No............)

Colour: Blue Roan. Height 12·2. Foaled 1896.

SIRE: EIDDWEN FLYER II. by EIDDWEN FLYER by WELSH FLYER (856), the celebrated one-eyed Cardi Trotting Cob.

DAM: WELSH MOUNTAIN PONY by CYMRO LLWYD (out of the famous TROTTING NANCY), the "Denmark" (177) of Welsh Ponies.

PRESS NOTICES.

LIVE STOCK JOURNAL, 28th June, 1901.

WELSH MOUNTAIN PONIES, CARDIFF ROYAL SHOW.

"Messrs. Parry and Jones coming second with the blue-roan Eiddwen "Flyer III. by Eiddwen Flyer II., a very sweet-headed five-year-old, with lots "of substance and big quarters, rather of the harness type."

FARMER & STOCKBREEDER YEAR BOOK, 1902.

PONIES IN 1901. (Royal Show, Cardiff.)

"The real Welsh Classes were very good as respects the few leading "specimens. Messrs Parry and Jones's Eiddwen Flyer III., a blue-roan of "quite remarkable build, substance and action, and a hard one to beat, was "placed second."

JOURNAL OF THE ROYAL AGRICULTURAL SOCIETY.

Vol. 62. 1901.

WELSH MOUNTAIN PONIES.

"This was a good class. The Second Prize Pony (Eiddwen Flyer III.) was "of great merit, but of rather a stronger character" (than Starlight).

SERVICE FEE (Tenant Farmers) - ONE GUINEA.

Grass Accommodation for Mares, 2/6 per month.

TELEGRAPHIC ADDRESS—PARRY,

NEUADD, CROSS-INN,

LLANDYSSUL.

LEFT *Eiddwen Flyer III: stud card for 1902.*

in the catalogue (class 28) as 'For Sale mare and foal £100'. The foal was later registered as Llwyn Tyrant, sire of Revolt who sired Coed Coch Glyndwr, the leading section A stallion of the second quartile.

W. S. Miller judged at the 1906 WN Show (again at Aberystwyth) and placed the chestnut Golden Gleam (owned by J. M. Phillips, Treriffith, Cardigan) above Llwyn True Blue and the fashionable Hackney Berkeley George in the stallion class. Golden Gleam was of unregistered parentage but his grand-dam, Cymraes, was by Cardigan Comet II. Golden Gleam earns his place in history by being g-sire of Teify Pride, the g-dam of Teify Brightlight II, eight-times RW champion during 1953–64. A local mare with the rather unglamorous name of Bess, from Edward Jones, Gwarcwmucha, won her 12-strong class, beating another local mare, Lively Girl owned by W. R. Jones, Bryngwynmawr, with Mathrafal Sensation from Meyrick Jones third, followed by Evan Jones with Myfanwy, dam of the champion section A Greylight, and Charles Le Brun Powell (nephew of show secretary Sir Lewes Loveden Pryse) was fifth with Tregaron Lady Trustful who was also offered for sale in the catalogue that day at £100.

RIGHT *Lloyd Jones with Teifi Brightlight II, RW champion 1953*, 1955*, 1956, 1958*, 1960*, 1961, 1962*, 1964*. Photo: Wynne Davies.*

WPCS secretary J. R. Bache is to be congratulated for awarding the top prizes to good Welsh types Llew Llwyd and Llwyn Snowdrop in 1907. However he lost this admiration when he judged again in 1910 and gave the two red cards to the champion Hackney ponies Southworth Swell and Tanrallt Paula! The dun Llew Llwyd was foaled in 1901, sired by Trotting Flyer out of Gwesyn Girl by a son of Young Flying Comet out of a daughter of Cymro Llwyd. Llew Llwyd had been shown by his breeder, Hugh Davies of Abergwesyn, at the 1905 show in the aforementioned class 21 (won by Klondyke) under the name of Gwesyn Flyer and was registered in volume 3, WSB. He is quoted in the catalogue as 'price moderate' and was bought at the show by Thomas John Jones of Dinarth Hall who re-registered him in volume 5 as Llew Llwyd and sold him in 1906 to Tom J. Mathias who exhibited him at the 1908 show. Mr Mathias describes him on the stud card thus: 'His breeding cannot be excelled, being by popular consent the bluest and best Welsh Cob blood obtainable'. Certainly Llew Llwyd deserves his place in any Welsh pony history and his name will crop up again as g-sire of the 1936 champion, Vrondolay Chess, and sire of Clettwr Polly (foaled in 1907), dam of the Menai foundation mare Menai

LEFT *Peter Jones with Menai Lady Conspicuous, RW champion 1999. Photo: Eberhard Holin.*

Queen Bess (foaled in 1914) who is g-g-g-g-g-dam of the 1999 RW champion, Menai Lady Conspicuous.

The judge at the 1908 show was William Foster of Mel Valley, one of the foremost Hackney breeders of his day, who was not on the WPCS panel of judges and Hackney exhibitors turned up in hoards and swept the board! Albert Humphreys of Gainsborough won the stallion class with the London Hackney Show winner Tissington Goss, bred by Sir Gilbert Greenall of Warrington who bred some 200 foals every year, half of them horses under the Terrington prefix, the other half ponies under the Tissington prefix. Llew Llwyd was third in this class, with the four-year-old Total, owned and bred by John Thomas and sired by Klondyke, standing fifth. In 1909, Total sired the 1913 and 1914 champion, Temptation, and in 1910 he sired Seren Ceulan with whom my father won the female championship in 1926 and overall in 1928. Total was exported to Laurie Wilson of New Zealand in 1911. William Foster's choice for female honours was another Hackney, Naughty Naiad by Berkeley Model;

RIGHT *E.S. Davies with Seren Ceulan, RW champion 1926, 1928*. Photo: G. H. Parsons.*

she had been bought for 240 guineas as a yearling. Llwyn Snowdrop was fifth to four Hackneys.

The Hackney pony stallions Little Fire, Southworth Swell and Bobby Dazzler won their classes in 1909, 1910 and 1911 and the Hackney pony mare Tanrallt Paula, bred by Sir Gilbert Greenall, won three successive WPCS medals in those years. Their particulars and photographs are not included in this book as they have had absolutely no influence on the breed and were only registered in the WSB to enable them to compete for WPCS awards. My father would escape from London at every opportunity to stay with his aunt at Talybont where he spent all his spare time at Tanrallt Stud and was allowed to show the Tanrallt 'second string', such as Tanrallt Firegirl who was second to Paula, shown by stud groom Ted Sowerby in 1911. Tanrallt Paula could hold her own in any company throughout Britain and the Tanrallt stables were covered with impressive prize cards which, unfortunately, had deteriorated beyond rescue when my sister and brother-in-law bought the Tanrallt farm (where my nephew now lives) in 1950.

Having sold Greylight for 1,000 guineas to Australia the previous year, Evan Jones of Manoravon still excelled himself at the 1912 show in Swansea by winning the Cob stallion class and the Prince of Wales cup with Manoravon Flyer, the pony of Cob-type stallion class with Kismet and the Mountain pony stallion class with Dewi Stone. Kismet had the Welsh parents Towyvale Fashion and Betty Ddu. The winning mare, Lily of the Valley from Blackwood, Monmouthshire, was also of Welsh parentage, sired by Evolve who was a popular sire in south-east Wales, out of Ruby by Trotting Flyer and g-dam Maud by Caradog.

The chestnut stallion Temptation, foaled in 1909, won his class in 1913 at Porthmadoc for his owner/breeder John Thomas; his sire, Total, and dam, Lady Goldyke, were both sired by Klondyke. John Thomas sold Temptation at the Wrexham Sales to Marshall Dugdale of Llwyn for whom he won again in 1914 and he was then sold to W. H. Millspaugh of Ohio, USA in 1915. Second to Temptation in 1913 was the bay Lord Grip, foaled in 1904 and owned and bred by H. Williams, Garnuchaf, Bethania. Lord Grip was another true Welshman, sired by Trotting Flyer out of Nance by

RIGHT *Queenie, RW champion 1947, 1949, 1950*, 1951*, 1952*, 1957*, 1961*.*

Cardigan Flyer, g-dam by King Jack I. With Total and Klondyke, Lord Grip is one of the stallions remembered by Dafydd Edwardes in his article 'The Cob Pony' in the 1969 WPCS *Journal*. The influence of Lord Grip on the breed came into prominence 40 years later when his grand-daughter, Queenie, won seven RW championships.

The three mares competing in 1913 were local to the show site at Porthmadoc, William Hughes of Pwllheli winning with Rosey who is described in the catalogue as 'Hackney pony', Miss Eurgain Lort of Castellmai second with the Welsh Deryn Cochddu (the same exhibitor winning the Mountain pony stallion class with the four-year-old Revolt, sire of Coed Coch Glyndwr) and third was Brynhir Georgina, a piebald owned by Walter Glynn of Brynhir and the g-dam of Brynhir Black Star, dam of Tanybwlch Berwyn.

The 1914 show was held at Newport and another local winner won the mare class. This was H. G. Jenks of the Carpenters Arms, Rumney, whose son, Trevor Jenks, was a leading show jumper after the second war. Mr

ABOVE *Baedeker, RW champion 1926*. Photo: G. H. Parsons.*

Jenks's mare was Pinderfields Megania, sired by King Flyer (ceffyl Morgan y Gors), a 13 hands 2in stallion not to be confused with the 15 hands 2 in Mathrafal stallion King Flyer (cel Glandulais), Prince of Wales cup winner in 1913 and 1914.

When the show got under way again in 1922 at Wrexham after the interim of the war years, the judge was again J. R. Bache (secretary of the WPCS from 1909 to 1928), judging for the third time within nine shows, and he was to officiate again in 1929! The WPCS had tightened up its rules and, fortunately, the pure Hackneys stayed away. Dinarth Hall won the stallion class with Baedeker who was predominantly 'Hackney pony' bred with a dash of 'Welsh' but deserves his place in Welsh pony history as the pedigrees of many of our current champions contain his name. Baedeker was bred by Miss Eurgain Lort of Castellmai in 1910 and sold at her 1913 sale (lot 30) where lot 34 was Revolt the sire of Coed Coch Glyndwr. Baedeker was sired by Traveller's Joy, a full-brother to Sir Horry (sold to the USA) and Bobby Dazzler (the 1911 RW champion). In 1909, Traveller's Joy had been sold for 430 guineas to Australian Anthony Hordern (who then bought Greylight for 1,000 guineass in 1911). Baedeker was bought at the 1913 sale by Mrs Philip Hunloke of Wingerworth Hall, Chesterfield, Derbyshire for whom he won second prize to Penuwch Cymro Bach at the 1919 RASE Show at Cardiff. Sylvia Hunloke, who bred her first Welsh pony, Wingerworth Sunset (WSB volume 16), in 1902, brought a large show string from Derby to the RASE Show at Cardiff and won other prizes with a Suffolk stallion, three children's riding ponies ridden by her daughters, Alma and Joan, the Welsh section A filly Grove Dora and two hunters which she rode herself. Philip Hunloke, the renowned yachtsman to King George V, who sailed *Britannia* in all her races, was knighted in 1922 and Lady Hunloke continued to breed Welsh ponies under the

ABOVE LEFT *Myrtle Rosina, RW champion 1929.*

ABOVE RIGHT *Synod William, RW champion 1971*, 1977*, 1980*, 1981*. Photo: Idris Aeron.*

Wingerworth prefix, including the 1923 RW champion, Wingerworth Eiddwen. Joan (Mrs Philip Fleming who was chairman of the Show Hack, Cob and Riding Horse Association for a record 30 years, 1955–85) continued the Wingerworth prefix for her Welsh and Shetland ponies from Barton Abbey, Oxfordshire until her death in 1992. Baedeker reappeared at the 1926 RW Show, in the ownership of Tom James, to win the championship from my father with Seren Ceulan. Baedeker was greatly admired by Alfred Williams of Blaentwrch who, in 1924, bred Blaentwrch Firelight by him; Firelight is the dam of Lady Cyrus, g-g-dam of the section B Downland Chevalier. Baedeker is also the sire of Myrtle Rosina, RW champion in 1929 and g-g-dam of Synod William, four times RW champion between 1971 and 1981.

To return to 1922: Major Dugdale won both top mare awards with Llwyn Coralie by Llwyn Cymro and Llwyn Tempter by Temptation. Coralie competed in this class for the next few years; Tempter was mainly put to Mountain pony sires and was a very successful breeder, including Llwyn Satan (by Kilhendre Celtic Silverlight) the 1926 RW section A champion who was g-sire of Coed Coch Glyndwr on his dam's side. Miss Beryl Chapman of the Kilhendre Celtic Stud was third with the strangely named Dilys Dilys, a daughter of Klondyke and bred by David Jenkins (Caran) of Welsh Black cattle fame.

Mr Tom James, Myrtle Hill judged at Welshpool in 1923 and Lord Howard de Walden of Chirk Castle won the championship with the stallion Wingerworth Eiddwen, a son of Baedeker, from my grandfather L. O. Williams with the dun Cream Bun whose dam, Aeronwen Ceulan, was also dam of my father's Seren Ceulan. Cream Bun was then sold to Dinarth Hall and won the RW championship for them in 1925. The winning mare in 1923 was Thomas Davies's Cilwen Lady Lilian (Trotting Jack x Myrtle Lady Trustful) who was then bought by the judge and, put to Baedeker, in 1925 produced Myrtle Rosina the 1929 RW champion. Cilwen Lady Lilian was later bought by Dinarth Hall and was again female champion in 1930, 1932 and 1934 (the latter twice to Ceulan Comet) and overall champion in 1933. The Dinarth Hall show string of Ceulan Comet, his son Dinarth Comet and Cilwen Lady Lilian accounted for a total of eight RW Show championships.

ABOVE *Tom Thomas with Cilwen Lady Lilian, RW champion 1923, 1930*, 1932, 1933*, 1934.*

There were very few true Welsh ponies of Cob-type at the 1924 RW Show. The stallion winner and champion was Howell Richards's Criban Shot who was registered in the WSB volume XXIV section A part II, and his breeding was Mountain pony with the Richards's Criban, Ystrad and Vaynor prefixes for their three hills or the Thomas's Pentre prefix from the adjoining hill back for eight generations apart from Klondyke being a g-g-sire on the dam's side. Criban Shot (foaled 1920) is best known as the sire of Criban Socks (foaled 1926), still regarded as the epitome of the Welsh Mountain pony. The winning mare, Teify Pride, was a true Welsh pony of Cob-type. Sired by the highly successful Ceitho Welsh Comet, her dam was Camddwr Pride III by the 1906 champion Golden Gleam and the g-dam was Camddwr Pride II by Evolution. The Show President, Lord Davies, MP, MFH, offered £200 prize money for a 'County Championship Competition' for national breeds and Cardiganshire won this competition for Welsh Ponies of Cob-type with 195 points from Glamorgan with 180.

The Cardiganshire group consisted of winning yearling colt, Ormond Comet owned by S. O. Davies of Lampeter; Penlan Pride (daughter of Teify Pride), winning two-year-old filly, owned by John Morgan of Abermeurig; Teify Pride, owned by Peter Davies of Llanio Road; and the second-prize mare, Fronlas Model,owned by Bodvel Morgan of Talybont.

By 1925, my grandfather had sold Cream Bun (second stallion in 1923) to Dinarth Hall where he was first and champion from Royal Welsh Jack, making the first of his six RW appearances; both stallions were sired by Llanio Trotting Comet. Blaentwrch Welsh Challenger, son of the aforementioned Blaentwrch Firefly, was third and the well-known Bethania stallion, Eiddwen Gleam, was fourth. The winning mare was the three-year-old Kerry Queen by Mathrafal Brenin

ABOVE *Cardiganshire winning County Group of Welsh ponies, RW 1925. From left: Seren Ceulan, Kerry Queen, Ormond Welsh Comet and Ormond Satisfaction. Photo: W. H. Bustin.*

OPPOSITE TOP *Cardiganshire winning County Group of Welsh ponies, RW 1924. From left: Ormond Comet, Penlan Pride, Teify Pride and Fronlas Model.*

OPPOSITE BOTTOM *D. J. Jenkins with Royal Welsh Jack, RW champion 1928, 1929*, 1930. Photo: G. H. Parsons.*

and my father's Seren Ceulan (who had won a WPCS medal at various shows every year since 1916), on her RW debut, was second, with Teify Pride third and Pride's daughter, Meurig Pride, fourth. Cardiganshire again won the County Group Competition with Seren Ceulan, Kerry Queen, Ormond Welsh Comet and Ormond Satisfaction (yearling).

Dinarth Hall had sold Baedeker to Tom James and he had his revenge at the 1926 show by beating Cream Bun with Royal Welsh Jack third. Seren Ceulan, with her colt foal Ceulan Comet at foot, won the mare class and her first RW WPCS medal from Teify Pride with Dinarth Hall's Kittiwake by Revolt third.

The 1927 classes were the strongest seen for many a year, starting with six stallions, all of them winners somewhere or other. Cefncoch Country Swell won on his RW debut from the former youngstock winner Ormond Welsh Comet, another RW newcomer, Paith Flyer II, was third, followed by Baedeker who was fourth, Mab-y-Brenin (owned by my grandfather and later to become sire of the famous section D RW champion Mathrafal) was fifth and Royal Welsh Jack was sixth. Kerry Queen won the mare class for the second time from the grey Flemish Cymraes by Ceitho Welsh Comet, then Cilwen Lady Lilian, Teify Pride and Brynhir Lightning by Bleddfa Shooting Star. The two-year-old filly Myrtle Rosina won the first of her many RW triumphs.

The mare class at the 1928 show turned out to be a 'battle of the giants', with five former winners present, headed by Seren Ceulan in her proudest moment, followed by the Bryncipill sisters, Flemish Cymraes and Flemish Eiddwen, daughters of Flemish Sunshine by Klondyke, then Cilwen Lady Lilian, Kerry Queen and Dinarth Maid. Royal Welsh Jack won the stallion class from the cream Wild Buck. In addition to two WPCS medals (one for champion male and one for female), in those days Prince of Wales medals were given to the champion exhibits of Welsh Ponies and Cobs, cattle, sheep and pigs, so Seren Ceulan won another two medals that day.

BELOW *Welsh pony brood mare class, RW 1928. (from left) Seren Ceulan, Flemish Cymraes and Flemish Eiddwen. Photo: G. H. Parsons.*

Former WPCS secretary J. R. Bache judged for the fourth time at Cardiff in 1929. David Jenkins, Ffrwdwenith, Aberporth, owner of Royal Welsh Jack, wrote to my father on 7 June offering the stallion (still only 11 years old) for sale at the surprisingly low figure of £15 and by the show, in August, he was owned by Tom James and won the £10 first prize and the two silver championship medals. Tom James also won the mare class with Myrtle Rosina, with Flemish Cymraes placed second.

Ponies of Cob-type or Riding-type could compete in the same classes at the 1930 show at Caernarfon and Royal Welsh Jack won another £10 and WPCS medal to more than repay his purchase price of £15 the previous year. Ceulan Comet appeared at the RW for the first time since his foal days and was second, and grandfather's Mab-y-Brenin was third, with the riding-type Tanybwlch Berwyn fourth. Cilwen Lady Lilian won the mare class and the two medals for Dinarth Hall from her daughter, Myrtle Rosina, and Teify Pride.

LEFT *Tom Thomas with Ceulan Comet, RW champion 1931*, 1932*, 1933 and 1934*, after which he was exported to Australia. Photo: G. H. Parsons.*

1931 saw the start of the Ceulan Comet supremacy; Mr Jones of Dinarth Hall awarded him the championship and bought him at the show and he won another three consecutive male championships for Dinarth Hall, twice overall and reserve overall to Cilwen Lady Lilian in 1933, who was also champion four times for Dinarth Hall. At the 1934 show Ceulan Comet was sold to Australian Anthony Hordern and his daughter, Lady Creswick, attributes the good bone and movement in her stud 70 years later to the influence of Ceulan Comet. In 1934, stallions of Cob-type and Riding type competed in the same class but the mares were separated. However, in those economically depressed times the numbers registered in the WSB and competing at shows reached an all-time low. All three Cob-type females were owned by Dinarth Hall and they comprised Cilwen Lady Lilian, her four-year-old daughter, Dinarth Dora by Master Shot, and her three-year-old daughter, Dinarth Lady Eiddwen by Mathrafal Eiddwen.

RIGHT *David Davies with Croten Ddu O Tremain, RW champion 1935. Photo: G. H. Parsons.*

The 1935 Cob-type mare class brought forth a breath of fresh air in the appearance of a newcomer, the eleven-year-old Croten Ddu o Tremain. As her owners/breeders, the Davies family of Blaenpistyll, had been such well-established show exhibitors since the start of the WPCS, one wonders why Croten Ddu had not graced a show ring earlier in life and, afterwards, why she did not appear in later life. Croten Ddu was sired by Sant Deinol out of Pistyll Girlie (foaled 1909) by Cardigan Meteor (bred at Blaenpistyll in 1892) out of Puss by Trotting Briton. The other mares were Peter Davies's Dewi Pride (dam of Teifi Brightlight II) and Myrtle Rosina, in the ownership of Tom Wood-Jones, and Rosina's daughter, Heather, whom Mr Wood-Jones had bred in 1932 by Royal Welsh Jack. The stallion class was cancelled due to insufficient entries.

In 1936, the situation with the pony of Cob-type was critical which resulted in a revision of the schedule, the stallion class was cancelled in favour of a youngstock class for ponies of Riding-type, and only two of the three entered Cob-type mares turned up. The Dinarth Hall string was absent due to their owner judging sections A and D and Mr Llewellyn Richards judged the sections B and C. The winner was Vrondolay Chess, an FS mare by Myrtle Welsh Flyer out of Blodwen by the 1907 champion Llew Llwyd, and the other was a daughter of the 1927 champion, Cefncoch Country Swell, Hendre Betsan out of the Northwood family's foundation mare, Hendre Gwen (foaled 1923), whose descendants are still at the stud 80 years later.

Only one mare who could truly claim to be of Cob-type was present at Newport in 1937 but she became very important in the history of the breed. This was Alfred Williams's Welsh Homage, foaled in 1934, sired by Ceitho Welsh Comet out of Blaentwrch Firefly, a daughter of Bleddfa Shooting Star. Two years later, Welsh Homage produced Welsh Patriot, one of only two Cob-type stallions in the world after the war.

There was no RW Show in 1938 due to the RASE being held at Cardiff where extra classes were laid on for the Welsh breeds. Three Cob-type mares were entered and Captain Howson placed them in the order of Myrtle Rosina (now owned by Joseph Lewis; she had her filly foal Dyffryn

Rosina at foot), Dewi Pride and Welsh Homage. Dewi Pride's two-year-old son by Bowdler Brightlight was placed third in the youngstock class of Riding-type; he was named Teify Brightlight. Her famous son Teify Brightlight II was born 13 years later.

Joseph Lewis was one of only two Cob-type exhibitors in 1939, winning with Myrtle Rosina and second with Rosina's grey five-year-old daughter, Dyffryn Moonlight by Bowdler Brightlight, the only other entry being Seren Cwnlle by Ceitho Welsh Comet.

When the RW Show started again after the war in 1947, the Welsh ponies of Cob-type were allocated two classes, but by 1952 this was reduced to one class in with the Cobs and they could muster only one entry (Queenie). In 1957 there was still only one class but the Welsh ponies of Cob-type were allocated a separate section. This was increased to two classes (separate male and female) in 1961 and entries increased to nine which, by 1967, had increased to 11 which warranted three classes and entries responded with a total of 25 in 1968. This gave great encouragement to the organisers who allocated four classes in 1969, plus a progeny competition (which continued until 2002). The increase in entries continued, so five classes were offered in 1973 and attracted 51 entries (seven stallions, 11 mares, seven foals, 15 young fillies and 11 colts). This was altered to seven classes the following year, with colts and fillies being split, and this remained until 1984 when a barren mare class was introduced and entries had now reached 110. The next change was in 1989 when the mares were divided into novice and open, with the wording changed to '4– 7 years' and 'eight years old and over' in 1996 and separate classes provided for two year olds and three year olds, bringing the situation up to the current total of 11 classes.

Greater emphasis has been given in this chapter to some individuals whose bloodlines are responsible for the survival of the breed through the years of the Second World War. These include Welsh Homage, dam of the 1947 RW champion, Welsh Patriot; Teify Pride, g-dam of Teify Brightlight II , eight times champion from 1953 to 1964, and Lord Grip, g-sire of Queenie, champion seven times from 1947 to 1961. Queenie was dam of

ABOVE LEFT *Cerdin Jones with Gerynant Rosina.*

ABOVE RIGHT *Lyn Cwmcoed, RW champion 1966*, 1967*, 1968, 1969*, 1970*, 1972, 1973, 1974.*

LEFT *Miss Amanda Jones with Lili Cwmcoed, RW champion 1966, 1968*, 1969, 1973*. Photo: Ceri Davies.*

the 1967 and 1970 champion, Brondesbury Welsh Maid, the 1950 champion, Gwenlli Valiant, and Gwenlli Merry Boy, sire of the 1971 champion, Gwynau Dolly. Finally, and most importantly, Dyffryn Rosina, dam of Gerynant Rosina (dam of Synod William) and Dyffryn Rosina, is also dam of Piercefield Lady Lilian, dam of the eight-times champion, Lyn Cwmcoed, and the four-times champion, Lili Cwmcoed, and g-dam of the 1959 and 1962 champion, Pride of the Prairie, who is dam of the 1984 champion, Gwylfa Joyce.

It is surprising, almost uncanny, that of the total of 5,748 section C in-hand entries at the RW Shows from 1947 to 2003, those which have reached the greatest heights are 'carry overs' from the few big names which survived the war years.

There were only two or three section C exhibits at the RW Show annually from 1947 to 1960 and to increase the number of animals within this section, several section A mares were put to Cob stallions. Examples of RW champions produced in this way are the 1974 and 1975 champion, Cefn Moonlight (foaled in 1969) (Maylord Starlight x Cefn Princess by Ceulan Revelry), the 1977 and 1978 champion, Lleucu Queen (foaled in 1968) (Brenin Dafydd x Derwen Chess by Derwen Ike), the 1982 champion, Gurrey Brenhines (foaled in 1980) (Nebo Daniel x Gurrey Tulip by Grovehill Crusader), the five-times champion, Nebo Bouncer (foaled in 1981)

ABOVE *Colin Davies with Cefn Moonlight, RW champion 1974*, 1975*. Photo: Photonews.*

RIGHT *Owen Jones with Nebo Bouncer, RW champion 1985*, 1986*, 1988*, 1993*, 1997. Photo: Wynne Davies.*

ABOVE *Mrs Lisa Reed with Tyngwndwn Moonlight, RW champion 1987, 1989. Photo: Wynne Davies.*

(Nebo Brenin x Nebo Shani Lwyd by Bengad Snapdragon), and his three-quarter sister, Tyngwndwn Moonlight (Nebo Brenin x Nebo Shani, dam of Nebo Shani Lwyd), who was youngstock champion in 1983 and champion in 1987 and 1989.

Cefn Moonlight's daughter, Cefn Moonraise (foaled 1975, by Lyn Cwmcoed), was champion in 1981 and her photograph graced the front cover of that issue of *Horse and Hound*. Another daughter, Cefn Moonlady (foaled 1982, again sired by Lyn Cwmcoed), won her class in 1987 and she is dam of Popsters Loaded Weapon, the leading yearling of 1999.

Lleucu Queen was dam of the 1992 champion, Fronarth Red Rose (by Synod Roger), who had an illustrious career in youngstock classes. Her early death was a great loss to the breed.

Nebo Bouncer, foaled in 1981, won five RW championships between 1985 and 1997 and was HOYS Lloyds Bank qualifier at the 1988 RW Show which is a brilliant record for a foal whose dam died when he was only six

ABOVE LEFT *Owen Jones with Hengwys Tywysog, RW champion 1996. Photo: Bleddyn Pugh.*

ABOVE RIGHT *Dewi Jones and judge Colin Davies with Tremymor Sportsman, RW champion 2004*. Photo: Wynne Davies.*

BELOW *Wayne Groucott with Hafodyrynys Cariad, RW champion 2004. Photo: Sporting Prints.*

weeks old. Nebo Bouncer has topped the WPCS section C sire ratings ten times since 1990. His son, Hengwys Tywysog, was champion in 1996 and Tywysog's son, Starcrest Sovereign, was reserve male champion at the 1999 RW Show at three years old and then qualified at the 2003 Royal Bath and West Show for the Cuddy Breeders championship at the HOYS. One Bouncer son to boast being RW champion is Yarty Royal Bonus (son of Fronarth Rhian by Synod Roy Rogers) who was male champion at three years to Hywi Moonlight in 2000. Another Bouncer son, Tremymor Sportsman (foaled in 1998), was champion in 2004, his g-dam being Parktydfil Sunshine who was the foundation mare of the Tremymor Stud in 1972. A Bouncer daughter, Hafodyrynys Cariad (foaled in 1992, daughter of Poundy Carys by Poundy Brenin) was reserve female champion in 2000 and female champion in 2004, while Carys's son, Hafodyrynys Welsh Crusader (foaled 1996, sired by Nebo Brenin), was reserve male champion in 2000 and champion in 2003. With the RW progeny competition modified in 2003 to be based on points won at the show, in 2004 Nebo Bouncer won almost twice more than any other section C sire.

LEFT *Hafodyrynys Welsh Crusader, RW champion 2003. Photo: Carol Jones.*

Bouncer's three-quarter sister, the double champion Tyngwndwn Moonlight, was foaled in 1980 and her full-brother, Nebo Cracker (foaled in 1977), was reserve male champion as a yearling for Northleach Stud. The result of the close mating of Nebo Bouncer x Tyngwndwn Moonlight in 1993 produced Tyngwndwn Daylight, the 2003 RW overall champion.

An interesting variation was the 1993 champion, Cwm Lowri (foaled in 1982), who was bred the other way round, i.e. sired by the section A stallion Revel Classic out of the Cob mare Cwm Llinos. Cwm Lowri was bought by Ty'reos Stud for 300 guineas at the 1983 RW Sale and, after producing Ty'reos Lowri who won the foal class at the 1989 RW Show, she was sold for 3,800 guineas at the 1991 RW Sale and went on to win the RW championship in 1993 for her new owner. Meanwhile, Ty'reos Lowri kept the flag flying at Ty'reos, winning the barren mare class in 1993, the

ABOVE *Miss Nerys Davies with Cwm Lowri, RW champion 1993.*

novice brood mare class and reserve female championship in 1995, the open brood mare class and overall championship in 1997 and, as if that was not enough, she came back in 1999 and won under saddle!

Examples of Cob x Cob are the 1963 and 1965 champions Gwynau Boy and Gwynau Puss; they are all section D breeding, Brenin Gwalia, Llethi Valiant, Myrtle Welsh Flyer, Ceitho Welsh Comet, etc. back for many generations but registered in section C on height.

One has to study bloodlines very carefully if intending to breed a section C from a section B background but the 1983 champion, Coediog Dwynwen, bred in this way, was as true to type as any. She was sired by Golden Sunshine (sire also of the 1996 section D champion, Fronarth Welsh Model) out of Penucha Wennol whose g-sire was Coed Coch Blaen Lleuad. There are some current section B families which have lost their

ABOVE LEFT *Barry Abrey with Ty'reos Lowri, RW champion 1997*. Photo: Carol Maurer.*

ABOVE RIGHT *Eric Jones with Coediog Dwynwen, RW champion 1983. Photo: Horse and Hound.*

native characteristics but Blaen Lleuad was sired by Criban Victor who was a combination of the best section A and D strains and when Victor was shown by Lord Kenyon at the 1949 RW Show, he was entered in class 35 entitled 'Stallion of Cob-type' and he stood third to Welsh Echo.

WPCS registration regulations were altered in September 2004 and, as from 1 January 2006, it will not be possible to register foals from B x C or B x D matings.

It can be claimed that it was section A which saved section C during the early 1960s; we have already met Lyn Cwmcoed (foaled in 1960, Coed Coch Madog [A] x Piercefield Lady Lilian [C] by Brenin Gwalia [D]), and the other outcross was Menai Fury (foaled in 1963, Gredington Oswallt [A] x Menai Ceridwen [C] by Caradog Llwyd [D]) sire of the RW champions Synod William (foaled 1969) and Synod Roy Rogers (foaled 1982). Menai Ceridwen (second-prize mare at the 1964 RW) was also dam of the blue-eyed cream Llanarth Cerdin who was the second- or third-placed stallion at most RW Shows between 1961 and 1969. Llanarth Cerdin was bred at Menai but was sired by Llanarth Marvel whose g-sire on his sire's side was Llanarth Braint and whose g-dam was Llanarth Firefly (foaled in 1933), one of the foundation mares of Llanarth Stud. The section C championship went to Llanarth in 1965, with Llanarth Flying Saucer (foaled in 1951) sired by Llanarth Braint out of Llanarth Rocket by Llanarth Prince Roland who was a son of the same Llanarth Firefly. Flying Saucer is one of the most important names in the whole history of the WPCS but her influence was within section D which has already been dealt with in *The Welsh Cob*.

The influence of Lyn Cwmcoed has already been quoted when discussing Cefn Moonraise and Cefn Moonlady. Another influential family stems from Saltmarsh Belinda whose sire, Saltmarsh Cock Robin, and dam, Stremda Dymplin, were both sired by Lyn Cwmcoed. Belinda was the first

ABOVE LEFT *Neuaddparc Welsh Maid, RW champion 1988. Photo: J. de Rade.*

ABOVE RIGHT *Hywi Moonlight, RW champion 1996*, 2000. Photo: Wynne Davies.*

section C at Neuaddparc Stud; she was bought as a foal at the 1977 Llanarth Sale and her daughter, Neuaddparc Welsh Maid (foaled in 1984 by Nebo Daniel), was female champion in 1988 and another daughter,, Neuaddparc Rowena (foaled in 1989 by Rhosymeirch Prince), was overall champion in 1995. Another son of Lyn Cwmcoed, who continues his influence to the present day, was Poundy Brenin (1978–2002) who is the sire of the 1996 and 2000 champion, Hywi Moonlight, her dam, Talon Bobby Dazzler, being a g-daughter of Menai Fury.

Menai Fury, RW champion in 1976 after standing in second position on five occasions after the first time in 1967, earned his title as a sire for Menai Stud by siring the 1986 champion, the three-year-old filly Menai Rachel out of Synod Rachelian, daughter of Tydi Rosina who was also dam of Fury's illustrious sons, Synod Roy Rogers and Tydi Cerdin. Tydi Cerdin was reserve champion at the 1969 RW Show as a two year old and his death through grass sickness at four years was a great loss to the breed, especially when one considers that he was the sire of Synod Frolic, dam of the 1989 in-hand and many times harness champion, Gwelfro Tywysog. Another 'Menai' success was the 1999 champion Menai Lady Conspicuous whose sire was the Fury son, Menai Bonheddwr. One of the most successful outcrosses for other studs was with Cathedine Aggie Gwyn for Ty'reos Stud. Ty'reos Furietta (foaled in 1985, Menai Fury x Aggie Gwyn) was first

ABOVE LEFT *Cerdin Jones with Synod Roy Rogers, RW champion 1992, 1994*, 1995. Photo: Wynne Davies.*

ABOVE RIGHT *Tydi Red Rose. Photo: Popard.*

at the 1994 RW Show and twice overall champion in 1990 and 1998. Recently, Ty'reos Stud has acquired the established sire Merioneth Storm (foaled in 1983, Menai Fury x 1978 RW champion Chalkhill Dragonfly) to reintroduce Menai Fury bloodlines into the stud.

The most important event in the whole history of the Welsh pony of Cob-type must be the purchase of Gerynant Rosina (foaled in 1955, Valiant Flyer x Dyffryn Rosina) by D. I. Jones and Son, Castell Crugiau, Plwmp in 1960 at Llanybyther market for £72. Rosina, who started her show ring career by coming second to her niece, Pride of the Prairie, at the 1962 RW Show, then gave the Tydi Stud a good start by producing five fillies: Tydi Rosina (foaled in 1961) and Tydi Rosita (foaled in 1963) both by Meiarth Royal Eiddwen, Tydi Rosette (foaled in 1964) by Lyn Cwmcoed, Tydi Rosie (foaled in 1965) by Llanarth Cerdin and Tydi

OPPOSITE TOP *Cerdin Jones with Synod Reagan, RW champion 1983*. Photo; Wynne Davies.*

OPPOSITE BELOW *Len Bigley with Synod Rum Punch, RW champion 1999*. Photo: Eberhard Holin.*

Rosemary (foaled in 1967) by Hendy Brenin. Tydi Rosina had three foals by Menai Fury, two of whom, Tydi Cerdin (foaled in 1966) and Tydi Red Rose (foaled in 1967), died prematurely after an illustrious youngstock career. Then followed the great successes of Synod Roy Rogers (foaled in 1982) who was RW male champion in 1992 and 1995 and overall in 1994.

After producing the 'Tydi' fillies, Gerynant Rosina then produced two Menai Fury sons, Synod Cerdin (foaled in 1968) who was awarded the Brodrick Memorial award in 1977 for winning private driving classes at the three 'royal' shows for Mrs Deirdre Colville, and the greatest of them all, Synod William (foaled in 1969) who was RW champion four times, in 1971*, 1977*, 1980* and 1981* and who sired the winning progeny group at the RW no fewer than ten times. Synod William's most famous sons were produced out of his half-sister, Tydi Rosemary. They were Ranger (foaled in 1975), Roger (foaled in 1976), Reagan (foaled in 1980) and Rum Punch, foaled in 1990, the year before William died.

BELOW *Cerdin Jones with Synod Roger, RW champion 1978, 1979*, 1982*, 1984*, 1987*. Photo: A. Reynolds LBIPP, LMPA.*

Synod Ranger (who died in February 2001) won the stallion class for Persie Stud at the 1979 RW Show, then qualified for the ridden championships at Olympia and also sired Persie Ramrod who was stallion winner in 1991 and Olympia ridden champion in 1989, and also sired Waxwing Reward who was RW male champion in 1991 but, unfortunately for the breed, was gelded soon afterwards to embark on a ridden career. Another Synod Ranger son to gain prominence as a sire is Persie Renown (foaled in 1984, out of Persie Rebecca by Synod William) who is currently senior section C sire at Twyford. Renown's claim to fame is as the sire of the 1994 female and 2002 overall champion, Ashgrove Abigail (foaled in 1990 out of Brynmair Janet by Menai Fury out of Brynmair Blodwen by Fronarth Welsh

RIGHT *Rhys Davies with Ashgrove Abigail, RW champion 1994, 2002*. Photo: Carol Jones.*

Jack). The 2002 RW Show saw Abigail claim her fourth RW first prize and she was retired from the show ring that day.

Synod Roger was RW male champion in 1978 and overall in 1979, 1982, 1984 and 1987 and he was also the sire of Synod Replay (1984–96) out of the black Lyn Cwmcoed and Gerynant Rosina daughter, Tydi Rosette. Replay was steadily building up a reputation of being amongst the top sires ever, and his loss to the breed and to Parvadean Stud at only 12 years old was tragic.

Synod Reagan is probably the least well known of the quartet but was RW champion as a three year old in 1983, beating the stallion winners, Synod Roger and Persie Ramrod. Finally, Synod Rum Punch was champion in 1999, after winning the stallion class from Twmbarlwm Nimrod, son of Synod Replay and out of the Synod Ranger daughter, Persie Nanette, who was a good producer at Ceulan before she went to Twmbarlwm Stud.

Possibly the pick of the Synod William mares would be Synod Rally (foaled in 1982, out of Synod Ringlet, daughter of Tydi Rosette) and

Synod Sweet William (foaled in 1989) daughter of Synod Maggie May who was herself a daughter of Lili Cwmcoed. Synod Sweet William, with Synod Rally and Synod Roger, made up the 1989 RW winning progeny group for Synod William.

Synod William has been equally successful with the very few visiting mares who were allowed; one exceptional daughter being Rookery Flower Lady (foaled in 1983) out of Craven Fancy Lady who was sired by Nebo Dafydd out of Craven Ladyship by Criban Victor. Flower Lady was female champion to Nebo Bouncer as a two year old in 1985 and won the novice mare class in 1989. When Cwnlle Lily (by Lyn Cwmcoed) was mated to Synod William in 1975, she produced Paddock Lightning who was the sire of the 2002 champion, Thorneyside Bay Prince. Bay Prince's dam was the section D Thorneyside Glory but his g-g-dam, Thorneyside Flying Lady (dam of the two RW section D champions Thorneyside The Boss and Thorneyside Flyer), was sired by the section C Ross Black Prince.

In addition to their success with Persie Ramrod at the 1991 RW Show, Glynwyn Stud also won the female championship with Glynwyn Diamante whose sire, Isamman Dafydd (RW champion in 1975), and dam, Peris Blackie, were both sired by Brenin Dafydd. Their home-bred stallion,

LEFT *Stephen Heppenstall and judge Geraint Davies with Glynwyn Diamante, RW champion 1991*. Photo: Wynne Davies.*

Glynwyn Gideon (twice youngstock winner at the RW), is a son of Glynwyn April Dawn whose sire, Glynwyn Gwilym, and dam, Glynwyn Arbennig, are both out of the 1980 RW champion, Paddock Dawn (foaled in 1973, Fronarth Welsh Jack x Cwnlle Lily by Lyn Cwmcoed), Gwilym, sired by Persie Ramrod, and Arbennig, sired by Isamman Dafydd.

Only two champions from 1947–2003, Bodwenarth Red Spark (1990) and Tyas Eiddwyn (1998), are not directly related to the preceding families, Red Spark being sired by Cippyn Red Flyer (Nebo Black Magic x Felin Rosina) out of Bodwenarth Blodyn by Heliguchel Craddock, and Eiddwyn sired by Nebo Prince out of Y Ddol Bet by Farian Prince out of Beudog Peggy by Beudog Delight. Phil Sweeting of the Estoro Stud in Wakefield, West Yorkshire went to the Royal Welsh Brightwells Sale in 1983 with no intention of buying a section C but fancied the colt foal Bodwenarth Red Spark, described in the catalogue as 'should make useful stallion' and bought him for 120 guineas. Very soon after arriving home, Red Spark was supreme champion at the Yorkshire Foal Show and went on to win five WPCS medals and the RW gold medal in 1990. After the foal successes with Red Spark, Phil returned to the Brightwell Sale in 1984 and ended up buying his dam, Bodwenarth Blodyn, who produced one winner after another for Estoro Stud.

CHAPTER FOUR

The Welsh Part-bred Pony

CURRENT CHILDREN'S riding ponies, most of which have a dash of Welsh blood, are registered in the Stud Book of the National Pony Society (NPS) which was instituted as the Polo Pony Society (PPS) at their initial meeting at the RASE Show in Chester on 20 June 1893.

The preface to volume 1 of the PPS Stud Book (1894) states that the society will be formed 'for the improvement and encouragement of the breeding of high-class riding ponies'. In his presidential introduction Lord Harrington stated that: 'ponies which could have been bought twenty years ago for £30 are now worth £100 or more'. The preface to the Stud Book was written by John Hill of Marsh Brook House, Church Stretton, who was made an Honorary Member of the WPCS and also wrote the preface to volume 1 of the WSB in 1901. John Hill writes in the PPSSB:

> Living on the boundary of Wales and being intimate with its ponies all my life, I have no hesitation in saying that there is no safer or more appropriate foundation for the object which the Society has in view than this pure Welsh pony blood. The

> indomitable pluck, endurance and good temper of the Welsh pony, together with his substance and dash, will be found an invaluable cross for the Thoroughbred and Eastern bred ponies.

Many pure Welsh ponies and Cobs were registered in volume 1 of the PPSB, such as the Mountain pony stallion Tyrant (foaled in 1890) owned by W. J. Roberts of Church Stretton (sire of Bleddfa Tell-Tale, the little mare who was so influential in chapter 1) and the Cob stallions Trotting Briton (foaled in 1884) and Trotting Comet (foaled in 1887). Also registered in volume 1 were the part-bred mares Fanny (foaled in 1881) sired by the Thoroughbred Lampton out of a pure Welsh Mountain mare owned by C. W. Woosnam of Cefnllysgwynne, Builth Wells, and Decca (foaled in 1891) sired by Bombay Chief (an Arab imported from Egypt) out of the Longmynd Hill pony Darnford (foaled in 1882) bred by John Hill.

Soon afterwards enthusiasts of breeds previously embraced by the PPSB (with the exception of Shetlands) became anxious to achieve individual recognition and decided to form their own societies, such as the Welsh (1901), New Forest (1906), Dales (1917) and Dartmoor (1920).

In the early days of the WPCS, animals were accepted for registration even if they contained 'alien' blood, and Welsh farmers would take advantage of high-class stallions owned by wealthy landowners. Such was the case of Nance o'r Glyn , registered in the WSB volume 1, foaled in 1891, and bred by Jenkin Jenkins of Blaenplwyf, sired by J. C. Harford's TB Rameses out of the Mountain pony mare Polly by Welsh Jack. Nance became an almost unbeatable racing mare and, at the time of Mr Jenkins's death, when she was sold to Dinarth Hall for £52, she had won 217 races, been second 61 times, third 16 times and unplaced only eight times.

Another famous racing mare was Lucy Grey, foaled in 1930, sired by the Thoroughbred Spion Kop (winner of the Derby and sire of the Derby winner Felstead) out of Kittiwake who was champion Mountain pony at the 1927 RW Show for Dinarth Hall. Lucy Grey was bred by Captain Briggs of Mynachdy Mansion, Pennant and was bought by Dafydd Jones of Frongoy for £2 at a farm sale. Ridden by David John Jones (recipient of the WPCS Brodrick memorial trophy in 2000), Lucy Grey won over 400 races and died at Frongoy, aged 29. Spion Kop was also the sire of the TB Saleve who stood at stud in Cardiganshire in the 1930s at a stud fee of 3 guineas. Saleve (foaled in 1928) was a winner of races on the flat and over hurdles and was sold as a yearling for £6,100. One of Saleve's Welsh part-bred progeny was Ceulan Blue Moon (foaled in 1936) whose dam, Ceulan Silverleaf (reserve section A female champion RW Show 1932), in 1938 produced Ceulan Silver Lustre by Incoronax (an Arab bred by Lady Wentworth).

Ponies sired by TB and Arab sires out of Welsh mares were equally successful in children's riding classes within the principality. The 13-hand Dolly Grey of Coedparc, foaled in 1931, sired by the TB Shandy Gaff out of Parc Dolly Grey (foaled in 1913) by Trotting Jack, was a very hard act to follow when ridden by Sam Morgan, the 1978 WPCS President. A contemporary rider was David Davies of Ceulan who outgrew his 12-hand mount, The Imp, on which he won the best rider award at the 1933 RW Show. He was equally successful on the 14-hand Criban Spotless, foaled in 1933 and sired by the TB Criban Lally (bred by Mrs Pennell by the King's

LEFT *Criban Spotless with David Davies (1937).*

Gold Cup winner Gay Lally) out of the Mountain pony mare Criban Mulberry, grand-dam of Criban Victor (chapter 2).

A Polo pony sire owned by Dinarth Hall was Friar who won at the 1936 NPS and RASE Shows. At the Dinarth Hall dispersal sale following the death of Mr T. J. Jones in 1937, Miss Brodrick bought a filly foal for 8 guineas, sired by Friar out of the Welsh mare Bryn Candy (bought at the sale for 6 guineas by Mrs Sievewright) and she registered the foal as Friar's Balsam FS. Friar's Balsam won the section B youngstock class at the 1939 RW Show for Miss Brodrick and she was then sold to the Brookshaw family of Market Drayton, for whom she won the 13.2 hh ridden class at the first post-war RW Show in 1947.

Placed second to Friar's Balsam in this 13.2 hh class was another 50 per cent Welsh mare, Primula, owned by Mrs Agnes Hepburn, a great supporter of the Welsh Riding pony, who judged the section Bs at the 1959 RW Show when she was Mrs Price. Primula was sired by Jotham AHSB out of a former ridden winner, Craven Nell, by the strikingly marked Craven Black and White. Mrs Hepburn had been showing Welsh ponies under saddle since 1934 when she bought Tanybwlch Rhos for her ten-year-old son, her most successful pony being Coed Coch Powys who had been pulling a plough before she bought him in 1946. Powys subsequently won 43 championships (including the supreme at the White City in 1949), 17 reserve championships and 36 silver cups outright!

Political changes saw polo decline and, with it, a need for the purpose-bred Polo pony, giving way to a breeding policy for a more general purpose mount. Native stalwarts declared varying degrees of scepticism about the 'new cross-bred' pony, many feeling that the established native character, hardiness and temperament was being sacrificed for 'quality', speed and agility. However, over the ensuing one hundred years, native pony blood, especially Welsh, has been at the heart of breeding a pony of great beauty and versatility that knew no bounds and was admired the world over.

The two most influential Riding ponies, post Second World War, were undoubtedly the stallion Bwlch Valentino with his Welsh g-g-dam (dam of

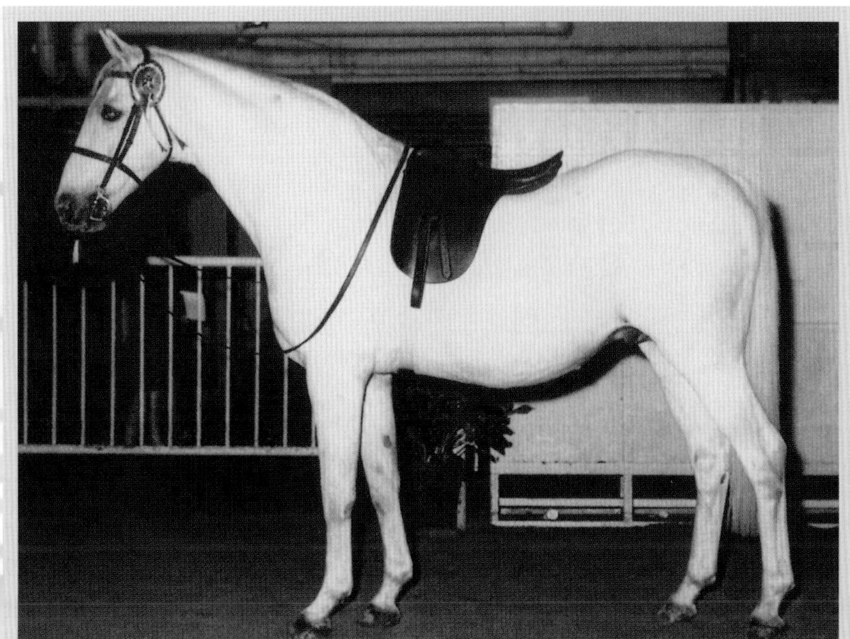

ABOVE LEFT *Bwlch Valentino, aged 18, at HOYS 1968.*

BELOW LEFT *Pretty Polly ridden by Davina Lee-Smith. Photo: Alex Gill.*

Cigarette) and the mare Pretty Polly, daughter of the Welsh Gypsy Gold. Mrs Nell Pennell of Bwlch (whose contribution to the WPCS is second to none) spotted Valentino's dam, Bwlch Goldflake (foaled in 1927), grazing near Oxford and bought her. Bwlch Goldflake was sired by Meteoric (a son of the Derby winner Sunstar) out of Cigarette who was a very successful 'flapping' pony. As an ageing mare in 1949, Bwlch Goldflake was sent to be covered by Valentine (by the Argentinian Polo pony sire Malice and out of the part-Arab mare Silver Spray) and Bwlch Valentino was foaled in 1950. Valentino was a somewhat gangly and plain youngster but had a rather special aura about him and, when shown by Dick Richards of Criban, he won the foal class at the Roehampton NPS Show with judge Count Robert Orssich. Valentino's only show ring outing in 1951, was at Llandeilo where Count Robert Orssich, along with Horace Smith of the Cadogan Riding School, Maidenhead (who taught HM the Queen to ride) judged every horse and pony class at the show, starting with the Welsh ponies and Cobs, followed by pony breeding classes, ridden hunters, hacks and children's riding ponies, and ending up with the harness classes! What I remember about the 1951 Llandeilo Show was securing the first notch on the Evan Jones cup (which we won outright in 1953) and the harness class with Dinarth What Ho and Bwlch Valentino (shown by Miss Elspeth Ferguson) standing first and reserve riding pony breeding champion to Mrs Cuff's Craven Bright Sprite.

Valentino was not to become a show animal but a sire who left an indelible mark on the British riding pony. His breeding was mainly Thoroughbred but he inherited enough Welsh blood to retain and procreate 'pony' character and it was thought that his exceptional movement came from Malice.

Bwlch Valentino was leased to Llewellyn Richards of Criban as a three year old and produced three progeny: Criban Silver, Criban Dart (exported to the USA) and Criban Heather. Three more Criban foals who were tagged on to the end of the October 1954 Cui Sale were also sired by him, including the palomino filly Criban Fiesta for whom the Duchess of Rutland paid 60 guineas.

At this time Valentino was on offer to Keith Lee-Smith as a riding gelding, but then Mrs Pennell agreed a sale to Vivian Eckley of Cusop on the proviso that her favourite mare, Miss Minette, would be covered by him. Miss Minette, who was champion riding pony at the 1952 RW Show in the ownership of the Jackson family of Worcester, was just over 13 hands and was sired by the 'teaser' Malinen out of the equally successful half-Welsh riding pony Kavora Kismet. The matings of Miss Minette to Valentino produced the dynasty of stallions: Bwlch Zephyr, Zip and Zingaree, as well as the influential mare Bwlch Minuet who was the 1960 RW champion riding pony for Mrs John Reiss, with the Valentino daughter, Cusop Jittina, making her first appearance to stand reserve.

Valentino's offspring were certainly 'top drawer' and included four who captured the Pony of the Year titles: Cusop Quickstep (1962), Cusop Pollyanna (1963), Cusop Pirouette (1966) and Treharne Veronica (1970), Pony of the Year at the 1970 HOYS and daughter of the section A Hinton Skylark (Coed Coch Glyndwr x Criban Topsy). From this point in time the 'Val Experience' dominated pony classes. Often stallions breed good mares or vice-versa but Valentino was unique in that his prepotency passed to

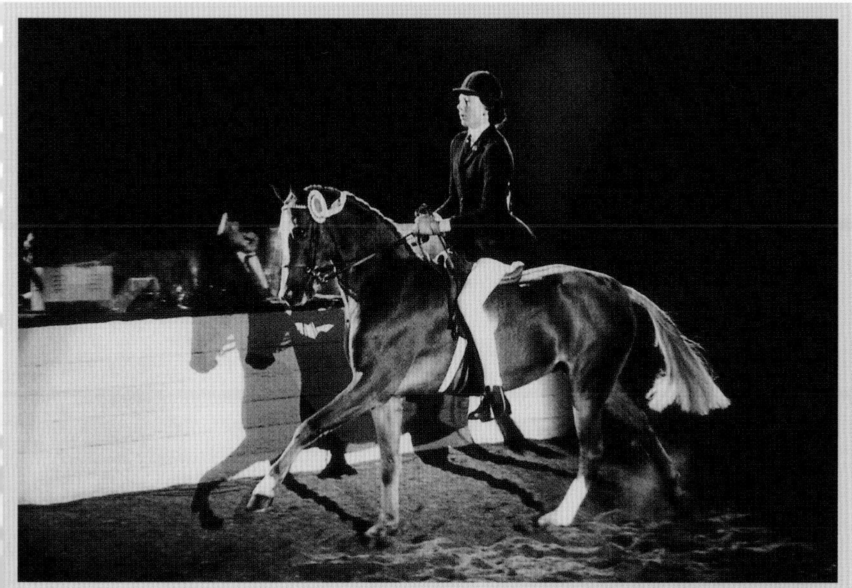

LEFT *Treharne Veronica ridden by Susan Rose at HOYS 1970.*

male and female alike. For more than three decades, Valentino progeny dominated the riding pony scene in the UK, to the extent that a winning pony not related to Valentino was a very rare animal indeed.

Although Mrs Pennell retained a service to Bwlch Valentino for her 'special' mare, Miss Minette, in 1960 she returned to Welsh blood and used Criban Victor, the resulting offspring being the lovely FS1 mare Bwlch Melody. At this time Mrs Pennell bought from Criban the much admired chestnut colt Criban Dash (foaled in 1960), sired by Bwlch Valentino out of Criban Red Heather FS (foaled in 1948) who was by Criban Loyalist (foaled in 1939) (by Silverdale Loyalty) out of Criban Heather Belle (foaled in 1943) (RW section B champion 1949) who was a daughter of Criban Bowbell FS by Silverdale Bowtint GSB. Criban Bowbell (foaled in 1939) was also dam of Criban Belle (foaled in 1945) who was dam of the noted riding ponies Criban Activity (foaled in 1949) and Criban Biddy Bronze (foaled in 1950), dam of Solway Master Bronze (chapter 2). In 1963, at the first Northleach Show, Criban Dash won the part-bred young-stock class of 26 entries and went on to win the overall show

RIGHT *Criban Dash.*

championship. A more important event for Welsh part-breds in 1963 was Criban Dash covering the two-year-old filly Bwlch Melody to produce Bwlch Mazurka. Mazurka became a top show mare for Mrs Jennifer Williams at Pendley, taking many titles, including the supreme in-hand award at the 1969 POB Championships.

The most important present-day influence of Bwlch Mazurka is via her grand-daughter, Pendley Birthday Girl (foaled in 1976), who is dam of Colbeach Salaman (foaled in 1996) and Colbeach Sensation (foaled in 1991), both sired by Willowbay Symphony. In the 128 cm class at the 2004 HOYS, Salaman was first and champion and Sensation was third. Birthday Girl's sire and dam, Enstone Artist and Pendley Maypole, were both sired by the WPB Pendley Model (foaled in 1967) who will be met

BELOW *Colbeach Salaman ridden by Samantha Dent. Photo: Real Time Imaging.*

later in this chapter in connection with the influence of the section B Solway Master Bronze who was his sire.

Many important Welsh part-breds were produced the 'other way round', i.e. using a Welsh sire on a non-Welsh mare. Criban Victor had many elegant ladies crossing his threshold, including the legendary Arden Tittle Tattle, to produce Gossip in 1965. The lovely Anglo-Arab hack Ermine Toes produced Minto (foaled in 1963), a very distinctive roan stallion with a beautiful 'pony' head who became a great stock-producer for Mrs Olive Weston at the Seaholm Stud in Lincolnshire. Criban Victor also established a line of noted part-breds under the Henbury prefix for Mrs Andrew of Macclesfield; these included the sires Henbury Sylvester, Limelight, Calypso and Mr Blandish.

The year 1949 will be remembered as a significant date by historians of riding pony development in the UK. With the war over, people experienced a real sense of liberation and enjoyment and riding for leisure was on the increase. Pressure was being put on the National Pony Society (the new name for the Polo Pony Society from 1910) to place greater emphasis on the riding pony and it was during a meeting at the NPS Offices in 1949 that the British Show Pony Society (BSPS) was formed. A founder member was Albert Deptford (a well-known breeder of Suffolk Punches) but, more significantly, his purchase of a mare, Pretty Polly, at the end of that year (after she had won the ridden championship at Dublin, ridden by Barbara Falloon), was to change the ridden pony scene for years to come. Pretty Polly was a four year old, bought from Billy Benson and bred by the Nicholson family at Kells, Co. Meath. She was sired by the Arab Naseel out of the Welsh mare Gypsy Gold. Produced by Keith Lee-Smith and ridden by his daughter Davina, Pretty Polly took the HOYS Show Pony of the Year titles in 1950 and 1951, as well as winning the championships three times at Richmond, the RASE, Peterborough, NPS and the White City and twice at Windsor. Pretty Polly was also a prolific breeder, especially when mated to Bwlch Valentino, producing Pollyanna (1963 Pony of the Year before being exported to USA) and Polly's Gem who, although never the star of the ridden ring, bred the 1971 Pony of the Year, Gem's

Signet (himself by Bwlch Hill Wind) who, in turn, sired the most consistent ridden pony of all time, Holly of Spring, winner of a remarkable four Pony of the Year titles from 1975 to 1978.

In 1959 Pretty Polly was sent to Criban to be covered by Bolgoed Automation, a section A stallion who had grown over height. The resulting colt foal was sold to Vivian Eckley of Cusop and registered as Cusop Policy. Among his many offspring Policy sired Caerloew Planet (foaled in 1966) from the section B mare Trefesgob Stardust. Planet was an outstanding Working Hunter Pony, culminating with the BSPS Peterborough title in 1975, ridden by Sally Lord from Pembroke. Sally and Planet later appeared at Wembley in the personality parade.

A prefix with high profile in chapters 1 and 2 and already mentioned in this chapter is 'Criban' who held breeding records of their ponies going back 200 years before the formation of the WPCS. The Criban ponies were not for looking at; they were integral to the farming policy. They were regularly used as shepherding ponies, having a good length of rein, with limbs, bone and feet of the best, and capable of carrying a man all day. The same pony was hunted with the local pack and the fastest of them competed in local 'flapping' races.

The Richards family of Criban always inclined towards a more active riding type of pony, rather than the 'pitter' type which served the industrial needs of the adjoining areas of Merthyr Tydfil, Dowlais and Cefn Coed. This is undoubtedly the secret of the phenomenal success of the Criban ponies. The Richards family were riding men through and through. Howell Richards (President of the WPCS in 1938 and 1948) was photographed riding Criban Mog in 1960 when he was 95 years old and he had ridden in the Llanfihangel point-to-point in 1945, aged 80! Originally, the prefixes 'Ystrad', 'Vaynor' and 'Torpantau' were used, named after the mountains where they had three farms, Abercriban, Coed Hir and Ystrad in the Taff Fechan valley on the south side of the Brecon Beacons. After 1918, a partnership was formed with the three sons, H. Llewellyn (Criban), Richard J. (Criban R) and William R. (Cui). Advantage was often taken of stallions (such as Klondyke, chapter 3) at W. S. Miller's Forest Lodge Stud to where the Richards brothers would ride their mares to get them covered. Criban Socks (foaled in 1926), still regarded as the epitome of the Welsh Mountain pony, was, in fact, bred at Forest Lodge, sired by a Criban stallion out of a Forest mare.

When the height limit of Polo ponies was raised from 14 hands 2 in to 15 hands, the small, old type of Polo pony stallions lost favour. However, Llewellyn Richards saw an opportunity to move forward in his quest for the versatile riding pony and he bought Silverdale Loyalty (foaled in 1923, Prince Friarstown x Silvery II), Silverdale Bowtint (Cherry Tint x Bowden by Bowery), whom Mr Richards sold to Mr Kiddie of South Africa, and Silverdale Tarragon (another son of Bowden) from Herbert Bright who had taken over as the leading Polo pony breeder from Tresham Gilbey. When 90 Criban ponies were sold at Brecon Cattle Market in May 1937, the Mountain ponies came from the Brecon Beacons and the 22 riding ponies (mainly sired by Criban Lally or Silverdale Bowtint) came from Oundle, Northamptonshire where Llewellyn Richards lived at that time. At the November 1946 sale of 44 ponies, also at Brecon Cattle Market (Llewellyn Richards now having returned to live at Pontsticill), Mrs Cuff bought Criban Victor for 40 guineas and the six-year-old Criban Loyal Lass, by Silverdale Loyalty, for 45 guineas. Loyal Lass was dam of Downland Lavender (foaled in 1950), RW section B champion in 1960 and dam of many good section Bs at Coed Coch. Also at this sale were eight foals sired by Criban Loyalist a 13-hand son of Silverdale Loyalty out of Criban Harpist. At the May 1952 sale of 65 ponies at Talybont-on-Usk Market, Mrs Cuff bought the thirteen-year-old Criban Bowbell, by Silverdale Bowtint, for 47 guineas, Bowbell being dam of Criban Heather Belle (foaled in 1943) with whom Mrs Cuff had won the section B championship at the 1949 RW Show. Heather Belle was dam of Downland Dragonfly, dam of Downland Dauphin (chapter 2). Bowbell was also grand-dam of the noted riding ponies Criban Activity and Criban Biddy Bronze and she was sold to Mrs Joan Bullock of the Sintoncourt Stud in 1963. Some Criban yearlings and foals were sold at the end of the October 1954 Cui Sale and they were sired by Silverdale Aquila, Bwlch Valentino and Loves Romance (TB).

The second-highest price (66 guineas) at the 1952 Criban Sale was paid by Mrs Pam Cuninghame (niece of the Richards family) for the two-year-old filly Criban Topsy (Criban Priority x Criban Hazel) who had won a WPCS medal at Brecon Show as a yearling. Topsy went to Hinton Stud to join Criban Posy (foaled in 1939, Criban Cockade x Criban Carnation) who was regarded by many as the best section A pony bred at Criban. Mrs Cuninghame was a staunch supporter of Coed Coch Glyndwr and sent both mares to him in turn, Topsy producing Hinton Skylark in 1955 and Posy producing Hinton Gentian in 1957. Hinton Gentian was sold to Mrs Robina Mills in 1960 and produced several good section As, including Rookery Jasmin (foaled in 1963, by Gredington Rheiol), dam of the popular stallion Rookery Juniper (foaled in 1968, by Criban Bantam). However, the most famous of this line at Rookery was Rookery Jigsaw from the mating of Gentian to the roan part-bred Silver Spray. Silver Spray (foaled in 1956) was sired by the Glamorgan HIS stallion The Admiral out of the section A mare Revel Tangle and he was supreme at the 1960 Ponies of Britain Show. Rookery Jigsaw was an outstanding 13-hand working hunter pony, taking the BSPS Working Hunter Pony of the Year title at Peterborough in 1977.

LEFT *Rookery Jigsaw ridden by Gordon Harley.*

Criban Topsy's claim to fame is as Hayley Mills's mount in the film *Tiger Bay*. Her daughter, Hinton Skylark, was bought as a foal by Mrs Patsy Egerton when she was forming her Welsh stud after previous experience with Thoroughbreds. Mrs Egerton was very conscious of sound, correct conformation and, realising that studs would not part with their best breeding mares, she bought youngsters, often foals. She was also a great admirer of Coed Coch Glyndwr and at one time had 11 Coed Coch Glyndwr daughters breeding at Treharne. It was her friend, Anne Hammond (Millfields), who sowed the seed that these Glyndwr mares would cross well with Bwlch Valentino and soon Treharne mares were regular visitors to Cusop. The cross was an outstanding success, producing a riding pony of sound construction and excellent movement, with a temperament suitable for a child to ride. The best of them were Treharne Veronica (foaled in 1964) and Treharne Valencia (foaled in 1973), both out of Hinton Skylark. Valencia took Edward Jackson to the top in 12.2 hh classes before becoming an outstanding brood mare, taking titles across the country, including the supreme at the NPS Championships.

Another Coed Coch Glyndwr daughter at Treharne was Solway Summertime. Although registered as section A, she was a full-sister to the famous Solway Master Bronze. In 1972 Summertime produced the chestnut colt Treharne Talisman (also by Bwlch Valentino) and he was exported as a three year old to Australia where he was an immediate success, winning 45 championships in his first three years and later siring many Royal Show and Australian Pony of the Year winners. Talisman was still siring foals in Australia at the age of 29.

Following the death of Mrs Anne Bullen of Catherstone Stud, Mrs Egerton bought Criban Viola (foaled in 1956, Bwlch Valentino x Criban Red Heather) who had taken Jane Bullen to the top in ridden classes, including the Royal International where she beat Arden Tittle Tattle. Because Viola was inspected as FS, even though sired by Bwlch Valenino, she was eligible to breed section B ponies, but her full-brother, the 1963 Northleach champion, Criban Dash, would have to be registered in the 'part-bred' appendix to the Stud Book. Viola's sisters were Criban Joy (dam of the successful riding pony stallion Knowle Lightning), Harebell and Heather (sold to Cusop and dealt with later). Viola was mated to both the section A and section B stallions at Treharne; to Treharne Minstrel (foaled in 1960, by Marsh Crusader) she produced Treharne Pamela and the Royal riding pony breeding champion Treharne Maxine.

ABOVE *Bwlch Hill Wind.*

In 1963 Criban Red Heather was sold to Mrs Pennell and in 1964 she produced Bwlch Hill Wind who matured to only 12 hands 3 in and was therefore rarely shown. Hill Wind was sold to Mr Durham Wells and stood at stud with his illustrious sire, Bwlch Zephyr, at Miss Elspeth Ferguson's Rosevean Stud near Worcester. When Mr Durham Wells was dispersing his pony interests, he refused a huge offer for Hill Wind to go to the USA, preferring to see him remain at Rosevean. Hill Wind duly earned his place in the pony 'hall of fame' through offspring of the calibre of Rosevean Eagle's Hill, Lloyds Bank HOYS champion as a yearling in 1976, champion again in 1978 (from Glenfield Chocolate Soldier and Pendley Maypole) and third in 1979 to Llanarth Flying Comet and Glenfield Chocolate Soldier. Other progeny of Hill Wind included the 1971 Pony of the Year, Gems Signet, the 1982 Pony of the Year, Runnings Park Hill Star, and Trellech Gizelle, a legend in the pony brood mare ring but sadly never able to capture the elusive HOYS title although qualifying for it at Royal Norfolk in 1980, Newark and Notts in 1984 and 1987 and East of England in 1986. However, her daughter, Rotherwood Rhapsody, won the title for Mrs Renita White in 1985, having qualified at Newark and Notts and then qualifying again later in 1986 at the Royal Norfolk.

Another Welsh part-bred to take this prestigious Wembley in-hand title was Rosevean Honeysuckle in 1990. Foaled in 1981, Honeysuckle was out of the riding pony mare Rosevean Honeypot by Coed Coch Ensign (Bwlch Zephyr x Coed Coch Penwn). Coed Coch Penwn was also dam of

ABOVE *Rosevean Honeysuckle.*

Coed Coch Hillstream (foaled in 1971, sired by Bwlch Hill Wind). A champion at NPS as a yearling, he was exported to the USA from the 1978 dispersal sale for 1,800 guineas. Kingvean Gypsy Star (foaled in 1998), who qualified for the HOYS Breeders In-hand championship at the New Forest in 2000, was reserve champion for the Cuddy In-hand championship in 2003 and champion in 2004, is descended from Rosevean Honeysuckle on both sides, through her sire, Sufton Romany Lore (exported to Australia), and her dam, Celebrity of Rendene.

Another Bwlch Hill Wind star was Sinton Samite, foaled in 1966. Following a very successful in-hand career, including the part-bred championship at the 1969 RW Show, she continued to be a favourite of the ridden judges, produced by the Gilbert-Scott family. As a four year old she was reserve riding pony champion at the Ponies of Britain Show. However, for the supreme award of the show there were three judges, Mrs Staveley, Mr Dick Richards and Major General Aizlewood, who reversed the decision of the riding pony judge and, unhesitatingly (according to Mrs Glenda Spooner writing in the POB journal), awarded Samite the supreme title. In five outings as a brood mare in 1972, Samite won five supreme championships. Sinton Samite was from another successful 'Criban' family, her dam was Criban Chiffon (purchased by Sinton in 1961), daughter of the good ridden winner Criban Ninon, herself a daughter of Criban Nylon, daughter of Criban Heather Bell.

ABOVE *Twyford Gone Away.*

Mrs Alison Mountain of Twyford also shared in the Criban success story. Llewellyn Richards had been given the TB mare Go Swiftly by Herbert Bright of Silverdale, but she could not withstand the harsh Breconshire winters and was given to Mrs Mountain carrying a foal by Criban Loyal Grey by Criban Loyalist (son of Criban Harpist, section B foaled in 1923) and g-sire of Criban Red Heather. That foal was Twyford Gone Away who became a leading 14 hands 2 in show pony, firstly with Sir John and Lady Reiss and later with the Durham Wells family. He won many titles before being exported to the USA. Go Swiftly bred seven foals at Twyford, all colts!

Vivian and Pat Eckley also found 'Criban' lines to be crucial in the setting up of the Cusop Stud which was later to become one of the most influential in the development of the riding pony in the UK. The three-year-old filly Criban Activity was bought for 48 guineas at the May 1952 Criban Sale as a riding pony for the Eckley daughters. After winning the ridden section A trophy at the RW Show outright (three times in succession), she went on to found the Cusop 'A' line but, sadly, bred mainly colts. Activity was then given to their daughter Jocelyn as a wedding present, subsequently changed form and bred a line of fillies, including Courtway

Actress. Activity's dam, Criban Belle, had been given to neighbouring farmer Will Thomas (Will Coity Bach) but was bought back by Llewellyn Richards when he realised her potential after she produced Criban Biddy Bronze in 1950. The TB stallion Loves Romance was owned by Vivian Eckley and Activity produced his foal, Cusop Belle. It was Loves Romance's sudden death in 1954 which prompted Vivian Eckley to persuade Mrs Pennell to sell Bwlch Valentino to him rather than accept a very tempting offer for him to go as a riding pony. To Bwlch Valentino, Cusop Belle produced Cusop Vagabond who tragically died at four years but not before leaving the prolific sire Lennel Strolling Minstrel who was owned and bred by Mrs Betty Sitwell and spent most of his life at the Whalton Stud of Mrs Joanna Macinnes.

Vivian Eckley also bought Criban Heather (foaled in 1954) from Llewellyn Richards. She was one of Bwlch Valentino's first daughters and her dam was Criban Red Heather. She became responsible for the Cusop

RIGHT *Cusop Heiress.*

'H' family, producing many noted winners, including Cusop Hostess (by Cusop Policy: Bolgoed Automation x Pretty Polly) who, although successful when ridden, proved her real worth as the dam of Cusop Heiress, a tremendous ridden winner for the Gilbert Scott family.

Several part-bred females at Cusop were entered into the Welsh FS register and upgraded using registered Welsh sires. Cusop Rhapsody, by Loves Romance out of a dam of unknown breeding, started the 'R' line, including Cusop Rhyme by Revel Newsreel and Cusop Rhythm out of Rhyme by Solway Master Bronze. A successful ridden winner was Cusop Request, sired by Cusop Dignity out of Rhyme. Finolla, foaled in 1946, by Potato, was another to gain inspection into the FS register and produced the 'F' line. The 1968 RW ridden champion, Cusop Jubilation, had different origins. By the 1965 and 1967 RW section B champion, Cusop Hoity Toity, she was out of the Valentino mare Cusop Jittino, a daughter of the superb TB Jittabug. Jittino had a glittering row of successes in the ridden classes at the RW Shows. She was reserve champion on her first appearance in 1960 to another Valentino daughter, Bwlch Minuet, then champion in 1961, 1963 and 1964 and reserve to Cusop Serenade in 1962! At the 1963 RW Show, Jittino won the 14.2 hh class and championship, Cusop Agility (out of Criban Activity) the 12.2 hh class and reserve championship and Cusop Felicity, sired by Revel Newsreel (section A out of the 1951 RW section B champion Revel Nance) won the 13.2 hh class and stood third in the championship line up! All subsequent Cusop 'J' ponies are descended from this line, including Cusop Journal, Just So and Junior.

For a long period of time, more Cusop prefixed ponies qualified for HOYS than any other prefix, a vindication of the successful breeding policy in which Vivian Eckley placed great value on Welsh blood.

At the Cui reduction sale of 177 ponies on 1 October 1954, following the death of Mr Willie Richards, Mrs Glenda Spooner of the Ponies of Britain Club bought a filly foal, Cui Bracken, for 10 guineas on behalf of Mrs Daphne Alexander of the Forge Stud, Malborough, Wiltshire. Bracken's dam, Cui Moonlight (foaled in 1951), sold for 15 guineas to Mr Emrys Griffiths of the Revel. I bought Moonlight's sister (two years younger), Cui Moon Flicker (whom I exported to the USA in 1956) and another sister (three years older), Cui Moonbeam, who followed to the USA in 1958. Moonlight's dam, Cui Blue Moon, sold for 36 guineas to Dr Mullen of Cardiff who owned Sengoran, one of the top Arab stallions in the UK at that time. Blue Moon's dam was the lovely Cui June (foaled in 1938, Mathrafal Tuppence x Criban Carnation), one of the five mares retained by Mrs Betty Richards in 1954 to continue the Cui Stud. Cui Bracken became a very successful producer of part-bred ponies at Forge Stud with the sires McGredy, Rosevean Pippin, Forge Pipkin and Bwlch Zephyr, the most successful of which was Forge Sweet Gale foaled in 1965 and sired by Bwlch Zephyr.

Forge Sweet Gale became one of the best young ponies of her height, taking the 12.2 hh championship at NPS and Ponies of Britain as a two and three year old. Sweet Gale was produced by Mrs Davina Whiteman as a four year old before going to be produced by Angela Massarella when,

RIGHT *Forge Sweet Gale. Photo: Monty.*

again, she was one of the most consistent winners of her height. Sweet Gale returned to Forge Stud for brood mare duties and, as an eight year old, she took the Ponies of Britain novice brood mare title, after which she was gifted to the Massarella family to continue as a brood mare. Cui Bracken's other part-bred progeny included Forge Tiki, Sweet Briar and Harebell, all sired by McGredy and all of whom turned out to be very successful riding ponies.

The champion section B at the 1950 RW Show at Abergele was Gem IV, bred and exhibited by Mrs Eddie Griffith. Gem (foaled in 1948) was sired by Tanybwlch Berwyn and out of Kinkie who was of unknown parentage. Gem deserves her place in this text, not as a RW champion but as the dam of two exceptional part-breds. Gem was twice put to the fashionable TB stallion Gay Presto (a twin, sired by Precipitation out of Joyette) and produced the two outstanding females, Promise (foaled in 1956) and Prudence (foaled in 1959), and both looked predominantly TB rather than 'Welsh'. Despite lack-

BELOW *Promise II with E. G. E. Griffith, reserve champion RW 1963. Photo: Sport and Country.*

ABOVE *Mirth, Best in Show, Ponies of Britain Show 1969. Photo: Pony magazine.*

ing pony-type heads, they were both extravagant movers and deep-bodied, with lovely quality limbs. Miss Elspeth Ferguson showed Promise successfully, winning the over 13.2 hh WPB class at the 1963 RW Show (the first time that WPB classes were staged) and reserve champion to the under-13.2 hh winner, Henbury Bouquet (by Criban Victor), who had also been placed under saddle. Henbury Bouquet was reserve WPB champion in 1964 and 1965. The judge on that occasion was Mr Dick Richards who commented on Promise's free movement. Promise 'clicked' very well with Miss Ferguson's resident stallion, Bwlch Zephyr, producing that wonderful trio, Mirth, Chuckle and Titter who was sold to an Australian syndicate. To many enthusiasts, Mirth was the ideal show pony and appeared to ooze quality from every sinew. Shown as a riding pony by Mr and Mrs P. T. Pratt, her moment of crowning glory was at the 1969 POB championships where she was Best in Show from the champion brood mare Bwlch Mazurka and the overall youngstock champion Chirk Catmint, all three being Welsh part-breds. Tragically, Mirth's career was cut short by a freak accident. Chuckle produced the 12 hands 2 in stallion Rosevean Merry Mountain (foaled in 1972, by Bwlch Hill Wind) so Merry Mountain had the Welsh Criban Heather Belle, by Criban Cockade, as g-g-dam on his sire's side and the Welsh Gem IV, by Tanybwlch Berwyn, as g-g-dam on his dam's side. Merry Mountain was one of the best limbed ponies of his day.

Prudence was three years younger than Promise and was bequeathed to Mrs Ailsa Pease by Mrs Griffith in her will. Like Promise, she also contested the matron classes and gained the supreme title at the 1969 RASE Show. Prudence was also an exceptional breeder but Mrs Pease crossed her with TB blood to produce larger animals. Most successful was the cross with Commandeer which resulted in the dual Hack of the Year title winner, Lemington Moonriver, owned by Mrs Profumo and ridden by Jennie Lorriston Clark. Sadly, Prudence died as a result of a road accident while still relatively young.

Mrs Ailsa Pease continued her interest in Welsh bloodlines by upgrading from her original riding pony, Winkie. It was Miss Brodrick who admired Winkie's Welsh type and persuaded Ailsa Pease to register her in the FS appendix. Winkie was first crossed with the Arab Rukaban to produce Lemington May Day who, in turn, was mated with the French TB Golden Cross. The resultant offspring included Lemington Entre, reserve supreme at the 1974 POB Show, Lemington Happy Ending, champion at Dublin, and Lemington Buckaroo who stood at stud at Gredington with Lord Kenyon. The most recent star bearing the Lemington prefix is Lemington Cliquot, a grey 122-cm gelding who has twice swept all challenges before him to take the Ponies (UK) supreme titles in 1999 and 2000. Cliquot was sired by the section B Brockwell Chipmunk, admired by Ailsa Pease for his 'trueness to type and amazing action behind'.

Another northern breeder to find success with Chipmunk was Mrs Leahy of the Ocean Stud, Pateley Bridge, Yorkshire who bred the 1979 Pony of the Year, Ocean So Fair, foaled in 1974 out of the part-bred mare Set Fair of Oakley.

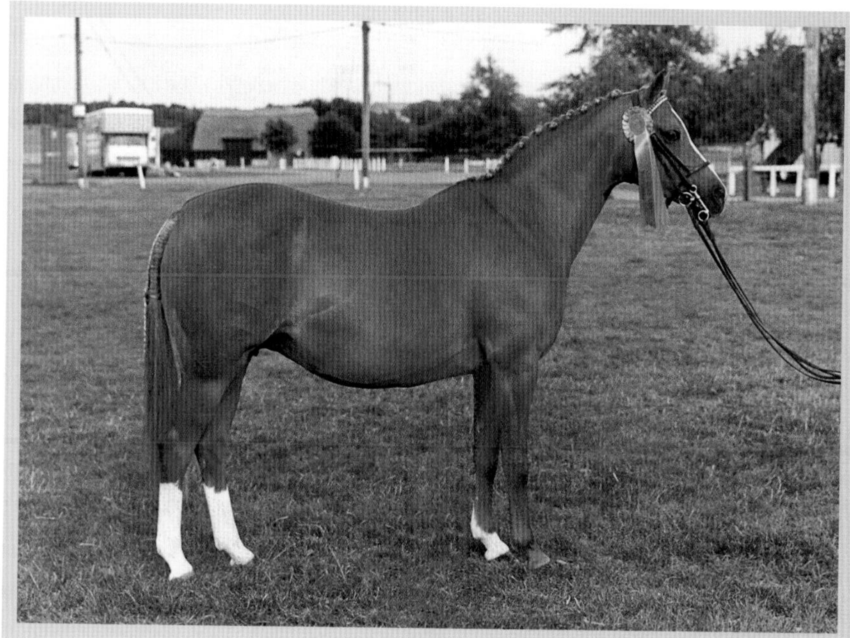

LEFT *Ocean So Fair. Photo: Carol Gilson.*

We have already looked at the phenomenal success of Solway Master Bronze as a section B sire in chapter 2, but he also found favour with riding pony breeders. Miss Miriam Reader of Elphicks had already requested first refusal on Master Bronze before he was born, owing to the brilliant ridden career of his dam, Criban Biddy Bronze, and the fact that his sire, Coed Coch Glyndwr, would have been 24 years old when Master Bronze was foaled in 1959 and Glyndwr's sire, Revolt, was even older (26 years) when Glyndwr was born in 1935. Miss Reader was delighted when her offer for Master Bronze was accepted and he remained at Elphicks until he was 14 (when the farm was sold) before moving to the Hon Mrs Ponsonby's Lechlade Stud for his last eight years.

Many famous riding pony mares visited Master Bronze at Lechlade, usually mares much bigger than Master Bronze himself. Mrs Sybil College brought Bubbles, producing her prolific sire, Oakley Bubbling Over. Mrs Jennifer Williams took her stylish TB Pendley Lady Precious Stream in 1966, to produce Pendley Model. Model also became a prolific sire, including, from his first crop, Enstone Artist, bought as a foal by Mrs Williams when still on his mother, Enston Delight (by Bwlch Zingaree out of Coed Coch Bwlbwl by Coed Coch Madog). Pendley Model was also shown with great success; the overall supreme at the 1969 POB Show at Ascot rating as one of his highlights. The palomino Gaulden Gadabout (foaled in 1963, out of Marilyn) was WPB champion for Mrs Cottrill at the 1964 RW Show and the Hon Mrs Ponsonby herself bred the 14-hand Lechlade Larkspur out of Lechlade Zinnia. Larkspur won 21 SHP championships in one season.

The name of Mrs Kathleen Cuff has become legendary in terms of the development of the modern section B ponies. However, prior to her successful launch into section Bs, Mrs Cuff was a leading exhibitor of children's riding ponies ridden by her own children, Andrew, Gillian (mother of international show jumper Andrew Davies) and Rosemary (Small-Land Stud). At the first post-war RW Show at Carmarthen in 1947, Mrs Cuff won first and third prizes in a class of 17 12 hands 2 in ponies with The Nut and Pip (of unknown parentage) and third and sixth in the

13.2 hh class with Twinkle (bred in Abergele) and Coed Coch Meteor (sired by Tanybwlch Berwyn out of Miss Brodrick's hunter mare First Flight). The Nut was first again in 1949, with Mrs Cuff's Craven Mona second and Reeves Crystal (bred at Ceulan and g-g-dam of Ceulan Cariad) third, and Mrs Cuff was second and third in the 13.2 hh class with Downland Pheasant and Berwyn Grey Lady. Mrs Cuff had acquired Criban Heather Belle for the novice ridden class where she was placed fourth to Mrs Hepburn's Jolagh, Mrs Cuff's other Berwyn Grey Lady and Ceulan Silver Lustre. The previous day Criban Heather Belle had won the in-hand section B championship from Berwyn Beauty (dam of Berwyn Grey Lady, Coed Coch Berwynfa, Coed Coch Blaen Lleuad, Brockwell Berwyn, etc.), Craven Nell and Ceulan Silver Lustre. Criban Heather Belle altered the course of section B history by being the dam (in 1955) of Downland Dragonfly who was the dam (in 1959) of Downland Dauphin, sire (in 1962) of the great Downland Chevalier.

Apart from Dauphin, Downland Dragonfly had a big influence on Welsh part-bred breeding, the other influence being via her 1963 daughter, Downland Demoiselle, a son x mother mating, Dauphin x Dragonfly. Demoiselle was a very successful 12 hands 2 in ridden pony before becoming a brood mare. The best known of her progeny was Longnewton Maestro, a ridden 'best of breed' at Olympia and also sire of Mrs Marie Claire Nimmo's dynasty of part-breds, including the black Duntarvie Catamount, champion WPB at the RW Shows in 1993, 1994 and 1995 and HOYS In-hand qualifier at PUK in 1998, followed by another Maestro son, Duntarvie Cat Burglar, champion in 2002 and HOYS qualifier at the Royal Highland.

BELOW *Duntarvie Catamount, RW champion 1993, 1994, 1995. Photo: Real Time Imaging.*

Tragically, Dauphin's life was cut short by grass sickness but fortunately not before producing Chevalier (foaled in 1962) and Downland Starletta (foaled in1965). Starletta was out of the TB Ashby Star bred by Rodney Mansfield (a very accomplished jockey of his day) and his father at Ashby-de-la-Zouch. Though a winner of two races on the flat, it was felt she was too small to make a big impact on the track so she was sent to the sales where she was spotted by Mrs Cuff. Sadly, Ashby Star bred only one foal but Starletta made a major impact on part-bred breeding, especially through her son, Downland Folklore (foaled in 1977), the flagship of the much-admired Dutch Welsh part-breds where they are allocated section K of the Stud Book. The Welsh part-bred ponies in Holland are of a firmly established type that almost makes them a breed. They are in great demand as sports ponies for dressage, show jumping and eventing disciplines across mainland Europe.

In chapter 2 we saw the dominance of Downland Chevalier in the section B world when he topped the sire ratings ten times between 1968 and 1981 (once jointly with his son, Downland Mandarin, foaled in 1969), followed four times by Mandarin's son, Keston Royal Occasion (foaled in 1972), then nine times by Keston Royal Occasion's son, Rotherwood State Occasion (foaled in 1979). Despite being exported to Australia, Keston Royal Occasion had a major influence on part-bred breeding through his sons Westacre Concerto, sire of the 1996 RW champion, Rotherwood Peter Pan, the 1983 RW champion Fairley Rembrandt (foaled in 1980) sire of Fairley Tempest, and Sandbourne Royal Ensign (foaled in 1981) who broke all records as sire of four Wembley ridden show pony champions and also as sire of Deanhills Royal Portrait (foaled in 1996, out of Bradmore Nutkin) so that he is three-quarter brother to Bradmore Catkin, the 1998 Wembley ridden Show Pony of the Year.

ABOVE *John Careless with Fairley Rembrandt, RW champion 1983. Photo: Carol Gilson.*

Downland Mandarin spent time with several studs, including the Meyers of Keston, Mrs Olive Weston of Seaholm and Renita and Norwood White of Colbeach. He was a popular sire and had the distinction of siring all the section B winners at the 1979 West Midland Stallion Show. At

ABOVE *Sandbourne Royal Ensign. Photo: Dalveen Gregory.*

Colbeach he sired probably his best part-bred, Colbeach Martina, foaled in 1989. This charismatic 12 hands 2 in mare loved the big occasion and big ring. Her many championships included the Keith Lee Smith Gold Cup at the East of England Show.

Without doubt, Mandarin's legacy to the pony world was through his greatest son, Keston Royal Occasion. Bred by James and Janet Meyer, he did stud duties with Lady Irene Astor at her Hever Stud before passing to Elizabeth and Rodney Mansfield at Rotherwood where, in addition to the exceptional Rotherwood residents, his visiting harem included some of the best mares in the UK. One often ponders why certain stallions are so successful, but with Keston Royal Occasion there was immediate admiration: an exquisite head with wide forehead, big bold fluid eye, free flowing movement and gaily carried tail. However, in terms of part-bred breeding, he also had a superb length of front and a natural 'turn' at the poll which he passed to his stock, setting them aside from the rest. He certainly stamped his offspring with his special hallmark.

John Careless of the Fairley Stud was early to appreciate the value of Keston Royal Occasion as a 'crossing' sire to cover his prolific broodmare, Fairley Melissa, in 1979. The resulting Fairley Rembrandt won championships at the RASE and RW Show in 1983. At four years Rembrandt appeared under saddle, winning the ridden stallion classes at the West Midlands and POB Shows. As a sire Rembrandt has been 'top drawer', producing winners in both the performance field and show world. In 1998 his son, Fairley Leonardo, swept all before him at the BSPS Championships to claim the top WHP title.

Rembrandt's greatest claim to fame is as sire of Ardenhall Royal Secret (foaled in 1987), three times 12.2 hh Pony of the Year and twice overall champion Pony of the Year. Two Downland mares were purchased from Mrs Cuff in 1980, Downland Seasong (out of Downland Starletta) and Downland Glissade (out of Downland Honeysuckle by Downland Chevalier). Both mares proved ideal matrons for Rembrandt, Seasong providing the stud with the next generation stallion Fairley Tempest who became a leading sire in the UK and in Australia (via frozen semen) and was later exported to the Lloyd Scott establishment in Australia.

In 1981 another Keston Royal Occasion colt was foaled who was to transform pony breeding over the next two decades. He was Sandbourne Royal Ensign . Chris and Hilary Sandison had acquired the riding pony mare, Cusop Anita, after she had been sadly measured out of 12.2 hh classes. Anita was by Cusop Dignity and out of Cusop Actress, daughter of Criban Activity; Royal Ensign was her first foal. He was shown lightly as a youngster. His best placing came at the 1984 POB Stallion Show where he was champion colt. In 1984 he was bought by Robert Cockram,

ABOVE *Ardenhall Royal Secret ridden by Charlotte Dujardin. Photo: WPCS calendar.*

becoming the foundation of his Deanhills Stud. The rest is now riding pony history as he has etched his name in the record books of all-time successful sires.

Like his sire, Sandbourne Royal Ensign showed great ability in stamping his stock not only with his huge, elegant front, but with endless quality, coupled with the very best of temperaments. It is without doubt that his ability to pass on these desirable criteria has made him a leading sire of riding ponies of all sizes and type.

Sandbourne Royal Ensign has sired four Show Ponies of the Year at HOYS, Sandbourne Royal Emblem (148 cm in 1990), Drayton Penny Royal (128 cm in 1992), Bradmore Catkin (128 cm in 1998) and

Glenmoss Juliet (128 cm in 1999). His other HOYS successes include the 2001 Pony of the Year, Radway Flashdance (138 cm), and the 2002 SHP of the Year, Royalswood Pageboy (122 cm). It is not only the HOYS arena which has witnessed his successes; Bennochy Royal Ensign was SHP champion at both the PUK and BSPS championships, Firle Squirel Nutkin was mini champion at Royal International, his stock won the progeny class at RASE in 2001 and 2002, Lechlade Mistletoe (out of Ceulan Siwan) was the champion mini show pony at the Royal International and, at the very same venue, Whinfell Tom Kitten was the overall in-hand champion.

Sandbourne Royal Ensign has sired a total of 11 qualifiers for the prestigious HOYS In-Hand championships. His stock have also gained him the POB Overall Progeny championship no fewer than six times, the supreme youngstock championships at NPS Shows four times and the supreme PUK yearling championship five times, a record that must surely rate as one of the best in the annals of pony breeding.

His best-known son is Deanhills Royal Portrait, a son of Bradmore Nutkin (by Teilwood Scorpio), herself a RASE and RW champion. Royal Portrait was only shown as a yearling in 1997, proving to be very successful, winning the coveted Cusop In-hand championship at the NPS Show and reserve for the In-hand HOYS qualifier which he later won at NPS Area 4, the finals of which were won by the WPB Huttons Ambo Camelia (grand-daughter of Chirk Caradoc), with the section A stallion Trefaes Taran reserve.

Although still only a relatively young sire (2004), Royal Portrait's stock have proved to be exceptional. Already he has sired two HOYS In-hand finalists, supreme champion foals at NPS Shows in 2000, 2002 and 2003 and twice champion youngstock and champion foal at RASE. In 2003 his stock reigned supreme at shows the length and breadth of the country: Thornsett Royal Romance supreme British National Foal Show, Great Yorkshire and PUK, Henleydown Picturesque National supreme WPB Champion at Shrewsbury and Bradmore Catalena supreme champion at the Midlands Show.

ABOVE *Michael Hendine with Huttons Ambo Camelia. Photo: A. Reynolds LBIPP, LMPA.*

LEFT *Robert Cockram with Henleydown Picturesque. Photo: Wynne Davies.*

Again, like his father, Royal Portrait has also witnessed his offspring excel under saddle. Blaircourt Masterpiece, former in-hand qualifier, is a championship winner in SHP classes and Barnsbrook Royal Portrait (out of Waxwing Tansy, daughter of the champion section B Sparkler of High Tor) is a leading show pony. Both Royal Ensign and Royal Portrait have made their mark on the pony rings through their unquestionable ability to breed a distinctive type of quality pony which has a temperament to suit every occasion.

In chapter 2 we have already seen the brilliant success of Keston Royal Occasion as a section B sire at Rotherwood Stud, with such progeny as Rotherwood Penny Royale and Rotherwood State Occasion. Mrs Elizabeth Mansfield of Rotherwood was also proud to see his successful crossing on many of the glamorous riding pony mares who visited. One to catch her eye when he arrived with his dam in 1982 was Westacre Concerto. The minute he stepped off the ramp, Elizabeth Mansfield thought he was 'very special' and how right she was later proved to be. His dam was the FS1

RIGHT *Oldcourt Contata ridden by Alexandra Fowler.*

mare Twylands Crescendo by Chirk Caradoc and out of Bwlch Minuet who was herself the offspring of Bwlch Valentino x Miss Minette. Concerto was a prolific winner as a colt, twice claiming the POB supreme youngstock title, as a yearling and as a two year old. However, it is as a sire that we appreciate his contribution to the Welsh part-bred scene. Exactly ten years after his brother, Twylands Carillon, stepped forward to take the Show Pony title at the HOYS, Concerto's daughter, Oldcourt Contata, was in the same spotlight, also taking the 138-cm class and reserve overall. However, Contata's sister, Oldcourt Balilika, went further, taking the supreme Pony of the Year in 2002. Within weeks, Balilika was winging her way to Australia to resume her successful career down under. This family name was again to the fore at the 2003 HOYS when Mrs Ann Fowler's Broadgrove Chatterbox, a three-year-old daughter of Oldcourt Contata, claimed the Breeders In-hand title after qualifying as WPB champion at the RW Show, and it was Chatterbox's sire, Cusop Dimension, who took the RW Show HOYS ticket in 1997. Despite being only four years old in 2004, Chatterbox beat much more experienced mounts to win the 138-cm ridden show pony class at the HOYS ridden by Lucy Loughton, and then went on to win the reserve championship.

BELOW *Broadgrove Chatterbox. Photo: A. Reynolds LBIPP, LMPA.*

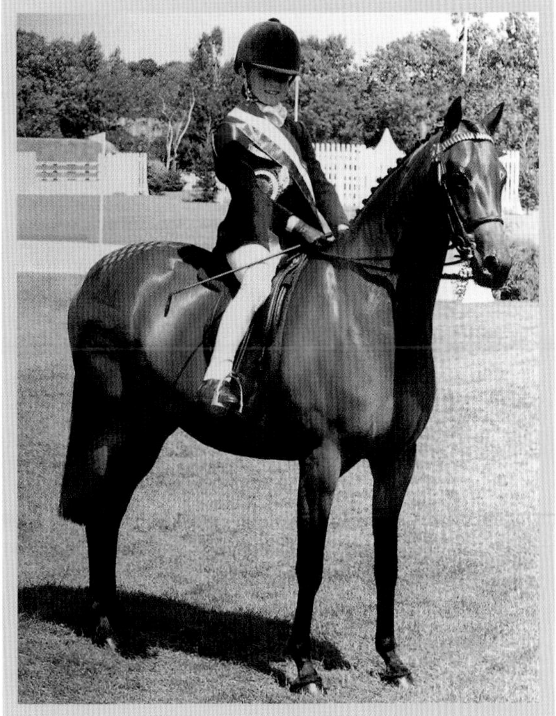

Interestingly, one of the first Concerto foals was Rotherwood Sonata from a female line similar to Concerto's, Sonata being out of Twylands Toccata, herself a daughter of Bwlch Minuet and by Criban Loyal Grey. Sonata's many successes included winning the Vincent Taylor championship at the 1989 NPS Show.

Another family line that proved very influential was based on the chestnut Keston Royal Occasion daughter, Katie's Dream. Bred by Peter Wilson, she retired to stud at Rotherwood and became an instant success breeding to

Westacre Concerto. A selection of the family 'best' would have to include the 1992 RASE champion, Rotherwood Day Dream, and the outstanding colt Rotherwood Peter Pan, foaled in 1994. As a yearling Peter Pan stood supreme at the RASE and a year later was reserve supreme at PUK and WPB champion at the RW Show. It was obvious from his first crop of foals that this double cross of Keston Royal Occasion was producing the goods. By the time Peter Pan was six years old he had seen two of his offspring take the youngstock in-hand title at the HOYS, Rotherwood Flamenco in 2000 and Greenbarrow Mr Smee a year later.

Mrs Pat Johns-Powell also used 'Keston' bloodlines to breed a very successful line of WPBs at Cottrell Stud, Bonvilston, Cardiff. She selected Keston Music (foaled in 1974) a chestnut 12 hands 2 in mare by Downland Mandarin (sire of Keston Royal Occasion) who was crossed with Rotherwood State Occasion (son of Keston Royal Occasion), producing a line mostly with a musical theme, e.g. Fanfare, Magic Flute, Rhapsody and

RIGHT *Cottrell Statement. Photo: Carol Gilson.*

Musical Occasion, but probably the best had no musical connection and was named Cottrell Statement. Statement was originally shown successfully in hand, and later came into his own, taking many 128-cm titles including some at the RW Show.

Another Downland Chevalier daughter, who started her own dynasty of champions, was Abercrychan Antonella, foaled in 1967, out of the FS mare Antonia by Reeves Golden Lustre. Antonia was foaled in 1955 at a time before Reeves Golden Lustre (bred at Ceulan in 1945) was accepted into section B and, therefore, although her dam, Sally, was inspected and passed as FS, Antonia also had to be registered as FS. She was sold to Abercrychan Stud in 1965. Antonia's daughter, Antonette of Highmoor FS1 (foaled in 1961), and Sally's daughter, Little Sally of Highmoor (foaled in 1960), came to Ceulan in 1971 along with Downland Grasshopper (originator of the Kirby Cane 'G' family) from Douglas Tovey's Highmoor Stud in Nettlebed, Oxfordshire. Abercrychan Antonella was shown nationally in 1968 and won at Shrewsbury and the East of England Shows. Consequently, when she was offered by Abercrychan Stud at the 1968 FO sale, she fetched the third-highest price (850 guineas), selling to Mrs Vivienne Appell and her father, Mr da Costa.

ABOVE *Harmony Bubbling Champagne. Photo: Carol Gilson.*

Antonella won in youngstock classes at major English shows before being put in foal to Bwlch Hill Wind in 1970, the resulting progeny being Anton of Harmony who won many championships under saddle, including Royal Windsor. Antonella had another 12 foals by such sires as Oakley Bubbling Spring, Gaulden Gamecock , Rosevean Eagle's Hill, Dawnway Minstrel Man, Westacre Concerto and Twylands Troubadour, the most successful of which were the 1983 HOYS Pony of the Year, Harmony Bubbling Champagne (foaled in 1974), and his full-brother, Harmony Bubbling Cliquot (foaled in 1984), who qualified for the HOYS a record eight times between 1988 and 1996.

The other famous Downland line is based on Downland Romance (foaled in 1961) who was the foal of Downland Love in the Mist (foaled in 1954) one year before she produced Downland Chevalier. Mrs Cuff was a staunch supporter of 'Craven' bloodlines and Love in the Mist was a daughter of Craven Sprightly Twilight and her sire, Star Supreme, was sired by the 1949 RW Cob-type champion, Welsh Echo (chapter 3) out of Lady Cyrus (foaled in 1947). Although she was section B female champion at the 1947 RW Show, Lady Cyrus was sired by Craven Cyrus (by King Cyrus AHSB) out of the Cob-type Blaentwrch Firelight by the 1922 RW Cob-type champion Baedeker. Whereas Chevalier was sired by Downland Dauphin (foaled in 1959), Romance was sired by Downland Roundelay (foaled in 1958) who was sired by the section A Downland Serchog (foaled in 1951) who was by Downland Dicon (foaled in 1947) by Revel Brightlight whom we had at Ceulan in 1951. Roundelay was gelded in 1960 after covering Love in the Mist and was sold to Miss Thomas of Abercrychan for whom he was placed sixth in hand (2- or 3-year-old section B filly or gelding) and fifth under saddle at the 1961 RW Show. Serchog's dam was the 'wild and wonderful' Criban Sweetly (foaled in 1934), daughter of the brilliant Criban Socks. Sweetly won the section A ridden class at the 1951 RW Show for Mrs Cuff just a few months after being bought off the mountains where she had lived untouched for 17 years and could only be viewed through binoculars! Roundelay's dam was Downland Red Heather (foaled in 1953) sired by Downland Imp (son of Craven Iona) out of Criban Heather Bell, dam also of Dragonfly, dam of Dauphin.

A great believer in the Romance line was Mrs Cuff's daughter, Mrs Rosemary Rees of the Small-Land Stud. In 1969 she covered her TB mare Gazelle with Romance to produce Small-Land Mayday whom Jack Edwards of the Weston Stud placed as WPB champion at the 1971 RW Show. A full-brother, Small-Land Otto, was foaled in 1971 and he topped the 1972 FO Sale at 900 guineas, then going to Weston Stud where he became a leading 14 hand 2 in show pony. Gazelle was then put to Romance's son, Downland Mohawk, with continuing success and in 1975 produced Small-Land Mambrino, one of the most influential riding pony stallions of the day. Mambrino was a tremendous stockgetter and remained fertile until he passed away at 28 years old in 2003. During this time he was responsible for many champions but probably his finest hour came when two of his sons took their respective championships at the 1993 Royal International Horse Show. Sion Brian won the hunter pony title, while Royal Bronze led the show ponies and, later, was supreme ridden of the show. This was the first time that a pony had taken the Winston Churchill cup. Mambrino also sired two Wembley winners and a reserve champion that year.

Later that year Sion Brian was reserve Show Hunter Pony at the HOYS – a far cry from when he was bought at the 1989 Llanybyther Sale by William and Marilyn Scale. At that stage they did not even know his breeding but it turned out that his dam was a brilliant jumping pony, the Welsh section B Deiniol Sian, foaled in 1974, sired by the section B Trefach Prince (by Menai Shooting Star) out of Ffoslas Susan (one of the rare section Bs bred at Ffoslas) by Treharne Peregrine. Sion Brian was bred by Mrs Cynthia Higgon, long-serving steward at the RW Show and secretary of the All-Wales Point-to-Point committee for 32 years. Further testimony to the value of Small-Land Mambrino as a sire was apparent at the 1992 RW Show where he was sire of the champion show pony, Royal Bronze (out of Rookery Grania), champion WHP Small-Land Stormboy and the reserve champion SHP, Sion Brian. Mambrino stock could also prove their worth in the performance field, several becoming Advanced eventers, including Downland Chancellor and Small-Land Maymaster who also passed on his excellent conformation, especially regarding limbs and substance, resulting in animals with much appeal in the Show Hunter Pony ring. Two such animals have taken the SHP of the Year title, Small-Land Moonwalk in 1994 and Touch of the Tobies in 1999.

A completely different type was the Mambrino son, Small-Land Mascot. Foaled in 1979, he was out of Small-Land Mayday and was of true show pony quality. Mascot had the perfect pony head, with charisma and presence to spare; his conformation could stand the closest scrutiny. Mascot was the RW WPB champion at two and three years old. Like his sire, he had the ability to breed both hunter and show ponies. His ridden champions included the 13 hands hunter pony Small-Land Arabella and the 1991 RIHS show pony champion, Talacharn Wedding Chorus, while in

ABOVE *Small-Land Mascot. Photo: WPCS Journal.*

hand he sired the 1997 Templeton HOYS champion, Huttons Ambo Camelia. Mascot was exported to Eric Dudley in Victoria, Australia in 1995 but, sadly, sired only two crops of foals before he died in 1997.

Downland Mohawk (section B champion RW 1971) was the sire of the 1977 and 1982 RW champion, Rosedale Mohican, who, in turn, was sire of Orielton Aristocrat (foaled 1977, out of Hollytree Bettryn by Kirby Cane Guardsman whom I exported to Sweden in 1969), one of the most successful sires of the smaller riding pony. After spending time with Mrs Barbara Grant-Parkes, where his offspring included Twylands Prose (a leading sire at Chinook Stud), he moved to Mrs Annie Smalley's Barkway Stud where his stock have been equally successful. His HOYS champions have included the part-breds Barkway Happy Returns and Barkway Black Magic and the pure-breds Colne Heiress and Nantcol Lady Julia , all with wonderful temperaments.

Orielton Aristocrat also sired Twylands Arielle who was bought from Twylands by Mrs Sue Chance as a three year old. Soon her progeny, bearing the Spinningdale prefix, were gracing the show rings. The best was undoubtedly the 14 hands 2 in mare Spinningdale Arabella who first qualified at the 1991 Royal Cornwall Show as a yearling for the HOYS Creber championship where the reserve was the section B Thornberry Royal Gem. Arabella then qualified for the HOYS every year in which she competed under saddle, winning the Pony of the Year title in 1996. At the 1997 HOYS, Twylands Arielle made her entry into the record books when four of her progeny qualified in four different classes, Spinningdale Araminta, Octavious and Arabella in each of the show pony classes and Anastasia as an SHP.

Although many think of the Rookery prefix in terms of sections A and C, a very influential line of part-breds was also founded on the TB mare Cambusmore. Cambusmore was owned by Mrs Robina Mills's mother, Mrs

ABOVE *Rookery Grana with Rookery Grateful at foot.*

Robin Grosvenor of Chaddleworth, Berkshire, and, despite being the dam of three winners on the flat, the decision was made in 1964 to cover her with the part-bred Shalbourne Monseigneur by Coed Coch Glyndwr. The resulting foal was named Grana. Grana was put to a variety of Welsh stallions, producing Rookery Grace (foaled in 1968) by Cusop Hoity Toity, Rookery Grouse (foaled in 1970) by Chirk Crogan, and Rookery Granite (foaled in 1969), Graduate (foaled in 1973) and Grateful (foaled in 1974) by Gredington Mynedydd. Graduate, Grace and Granite were all RW winners, with Graduate also winning the reserve championship when I judged in 1974, while Grateful took the part-bred championship at Northleach in 1984. Other Grana progeny included Rookery Gretel (foaled in 1972) by Springbourne Blueberry, Greyling (foaled in 1975) by Gredington Mynedydd, Grebe (foaled in 1976) by Gorsty Firefly, Gremlin (foaled in 1980) by Lechlade Red, Greensleeves (foaled in 1981) and Grandee (foaled in 1982) by Sintoncourt Peregrine.

Rookery Grand Duchess (foaled in 1977), by Solway Master Bronze out of Grana, was reserve champion WPB at the 1978 RW Show before being exported to Mark Bullen's Imperial Stud where she was entered into the Australian Welsh FS register, won Welsh championships and bred a

RIGHT *Royal Bronze.*

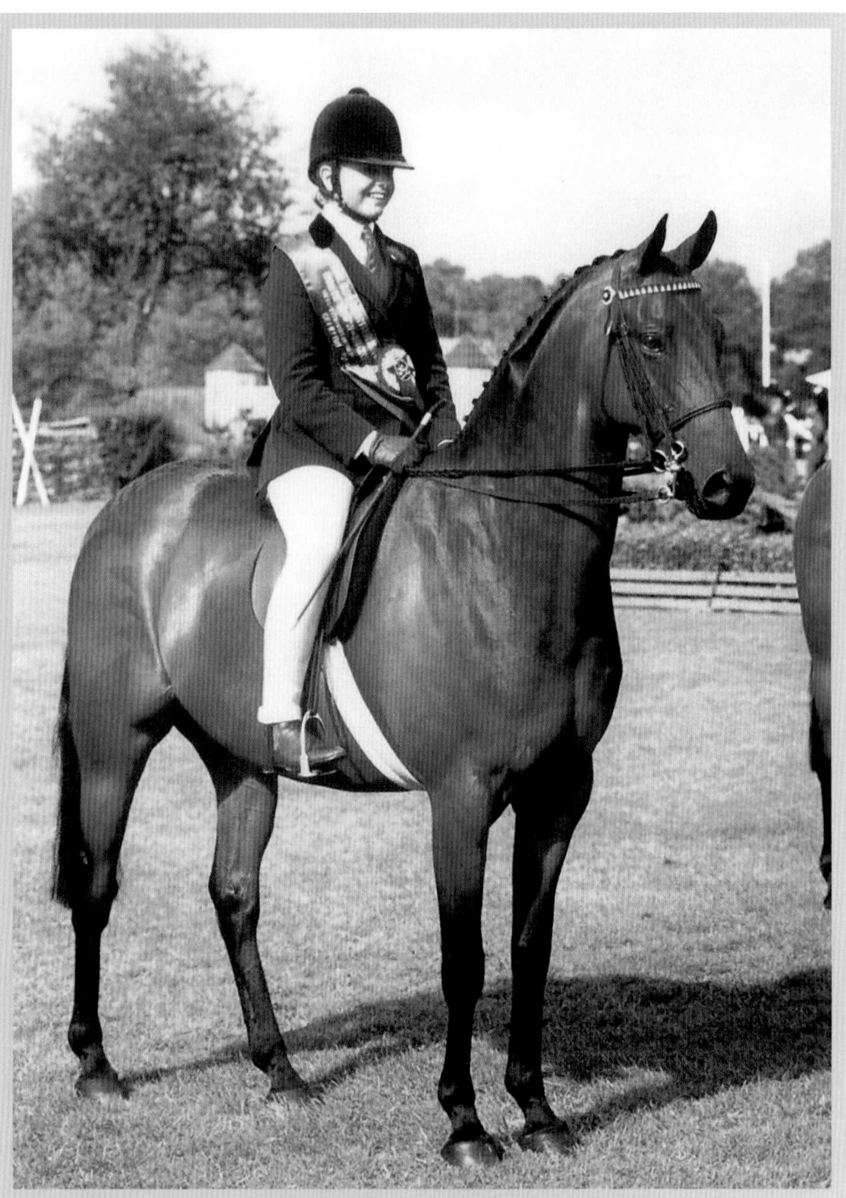

string of winners. When I judged in Australia in 1984, the champion section B was Imperial Lady Anne by Weston Chilo out of Rookery Grand Duchess. Grana was also covered by the riding pony Mischiefmaker (Bwlch Hill Wind x Arden Tittle Tattle, the winner of the first-ever In-hand HOYS championship in 1965), producing Rookery Grania who, in 1984, became the dam of Royal Bronze, the 1993 Winston Churchill cup winner at the RIHS. Royal Bronze also won the 14.2 hh class and was reserve champion at the 1993 HOYS for which he had qualified at the Three Counties. Royal Bronze was so named because he was much admired by HRH the Princess Royal as a very young foal at Pembroke County, shown by his owner Mrs E. L. Harries of Haverfordwest.

It was Lady Margaret Myddelton who described Chirk Caradoc as 'a terrible snob, much preferring his more glamorous ladies of other descents to his small woolly counterparts'! Caradoc always exuded that little bit extra which he passed on to his many offspring. One of Caradoc's fancied ladies was Lady Margaret's own Kitty's Fancy, a superb quality TB mare by Rajah II. The cross proved exceptional, producing the trio of females: Chirk Catmint (foaled in 1967), Caviar (foaled in 1970) and Cattleya (foaled in 1971), the 1974 RW WPB champion.

ABOVE *Chirk Catmint. Photo: Horse and Hound.*

Chirk Catmint was first shown by Lady Margaret before being sold to Miss Margaret Hinde for whom she bred Aristocrat and Contessa, both with the Flawforth suffix. Ron Hayes was the next owner and produced Little Aston Bayleaf and Tarragon. By now Catmint was an established brood mare and among her many titles was the British In-hand supreme in 1978. Later, in 1978, she was bought by Mrs Carolyn Bachman and her first progeny with the Carolinas prefix was Cat's Whisker (foaled in 1979) by Bwlch Zephyr. He was later exported to Australia where he became a leading sire. Others followed in quick succession, including Carolinas Catkin (foaled in 1980 by Erimus Typhoon), Pussycat (foaled in

RIGHT *Carolinas Pussycat. Photo: A. Reynolds LBIPP, LMPA.*

1981 by Bwlch Zephyr), Kitten (foaled in 1983 by Twylands Troubadour) and Cat's Eye (foaled in 1982 by Rosslyn Sandalwood).

Pussycat was a striking chestnut filly, winning the WPB championship at the 1984 RW Show where her half-sister, Kitten, was reserve. Pussycat also qualified for the HOYS at Devon County in 1987 and at the Three Counties in 1988. In 1985 Carolinas Cat's Eye was RW WPB champion and Kitten returned to be reserve for the second time in 1986. Cat's Eye also had a successful career as a hack before retiring to stud duties at Copybush Stud. Her three-year-old son, Copybush Catchphrase, sired by Trellech Courvoisier, was the HOYS Creber In-hand champion at the 1994 HOYS, having qualified at Newark where Mollegaard Spartacus was reserve, later to qualify at the South of England Show. Catmint died relatively young in 1984. In 1994, following the dispersal of the riding ponies at Carolinas, Pussycat became a resident riding pony brood mare at the Llanarth Stud. At Llanarth the family moved on a pace with successful crossing of the Cusop stallions based nearby. To Cusop Disciplin Pussycat produced the RASE champion Llanarth Catmint and, in 1992, she pro-

LEFT *Len Bigley with Llanarth Alleycat. Photo A. Reynolds LBIPP, LMPA.*

duced Llanarth Alleycat who was a HOYS finalist in 1997 at NPS and in 1998 and 1999 at the Midland Show. Alleycat has firmly established himself as a sire, one of his daughters, Merriment Pussycat (out of Oakley Baby's Fun), being the Templeton HOYS In-hand champion in 1998 at two years old, with her sire, Alleycat being placed seventh! The Pussycat line continues at Llanarth with a very attractive filly, Llanarth Kitty, sired by Cusop Dimension, and foaled in 2001. Unshown until three years old, she was reserve for the HOYS title at the 2003 Three Counties Show behind the section C Nebo Rachel.

Chirk Catmint's sisters, Caviar and Cattleya, were bigger, both contesting the 14 hands 2 in classes. The ridden scene was left to Caviar, where her length of stride and natural carriage made her a regular championship winner. She later became a successful brood mare with Mrs Rogers at Risinghoe. Cattleya, on the other hand, pursued an equally successful career through the youngstock and matron classes, starting with the 1974 RW Show where I awarded her the WPB championship. Another memorable occasion was at the 1978 POB championship where all the classes were won by Chirk Caradoc daughters, Chirk Cattleya, Chirk Catmint and Nantcol Arbennig, with Cattleya taking the championship over Catmint.

Cattleya gained further acclaim through her daughter, Chirk Windflower (sired by Solway North Wind), when she lifted the Lloyds Bank title at the 1986 HOYS as a three year old. Cattleya and Windflower both became resident at Rotherwood where Cattleya lived to the ripe old age of 33.

It was at Rotherwood that Chirk Caradoc produced another of the 'greats' of the part-bred world. At the 1964 NPS Sale at Newbury Racecourse, Mrs Mansfield bought a leggy yearling filly called Penhill Bo Peep, sired by Bwlch Zingaree out of a daughter of Cusop Celebrity. Ironically, that was the first time that Mrs Mansfield had ever bid at auction and she found herself sitting next to a gentleman who encouraged her to 'go on'. That gentleman was Vivian Eckley of Cusop and Mrs Mansfield had what she describes as 'the bargain of a lifetime' for 100 guineas. When it came to putting Bo Peep in foal, Chirk Caradoc was chosen, Mrs Mansfield being attracted to his movement and beautiful head. Bo Peep visited Caradoc three times, producing Rotherwood Peep Show (foaled in 1967), Peep Again (foaled in 1972) and Peep Shine (foaled in 1974).

BELOW *Rotherwood Peep Show ridden by Susan Rose. Photo: Monty.*

Rotherwood Peep Show had one of the most successful and complete careers of any pony. She started off as a very successful filly, winning the NPS youngstock title twice. She returned to the Malvern Show to take the ridden championship as a four year old (produced by Colin Rose) before, later in life, taking the brood mare title. Her first foray into brood mare classes was at the 1974 RASE Show where 'her feet never touched the ground' according to judge Mrs Joan Gibson when awarding her the Wembley Lloyds Bank ticket. But she was no stranger to the 'London lights', having been ridden pony champion at the 1972 Royal International Show.

Peep Show produced 11 colts and two fillies. Three of the colts were exported to Australia where they had a tremendous influence on the development of the ridden pony. The only living daughter is Rotherwood Bo-Peep (foaled 1988, sired by Solway North Wind), so named as she is the image of her grand-dam. Following a year under saddle, Rotherwood Bo-Peep returned to Rotherwood. Covered by Westacre Concerto, she produced the filly Rotherwood Peek-a-Boo, RW WPB champion in 1997 as a yearling. She was then supreme pony at the BSPS championships in 2002 and in 2004 and secured the Coronation Cup Supreme Championship for the first time ever for Rotherwood Stud. Peek-a-Boo occupies a special place at Rotherwood as she was born two days after the death of Peep Show and is her exact image.

In 1997 Rotherwood Bo-Peep produced another filly, named Rotherwood Take a Peep, sired by Strinesdale Matador. Sold as a foal to Pam and Bob Sowerby, Take a Peep was successfully shown to notch wins of the calibre of the £1,000 Red Rose Final. Take a Peep produced a foal as a four year old but headed for the ridden ring a year later, culminating with the BSPS Novice championship. However, this success faded into the

LEFT *Rotherwood Peek-a-Boo. Photo: Real Time Imaging.*

background at the 2003 HOYS when Mrs Elizabeth Mansfield achieved her life-long ambition to breed the Riding Pony of the Year. Take a Peep had only one thing on the agenda that day – to win – and she did it through a display of movement which left all the others in her wake.

Chirk Caradoc certainly had a lot to be proud of in this family but there have been others, although perhaps not through such established lines. Lady Margaret bred Chirk Seren Bach (foaled in 1965) by Caradoc out of Twinkle and he ended up champion at the 1972 RIHS, while Chirk Clwyd's Lad won the show hunter pony supreme at the 1988 SPS championships. Also at BSPS, the outstanding working hunter pony, the Caradoc grandson, Stambrook Pavarotti (foaled in 1992), gained the supreme in 2002. Pavarotti had also won the WHP titles at HOYS and the RIHS. Pavarotti's dam is the Chirk Caradoc daughter, Glansevin Pirouette, foaled way back in 1969.

Another successful Caradoc mare was Camelia of Flawforth. Bought as a weaned foal in 1971, she became the foundation of a small stud for Mrs Sue Hide, wife of the famous jockey Eddie Hide. As a broodmare she bred two HOYS in-hand finalists. Huttons Ambo Candytuft, who was British In-hand champion in 1985, qualified for the Lloyds Bank HOYS in 1986 at the South of England Show, the year that Mrs Mansfield's Chirk Windflower was champion. Candytuft had a full-brother, Huttons Ambo Checkerberry, who carried Jamie Osbourne to many victories in 14 hh WHP classes. Both were sired by Rudi but the Hides increased the 'Welsh' percentage by using Small-Land Mascot to breed the 1997 HOYS Pony In-hand champion, Huttons Ambo Camelia (foaled in 1989), who had qualified at the Scottish Horse Show under Mrs Renita White.

This chapter records the great strides forward and many major accolades achieved by Welsh part-bred ponies after a slow start in the 1950s when only nine were registered in ten years. In the WSB in 2003, 1,207 part-breds were registered, showing that they are now numerically stronger than section B (1,092 registered) and section C (902), section A being the most numerous (at 2,566) followed by section D (at 2,504).

CHAPTER FIVE

The Welsh Pony in Performance

THE WELSH breeds are world famous for their docile temperament, versatility and adaptability in performance in so many spheres. This chapter begins by tracing the increase in performance competitions at RW Shows.

At the first WN Show in 1904, there were 13 entries in three ridden classes, a far cry from 201 ridden section Cs and Ds in eight classes, 48 in four driven classes and 59 and 75 entries per class in HOYS qualifiers for sections A+B and C+D at the 2004 RW Show. Many of the 13 entries in 1904, although entered in the WSB to enable them to compete, were Hackney ponies from the leading British Hackney studs and, presumably, did not give very comfortable rides.

The next performance provision was a harness class for section As, first offered in 1928, and this was won every pre-war year (with the exception of 1937 when he was appointed judge to encourage other exhibitors!) by Mr Tom Jones Evans of Craven Arms. Mr Evans's winner in 1928 and 1929 was Craven Master Shot, and then Grove Sprightly was unbeatable seven times. Sprightly's biggest rivals in harness were Faraam Mercury (until he was exported to Australia in 1933), followed by Grove Will O'The Wisp and Bowdler Brightlight in 1934 and Faraam Mercury's son, Dinarth What Ho, in 1937.

When the RW Show resumed in 1947 after the war, Dinarth What Ho won every year for Ceulan Stud up to his death in 1953, including also twice winning the Tom and Sprightly competition which, in those days, was judged by a 'clapometer' instrument which measured popular applause. Placed second to What Ho in 1949, 1950 and 1951 was Ceulan Revelry (foaled in 1942, Ceulan Revolt x Ceulan Silverleaf) and in 1952 it was Revelry's full-brother, Ceulan Reveller (foaled in 1944), who was exported to the USA after a stint in Scotland and later at Cui Stud. From 1954 the main contenders were Bolgoed Atomic, Bolgoed Golden Glory, Glascoed Mervyn, Whitehall Sparklight and Criban Silver Sand. In 1956 a new face appeared in the form of Fronarth What Ho who was to remain prominent for 22 years. Atomic was given a good run for his money by Fronarth What Ho

ABOVE *Dinarth What Ho driven by E. S. Davies (1951). Photo: Modern Photo Service.*

RIGHT *Bolgoed Atomic driven by T. J. Thomas (1956).*

who was foaled in 1952 and sired by Dinarth What Ho out of the Cob-type mare Fronarth Queen Bee by Brenin Gwalia. Fronarth What Ho had a distinguished harness career at RW shows, winning 11 first prizes, including his final triumph in 1978 at the age of 26 years, and also, from 1963 to 1967, having to compete against Cobs in the same class. What a good investment the 10 shillings stud fee paid to me in 1951 turned out to be! Fronarth What Ho lived on to the ripe old age of 31 years, never having spent a day on grass after he was weaned.

It was not until 1968 that Cobs were allocated their own separate harness class. Fronarth What Ho was also second four times; to Cadle Starlight in 1962, to Gwynedd Gwyndaf in 1969, Whatton Pennaeth in 1970 and Fronarth Welsh Jack (section C) in 1972. Owing to insufficient entries, from 1972 to 1982 this harness class was for sections A, B and C, with section C being hived off to a separate class (just as it is in the present day) in 1983.

Another stallion with a formidable record was Grangelands Golden Gleam (foaled in 1966, Springbourne Fanfare x Orgwm Marian). In the absence of Fronarth What Ho in 1973, 1976 and 1977, Golden Gleam won

LEFT *Grangelands Golden Gleam driven by G. H. Carter (1973).*

in large classes consisting mainly of section Cs and he won again in similar company in 1983 and 1984 with seconds in 1979,1985 and, finally, in 1988 in the largest class of all time, including the invasion of Twyford Marengo (the winner) and Rollright Gallant from Holland.

From 1980 to 1982 the class was won by the section C stallion Gwelfro Tywysog (foaled in 1975, Brenin Dafydd x Synod Frolic) who then went on to win a further six times in the separated class up to 1989 when he was also in-hand champion.

REIGHT *Gwelfro Tywysog driven by D. J. Jones. Photo: Anthony Booth.*

Dyfrdwy Starlight (foaled in 1985, Aston Superstar x Dyfrdwy Difyrrwch), a full-brother to the 1991, 1994 and 2000 RW in-hand champions Dyfrdwy Seren Arian and Dyfrdwy Seren Fwyn, first won in harness in 1992 and then won a further six times up to 2002. When Mr Gwil Evans of the Dyfrdwy Stud judged in 1998, the winner was Silvester (who was sold to Holland for the top price at the 1993 Fayre Oaks Sale after winning the 1991 in-hand male championship but returned to the UK to compete at the RW). Mynydd Illtyd Dash from Belgium won in 1996. Second to

Dyfrdwy Starlight in 1999 was the in-hand male champion Trefaes Guardsman and these positions were reversed the following year. In 2003, Glyncoch Peter Pan won the harness class in the horse ring just a few minutes after winning a second prize in the main ring, this time for in-hand junior stallions.

After 1983, when section Cs were allocated their own harness class, Gwelfro Tywysog won six times up to 1989, to be followed by three wins for Leyeswick Gamecock. Animals with the 'Leyeswick' prefix of Mr Joe

LEFT *Dyfrdwy Starlight driven by G. E. Evans. Photo: Arthur Thomson BEM.*

Giles often scooped up the other prizes during this period; in fact, five out of the ten entries competing in 1986 boasted the Leyeswick prefix.

From 1994, this class was dominated by Mitcheltroy Black King who won seven times and was second to Garnfach Glyndwr in 1999. Black King had his revenge in 2003 when he won the class from Crossfield Glory, son of Garnfach Gerallt who is also the sire of Garnfach Glyndwr.

Section Cs also carried the flag successfully in private driving classes, Mrs Deirdre Colville's Synod Cerdin being awarded the WPCS Brodrick

RIGHT *Synod Cerdin driven by Mrs Deirdre Colville. Photo: Peter Rollinson.*

Memorial trophy in 1977 for winning the private driving classes at the three royal shows, the Royal Welsh, the English Royal and the Royal Highland.

Ridden classes for Welsh ponies at the RW Show were discontinued in 1922 but then the Country Life trophy was introduced in 1937 for the best registered Welsh pony within the children's riding classes. A photograph of the 1937 winner, Mrs Hepburn's Tanybwlch Rhos, is shown on page 73, along with the runners-up, Craven Bess and Pixie. Mrs Hepburn won it again in 1939 with Craven Nell and three times from 1947 to 1950 with Coed Coch Powys whom Mrs Hepburn discovered in Denbighshire pulling a plough!

BELOW *Coed Coch Powys. Photo: Rouch.*

When a separate Welsh ridden class was introduced in 1951, Mrs Cuff won all three top awards with Criban Sweetly, Downland Dicon and Craven Bright Sprite. To encourage the continuance of this ridden class, Mrs Mari Borthwick of the Trefesgob Stud offered a trophy to be won in three consecutive years by the same exhibitor. This trophy was won outright by Mr Vivian Eckley's Criban Activity in 1953, 1954 and 1955, and Mr Eckley re-presented it in 1956 as the 'Cusop' cup with the same conditions of outright winning and Activity won it again!

From 1957 to 1965 the ridden class was opened to sections A and B but with the Cusop trophy confined to the highest-placed section A. Noted section Bs to be placed during these years included Weston Lavender Blue, Downland Red Heather, Coed Coch Prydyddes, Miss Crimpy Peek-a-Boo and Downland Roundelay, sire of Downland Romance (chapter 2). Mr R. W. Thomas's Velvet (who had won the section A yearling filly class at the 1953 RW Show) won the Cusop cup outright in 1959, 1960 and 1961 and again re-presented it, this time as the 'Velvet' cup which Ceulan won with Betws Nans in 1962.

BELOW *Betws Nans (1962), ridden by Penny Rowland. Photo: Wynne Davies.*

ABOVE *Whitsand Warrior ridden by Jack Simpson. Photo: Real Time Imaging.*

In 1965 an experimental separation of section A and B ridden classes was tried out but because the section B class attracted only three entries (Coed Coch Nyddwr, Downland Dauphin, who had won the in-hand stallion class, and Ffawodden Llydan Star), the classes were recombined until 1972 when Talgarreg Bethan won the section As and Cusop Sequence the section Bs.

To date (2004) no section A has won the Velvet trophy three years in succession, although Arlwydd Martini won it in 1993, 1996 and 1997, Llanerch Sirius in 1991,1992 and 1994, Aston Heather in 1986 and 1988 and Whitsand Warrior in 1999 and 2003 after having been reserve champion over all breeds at Olympia in 2001.

The most successful of the section Bs is Baledon Commanchero (1987, 1988, 1991 and 1992), followed by the Judge family with the 1981 Olympia champion, Norwood Principal Boy, (1983) and Wharley Taliesin (1984 and 1985) and Gryngallt ponies with the 1990 RW ridden champion, Gryngallt Pageboy (1990), Gryngallt Picturesque (2000) and Gryngallt Perseus (2002). Pageboy (foaled in 1985) and Picturesque (foaled in 1992) are sons of the Gryngallt foundation mare, Bengad Rita. Perseus (foaled in 1998) is a son of Gryngallt Personality (foaled in 1994) who himself is a son of Bengad Rita. Personality qualified for the 2004 HOYS ridden M&M competition, while the most celebrated of all the

BELOW LEFT *Baledon Commanchero ridden by Wendy Evans. Photo: Mike Gash.*

BELOW RIGHT *Gryngallt Perseus ridden by Lara Hooper (2002). Photo: N. Hooper.*

brothers is Gryngallt Playsome (foaled in 1990) who was the 2002 HOYS WHP champion.

The ridden Welsh Cob or Welsh pony of Cob-type ridden class was introduced in 1956 when it was included within the section for ridden hacks and hunters and judged by the hunter judge. The class remained within this section until 1975 when separate judges were allocated and the class split into ridden section C and section D. Until 1975 never once did a section C win the class but the section C Llanarth Cerdin was third in 1968 and 1969 and fourth in 1970; Llanarth Firel was fifth in 1971 and Lyn Cwmcoed was sixth in 1973.

With section Cs competing in their own right, Llanarth Cerdin won in 1975, Isamman Dafydd in 1976 and Llanarth Cadel in 1977 and 1978. The other most successful winners were Menai Furious (1988, 1993 and 1994), Foxhunter Sentinel (1982 and 1986), Kingdown Rebekah (1981 and 1985),

LEFT *Parvadean Lotta Bottle ridden by Roy Wilmin. Photo: Wynne Davies.*

Persie Ramrod (1989, also fourth stallion in hand, and 1992) and Parvadean Lotta Bottle (1998 and 1999).

The WPCS Performance Competition was inaugurated in 1972 with, for example, 200 points awarded for a win in an unaffiliated three day event (or 500 if it was affiliated), to 25 and 70, respectively, for private drive and 20 and 60 for leading rein. The first organiser of this competition, who had the unenviable task of collating and adding up the scores, was Mrs Jill Rogers of the Willesley Stud, Tetbury, Gloucestershire, and such notables as the Duke of Beaufort often attended to present the trophies and rosettes. One of the most successful competitors in the early years was Miss Anne Muir of the Stoatley Stud in Haslemere, Surrey and she took over the organisation of the competition in 1982.

Miss Muir's successes during the first ten years included Stoatley Rhosyn (champion section A, with 1,315 points) and Stoatley Moonraker (champion section C, with 1,230 points) in the first year (1972), followed by Stoatley Venetia, champion WPB with 6,815; 6,375; 6,655 and 8,220 points in 1977, 1978, 1979 and 1980, the last occasion also securing the overall championship

The first animal to win its section championship four times was the section B gelding Millcroft Aries, foaled in 1967 and sired by Chirk Crogan (chapter 2). Aries increased his points from 4,845 in 1974 and 9,120 in 1975 to an enormous 14,490 in 1976, winning the overall championship each time. Aries was owned by the Thorp family and ridden by Mary Jane Thorp. Then, after seven years' rest, he reappeared, ridden by Frances Strong, and was champion again in 1984!

Another four-times champion was Twyford Bobbie who was section A champion in 1990, 1991, 1993 and 1994, his highest total being 7,655 in 1990. The only other four-times champions were Sarah Jane Cook's section C driving pair, Leyeswick Welsh Flyer and Leyeswick Bantam Cock, in 2000, 2002, 2002 and 2004.

The only animal to win five championships was Anne Brockie's section C mare, Glanteifi Nans, foaled in 1977, sired by Menai Fury and champion in 1984, 1985, 1986, 1989 and 1991. Nans was also overall champion, with

ABOVE *Leyeswick Welsh Flyer and Leyeswick Bantam Cock driven by Sarah Jane Cook.*

5,935 points, in 1989. Nans was the wheeler, driven in tandem with the section A Quickthorn Greylag as leader but each time Nans ended up with a few more points than Greylag, won in single harness.

Following the sudden death of Miss Anne Muir in 1989, Mrs Rogers stepped into the breach and resumed the organisation of the competition until a successor was found in the form of Mrs Kathleen James, an ardent supporter of the competition whose Highland Drummer Boy was champion in 1978 and Highland Jury champion in 2004.

Of all the thousands of ponies and Cobs who have competed in performance events over 33 years, some families are obviously more suited to performance than others. The section B gelding Harwel Wizard was over-

all champion, with 7,840 points, in 1997 and reserve overall, with 7,820 in 1998 and 7,050 in 1999. Wizard, who was the overall champion at Olympia in 1998, was sired by the 1988 Olympia champion, Marston Monsoon, who is a grandson of Marston Mirage, the overall champion of the very first competition in 1972. Wizard was amongst the prize winners at the 1999 HOYS for both M&M WHP and First Ridden competitions and again at the 2004 HOYS in the First Ridden class.

The 2004 Simpson Refractories HOYS ridden section A and B Pony of the Year was the seven-year-old palomino section B stallion Northlight Galliano, ridden by Danielle Waterhouse. Galliano had qualified for the

HOYS every year since 2001 and qualified for the NPS/Baileys championships at Olympia three times since 2002. His brilliant Olympia record was 'Best of Breed' in 2003 and reserve champion over 34 qualifiers (with 43/50 for ride and 41/50 for conformation) in 2004 to the Connemara Castle Comet. Galliano's dam, Douthwaite Bolero, was acquired by the Waterhouse family in 1988 and she died, still with them, in 2004, a few days before Galliano's victory at the HOYS. Bolero herself qualified for Olympia in 1993. Galliano's sire was Ernford Bellboy and he was Olympia Best of Breed three times. An interesting fact of breeding is that Bolero was sired by Tetworth Nijinsky and Bellboy was sired by Tetworth Mikado, both Nijinsky and Mikado being sons of Tetworth Czarina.

Another Tetworth stallion of similar Downland Chevalier and Solway Master Bronze breeding was Tetworth Tetrarch , foaled in 1980. He was the sire of Bushmere Tolomeo who qualified for Olympia three times. Tolomeo was the sire of Bushmere Eclipse who qualified for Olympia in 1998, ridden by Samantha Darlington. With Harwel Wizard proclaimed overall champion in 1998, with top conformation points of 44/50, Roseisle Holy Joe, ridden by Francesca Shuck, was top section A and third overall, with 40/50, equal to Eclipse, who was sixth overall (36/50 for ride), and Peasedown Party Popper, ridden by Jo Bartlett, was top section C, with 37/50.

OPPOSITE TOP *Harwel Wizard. Photo: Anthony Reynolds LBIPP,LMPA.*

OPPOSITE BOTTOM *Ernford Bellboy ridden by Roy Wilmin. Photo: Real Time Imaging.*

LEFT *Roseisle Holy Joe (A) (nearest), Sianwood Silvermine (B) and Gryngallt Pageboy (B) with Cusop Regal Heir (behind). Photo: Carol Jones.*

RIGHT *Heniarth Quip ridden by India Latter. Photo: R. Miller.*

Sunwillow Bernina descendants are particularly successful as mounts for children and four of them have qualified for Olympia in 2000–03. Whitsand Warrior, ridden by Jack Simpson, was sired by Sunwillow Niklaus (foaled in 1980), son of Bernina, and he was Best of Breed in 2000 and again in 2001, with the added distinction of being reserve champion overall, with riding marks of 45/50 and 44/50 for conformation to the section C Starcrest Discovery. Warrior was joined in 2001 by Springbourne Crusader, sired by Sunwillow Offenpas, Bernina's 1981 son. Crusader was nineteenth in 2001 and improved this position to tenth the following year, occupying equal position to Heniarth Quail, daughter of Sunwillow Quest. Quest, foaled in 1983, is a daughter of Bernina and she was top of the 1994 Fayre Oaks Sale at 4,500 guineas. Quail was sired by Gwynrhosyn Geraint whose full-sister, Gwynrhosyn Ellie, was Best of Breed at Olympia in 1992. Both Whitsand Warrior and Heniarth Quip qualified for Olympia in 2003 when Quip was placed eleventh and was Best of Breed, and Quip was again

LEFT *Roseisle Tudyr Melody. Photo: David Mathews.*

sixth in 2004. Quip was foaled in 1996. A son of Quest, he is also descended from Bernina on his sire's side, being sired by Dukeshill Magnum, son of Sunwillow Mutters, grand-daughter of Bernina.

Another prefix constantly amongst the best performers is that of John and Lindsey Milligan of the Roseisle Stud. Without ever having been champion section A in the WPCS Performance competition (due to leading-rein and first ridden classes generating only 70 points), Roseisle Tudyr Melody (foaled in 1992, Roseisle Pandytudyr x Moorcock Rhapsody) was second in 2000; fifth in 2002 and fourth in 2003. Tudyr Melody has an enviable HOYS record in M&M leading-rein and first-ridden classes, standing second in 1999 (the first year that these classes were staged at HOYS), second in both in 2000, first and champion in 2001, first and reserve champion in 2002 and qualified for the M&M first-ridden and open ridden in 2003 and 2004. Tudyr Melody has two full-brothers, Symphony (foaled in 1996) and Piccolo (foaled in

1997). Symphony qualified for the HOYS in 2002 and Piccolo in 2001, 2002 and 2004.

Roseisle Bridesmaid won the first ever HOYS leading-rein class in 1992 and her daughters, Roseisle Confetti and Roseisle Something Blue (both sired by Pandytudyr and foaled in 1996 and 1997), qualified for HOYS in 2002 and 2003. Roseisle Bridesmaid's grand-dam was Criban Chiffon who was dam of Sinton Samite (chapter 4), the supreme champion of the 1970 Ponies of Britain Show. Confetti qualified as a working hunter pony in 2002 and Something Blue was fourth in 2002 and sixth in 2003 in first-ridden classes. Two other progeny of Pandytudyr are the gelding Roseisle Holy Joe (foaled in 1989, out of Baledon Divine) who qualified for the HOYS in 1999, 2000 and 2001, and the mare Roseisle Bewildered (foaled in 1996, out of Cantref Let It Be) who qualified in 2002. Three other qualifiers to carry the Roseisle prefix are the gelding Roseisle Pannikin (foaled in 1988, sired by Cantref Glory) who qualified in 1992, 1993, 1994, 1995, 1999 and 2000, the mare Roseisle Samantha (foaled in 1998, sired by Rotherwood Spycatcher) who qualified in 2003, and another mare, Roseisle Tudyr Honour (foaled in 1990, out of Roseisle Maid of Honour) who was sixth leading-rein in 1998. The Roseisle Stud boasts an incredible total of HOYS qualifiers: three in 1999, three in 2000, four in 2001, six in 2002, three in 2003 and two in 2004.

Another stud which has concentrated on breeding leading-rein ponies is the Colne Stud of Mrs Overton-Ablitt in Colchester, with Colne Hollyhock (by Weston Best Man), Colne Tara (by Moorcock Bracken) and Colne Trisca (by Pendock Legend) qualifying for the HOYS in 2002, and Colne Nightflight, Colne Tantivy and Colne Trisca (all three sired by Pendock Legend) qualifying in 2003. These are all section As competing in M&M classes in addition to the section B Colne Heiress whom we shall meet later competing in the open BSPS classes.

Another section A to qualify for the HOYS leading-rein class four times is Bryndefaid Patsy (foaled in 1994, Friars Sprightly x Bryndefaid Pippa) who, despite a precarious start in life when she was rejected by her dam and had to be hand-reared, qualified for HOYS in 1999 (fourth), 2000

ABOVE LEFT *Colne Heiress. Photo: Barry Wilkinson.*

ABOVE RIGHT *Bryndefaid Patsy ridden by Catherine Scott. Photo: Summers Photographic.*

(fourth), 2001 and 2002 when she ended up mini-champion after which she retired to stud.

One Welsh family which has been able to hold its own against the best of the British riding pony stallions is the father and son combination of Rosedale Mohican and Orielton Aristocrat (chapter 2) who both lived to a good old age. Both Mohican and Aristocrat died in 2003, Mohican having been foaled in 1973 and Aristocrat in 1977. The HOYS successes of Mohican were achieved with Rosedale Mannequin in 1994, Rosedale Marionette in 1997 (reserve champion), 1998 and 1999 and Rosedale Maysong, also in 1998.

Aristocrat progeny to secure HOYS championship status are Nantcol Lady Julia (champion in 1995 and 1996 and dam of the 2004 reserve champion, Nantcol Sylphide), Barkway Happy Returns (2000 and 2002), Barkway Black Magic (champion Search For A Star 1998), while Colne Heiress (foaled in 1992, daughter of Colne Henol by Weston Best Man) was third in 1996 and 1997, champion in 1998, fourth in 1999 and 2000, champion and overall supreme Welsh champion of champions 2001, sixth in 2002 and 2003 and fourth in 2004. In addition to successes in the leading-rein and first-ridden classes, other progeny, such as Barkway Felicity and Twylands Humming Bee, have been amongst the placings in 128 cm open ridden pony classes. Between 1992 and 2004, Aristocrat progeny have won a staggering 64 HOYS qualifying tickets. Additional successes for the progeny of Aristocrat sons include the section B Rotherwood Statesman (also based at Barkway Stud where Aristocrat lived from 1986 to 2003 with his favourite companion, Ceulan Siwan, dam of the 1995 HOYS champion, Lechlade Melissa) and the part-bred Twylands Prose who sired 14 HOYS 'Chinook' qualifiers between 1998 and 2004.

The most exciting competitions at the HOYS are probably the under- and over-122 cm scurry driving pairs races for which a dozen qualifying rounds are held all over the UK. Initially, conventional vehicles were used

ABOVE LEFT *Miss Anne Muir driving Stoatley Moonstone and Stoatley Moonraker (C). Photo: Monty.*

ABOVE RIGHT *Mr John Marson driving Osborne Refrigerators Ltd Fine and Dandy (Ceulan Serchog and Ceulan Siabod). Photo: Welsh Pony and Cob Society.*

but they were rather prone to overturn at high speeds! Nowadays, specially constructed vehicles are used, with a track width of at least 130 cm, and wire spoked and/or pneumatic tyres are not allowed.

The first NPS-organised Mountain and Moorland ridden championships, sponsored by Equimix Feeds, was introduced into the Olympia schedule in 1978, with 29 qualifying rounds held all over the country. The finals are judged at the Olympia International Show Jumping championships which were established as a London pre-Christmas attraction in 1971. The Welsh section Bs captured the lion's share of 16 qualifying tickets in 1978, followed by five New Forests, three Connemaras, two each Dartmoors and Fells and one section A (Stoatley Hill Rise). Surprisingly, not one section C or D found favour in the first year.

With such a wealth of section Bs present, it was no surprise that Mrs Noelle de Quincey found her champion amongst this section; in fact, five of the top six. The champion was Major and Mrs Pritchard's Criffell Casper, an eight year old sired by Rhydyfelin Selwyn (chapter 2) who went to Sweden in 1959 but returned to Britain in 1970 and died on the Isle of Wight aged 34 years. Casper's dam was Criffell Cascade by Solway Master Bronze (chapter 2) out of Brenhines who was bred by the Dowager Lady Kenyon and sired by Coed Coch Siabod (chapter 2).

It was young Richard Pritchard who rode Casper when he qualified at the NPS Somerset Show but, in the meantime, Richard had also qualified another section B, Wilmar Georgie Girl, at Kent County and he decided to ride Georgie Girl rather than Casper at Olympia. Fortunately, a substitute rider was found for Casper and he romped away with the championship, ridden by Caroline Gilbert-Scott. Mrs Knowles's chestnut section B stallion, Burstye Kythnos, was second, ridden by Dominque Knowles, Mrs Jane Hill, riding her section B mare, Knighton Lullaby, came fourth, Mrs Elizabeth Mansfield's section B stallion, Keston Royal Occasion, ridden by Tardy Eyles, was fifth and Mrs Joan Bullock's section B stallion, Sinton Court Peregrine, came sixth.

With a Dartmoor champion in 1979 and a Connemara in 1980, it was Norwood Principal Boy who was next to fly the Welsh flag in 1981 after coming second in 1980. Principal Boy was bred in 1970 by Mrs Bates in Northumberland and was sired by Bwlch Star Quality out of Menai Fairy by Menai Shooting Star. Principal Boy was bought by the Judge family as a result of an advertisement in *Horse and Hound* in January 1978 and was ridden to many successes in show jumping, working hunter pony, hunter trials, dressage and ridden M&M by all three Judge sons, Richard, Philip and Timothy. As well as being Olympia champion, ridden by Philip Judge in 1981, he was also M&M Working Hunter Pony of the Year at Malvern and RW ridden champion in 1983. Principal Boy remained part of the Judge family until his death in 1997 at 27 years.

The Welsh Cobs Wiston Llwynog, Verwood Roger, Kentchurch Cloud and Kentchurch Request were champions in 1986, 1990, 1994 and 1996;

2004 WPCS President Mrs Anne Vestey of Kentchurch holding the record of the highest number (25) of Olympia qualifiers of any breed.

Persie Ramrod (chapter 3) (foaled in 1978, Synod Ranger x Synod Rowena) was the first section C to capture the Olympia championship. This was in 1989, the same year that he stood fourth in the stallion class at the RW Show to Gwelfro Tywysog, Parc Marvel and Synod Roger. The section C who qualified for Olympia the greatest number of times (five times, with four times 'Best of Breed') was Ryall Democrat who was bought by the Abrahall family as a two year old in 1985 and was still with them when he died in 2001. In addition to Olympia, Democrat qualified for the HOYS twice, was Ponies (UK) Ridden M&M champion Pony of the Year, reserve champion NPS WHP Pony of the Year, supreme ridden M&M NPS Championships, twice champion ridden sections C and D at the RASE and ridden champion and reserve supreme at Northleach, to list but a few of his achievements.

BELOW *Starcrest Discovery ridden by Debbie Baker. Photo: Wynne Davies.*

Harwel Wizard, the section B champion in 1998, has already been discussed in connection with his achievements in the WPCS Performance competition; his sire Marston Monsoon was Olympia champion in 1988 and Monsoon's grand-dam, Marston Mirage, was the first overall champion of the first WPCS Performance competition in 1972.

Section Cs returned to the forefront again in 2001, when the champion was Starcrest Discovery, foaled in 1995, sired by Pantyfid Toy Soldier out of Tywood Star Flight by Fronarth Rhidian. Tywood Star Flight was bought by Starcrest Stud in foal to Toy Soldier and Discovery was sold as a foal to Geoff and Debbie Baker. The Baker family sold him to go in harness as a three year old and he was gelded and proved very successful in that sphere. The Bakers then regretted parting with him and bought him back, broke him to saddle and, understandably after Olympia, will never part with him again. The sire, Pantyfid Toy Soldier, has been WHP champion at the WPCS Performance Show, ridden by David James of Sianwood Stud. The other progeny of Tywood Star Flight is Starcrest Sovereign (foaled in 1996, sired by Hengwys Tywysog), winner at the RW in 1999, Lampeter in 1997 and 2003 and Cuddy HOYS qualifier at the Royal Bath and West in 2003.

The WPCS has staged its own Performance Show since 1993, the 1993 and 1994 shows being held on the RW showground and, since 1995, at Felin-Newydd, Llandefalle, Brecon, home of Sir Martyn and Lady Jennifer Evans-Bevan.

Amongst the overall champions at Brecon, pride of place must go to Laura Collett of Cheltenham, overall champion with the section A Bockmer Winston in 1999, with the section B Baverstock Talissa in 2000, with the section A Glenwood Caradog in 2002 and again with the section A Penwayn Ryan in 2003. Bockmer Winston made his mark outside Wales at the 1999 HOYS when he was third in the WHP of the Year. Glenwood Caradog (foaled in 1993, Bengad Dogberry x Llanarmon Carys) was Brecon champion just a few months after being a hill premium stallion running out with his mares in the South Wales valleys, and was reserve Olympia champion in 2002. Ridden by Joanna Minns, Glenwood Caradog again qualified at Hickstead for the 2004 HOYS Show but was beaten by his daughter, Glenwood Dancing Queen, foaled in 1999, out of Cui

LEFT *1995 Performance Show champions. Photo: Wynne Davies.*

Miriam. The last of Laura's champions was Penwayn Ryan. Bought in 2002 at Brecon Market for £140, he was overall supreme in a few months at the WPCS Brecon Performance Show, followed later in the year by winning the £1,000 P(UK) overall championship and, to cap it all, supreme Pony of the Year at the HOYS over all the M&M ridden ponies, the open show ponies, the working hunter ponies (where he qualified), the show hunter ponies and the coloureds.

A consistent section C within the WPCS competitions was Sackville Nicky, foaled in 1987, sired by Synod Roy Rogers out of Ceulan Nesta by Synod Dafydd. Ridden by Nicola Hall, Nicky was reserve supreme at the Performance Show in 1997 and again section C champion in 1998. Within the Performance Competition, Nicky was section C champion in 1997, 1998 and 1999, being overall supreme in 1998 with the enormous tally of 9,770 points.

Being a competent performer certainly pays off when the animals are offered at sales, the 2003 section B Performance champion, Orielton Beamish, selling for £10,500 the following month at the Fayre Oaks Sale, while the section C stallion, Uphill Tom Thumb, sold at the Royal Welsh Sale the previous year for £14,500 after being ridden in the sale ring.

RIGHT *Sackville Nicky ridden by Nicola Hall.*

Appendices

ROYAL WELSH CHAMPIONS SECTIONS A AND B 1904 –2004

		Welsh Mountain Ponies			Welsh Ponies		
		Judge	Male Champion	Female Champion	Judge	Male Champion	Female Champion
Aberystwyth	1904	R Brydon	Greylight	Titw			
Aberystwyth	1905	D Rees	Greylight	Llwyn Nell			
Aberystwyth	1906	W S Miller	Greylight	Kerry Lassie			
Aberystwyth	1907	J R Bache	Greylight	Lady Starlight			
Aberystwyth	1908	W Foster	Grove Ballistite	Bleddfa Tell Tale			
Aberystwyth	1909	John Hill	Greylight	Lady Greylight			
Llanelli	1910	J R Bache	Greylight	Gwyndy Bessie			
Welshpool	1911	Tom James	Grove Ballistite	Towyvale Myfy			
Swansea	1912	Roger Howells Ben Davies	Dewi Stone	Grove Limelight			
Porthmadoc	1913	Evan Jones Rev.John Owen	Grove Ballistite	Nantyrharn Starlight			
Newport	1914	T J Evans Bennett Owen	Grove Arclight	Hawddgar Lady Starlight			
Wrexham	1922	J R Bache	Grove King Cole II	Grove Fairy Queen			
Welshpool	1923	Tom James	Llwyn Might Atom	Dawn of Bryntirion			
Bridgend	1924	Arthur Pughe	Llwyn Might Atom*	Ness Sunflower			
Carmarthen	1925	T H Vaughan	Llwyn Temptation*	Irfon Marvel			
Bangor	1926	T Jones Evans	Llwyn Satan*	Ness Daisy			
Swansea	1927	Major Dugdale	Grove King Cole II*	Kittiwake			
Wrexham	1928	Edgar Herbert	Craven Master Shot*	Caerberris Dazzle			
Cardiff	1929	J R Bache	Craven Master Shot*	Dawn of Bryntirion			
Caernarfon	1930	T E Jenkins	Grove Sprightly*	Clumber Miss Mary			
Llanelli	1931	T J Jones	Grove Sprightly*	Dunchurch Venus			
Llandrindod	1932	Meyrick Jones	Grove Sprightly*	Grove Ladybird			
Aberystwyth	1933	Matthew Williams	Grove Sprightly*	Grove Ladybird			
Llandudno	1934	T J Mathias	Grove Sprightly*	Grove Ladybird	T J Mathias	-	Grey Nymph FS
Haverfordwest	1935	T Davies Jones	Grove Sprightly*	Craven Jean	T E Jenkins	-	Dolly Grey FS
Abergele	1936	T J Jones	Grove Sprightly*	Craven Shot Star	T J Jones	-	Cuckoo FS
Monmouth	1937	Tom Jones Evans	Grove Will O The Wisp*	Criban Socks	T Jones Evans	-	Cuckoo FS
RASE	1938						
Caernarfon	1939	Matthew Williams	Grove Sprightly*	Vardra Sunflower	Matthew Williams	Craven Cyrus	Tanybwlch Prancio
Carmarthen	1947	J Morgan Evans	Dinarth What Ho*	Vardra Charm	J Morgan Evans, MBE	Criban Victor	Lady Cyrus
Swansea	1949	Capt T A Howson	Tregoyd Starlight*	Coed Coch Serliw	Capt T A Howson		Criban Heather Belle
Abergele	1950	Matthew Williams	Coed Coch Meilyr	Coed Coch Siaradus*	Matthew Williams	Coed Coch Siabod	Gem
Llanelwedd	1951	Mrs N Pennell	Coed Coch Madog	Coed Coch Siaradus*	Mrs C Darby	Coed Coch Siabod	Revel Nance*
Caernarfon	1952	Frank Preece	Dinarth What Ho	Coed Coch Siaradus*	J M Havard	Coed Coch Siabod*	Coed Coch Silian
Cardiff	1953	J R Berry	Coed Coch Madog	Coed Coch Siaradus*	Mrs Raleigh Blandy	Coed Coch Siabod	Verity*
Machynlleth	1954	A R McNaught	Coed Coch Planed	Ankerwyck Clan Snowdon	W J Thomas	Criban Victor	Verity*
Haverfordwest	1955	E S Davies	Coed Coch Madog	Coed Coch Siaradus*	J J Borthwick	Valiant	Coed Coch Silian*
Rhyl	1956	Mrs N Pennell	Coed Coch Madog	Brierwood Honey*	Dr Arwyn Williams	Criban Victor*	Gredington Daliad
Aberystwyth	1957	T Wilding-Davies, TD	Coed Coch Madog	Revel Spring Song*	Miss E Morley	Coed Coch Blaen Lleuad	Gredington Daliad*
Bangor	1958	G Mathias	Coed Coch Madog	Shan Cwilt*	Mrs T Price	Criban Victor*	Gredington Milfyd
Margam	1959	A L Williams	Coed Coch Madog	Revel Rosette*	Mrs N Pennell	Criban Victor*	Norwood Starlet
Welshpool	1960	T J G Price	Coed Coch Madog	Coed Coch Symwl*	A L Williams	Criban Victor*	Downland Lavender
Llandeilo	1961	Capt L B Brierley,MC	Bowdler Brewer*	Revel Choice	E S Davies	Solway Master Bronze*	Norwood Starlet

		Welsh Mountain Ponies Judge	Male Champion	Female Champion	Welsh Ponies Judge	Male Champion	Female Champion
Wrexham	1962	William Davies	Coed Coch Madog	Revel Jewel*	I V Eckley	Solway Master Bronze*	Gredington Milfyd
Llanelwedd	1963	R J Richards	Clan Pip	Revel Caress*	Mrs M Redvers	Solway Master Bronze*	Gredington Milfyd
1964		Mrs J Austin du Pont	Clan Pip*	Coed Coch Pelydrog	Mrs R J Richards	Criban Victor*	Coed Coch Penllwyd
1965		The Rt Hon Lord Kenyon	Coed Coch Siglen Las	Coed Coch Pelydrog*	Mrs B Crisp	Cusop Hoity Toity	Belvoir Tosca*
1966		H Ll Richards, MC	Coed Coch Siglen Las	Clan Peggy*	Lady Margaret Myddelton	Brockwell Cobweb	Coed Coch Priciau*
1967		Mrs G J Mountain	Treharne Tomboy	Clan Peggy*	R J Richards	Cusop Hoity Toity	Lydstep Rosetta*
1968		Sir Harry Llewellyn,CBE	Treharne Tomboy*	Ready Token Glen Bride	Mrs S Homfray	Springbourne Golden Flute*	Sinton Moving Charm
1969		T J G Price	Coed Coch Pryd	Coed Coch Swyn*	T Wilding-Davies, TD	Kirby Cane Scholar	Revel Glimpse*
1970		R A Swain	Treharne Tomboy*	Rowfant Prima Ballerina	Mrs B K Binnie	Bowdell Quiver	Rotherwood Honeysuckle*
1971		Dr Wynne Davies,MBE	Coed Coch Norman	Brierwood Rosebud*	D E Bowen, MRCVS	Downland Mohawk*	Gredington Blodyn
1972		W W Williams	Gredington Simwnt*	Dyfrdwy Midnight Moon	Mrs G A Furness	Brockwell Chuckle*	Weston Choice
1973		G E Evans	Gredington Simwnt*	Coed Coch Glenda	Mrs T Smalley	Moorfields Tarragon	Reeves Fairy Lustre*
1974		Mrs P A M Hambleton	Coed Coch Bari*	Bengad Love in the Mist	R A Swain	Cusop Banknote	Coed Coch Dawn*
1975		E Davies	Rondeels Pengwyn	Springbourne Hyfryd*	P Ward	Cusop Banknote	Weston Mary Ann*
1976		J A Edwards	Revel Cassino	Valleylake Breeze*	Mrs M C Williams	Cusop Banknote*	Weston Rosebud
1977		Mrs R Mills	Revel Cassino*	Cwmgarn Heidi	I V Eckley	Rosedale Mohican	Lydstep Ladies Slipper*
1978		T Parry	Aston Superstar*	Bengad Day Lily	Mrs Towers Clark	Baledon Squire	Rotherwood Honeysuckle*
1979		G Jones	Aston Superstar*	Coed Coch Ateb	Mrs P Egerton	Cusop Banknote*	Weston Picture
1980		D Garrett	Revel Saled	Crossways Merle*	Miss R Philipson-Stow	Glansevin Melick	Weston Glimpse*
1981		J G Berry	Glenfield Chocolate Soldier	Bengad Day Lily*	H C Chambers	Downland Goldleaf*	Rotherwood Lilactime
1982		W G James	Revel Japhet	Crossways Merle*	Mrs J Price	Rosedale Mohican*	Weston Glimpse
1983		C T Davies	Aston Superstar*	Cledwyn Seren Goch	Mrs A Berryman	Tetworth Mikado	Rotherwood Penny Royale*
1984		Mrs D Jones	Revel Japhet*	Llanerch Decima	Miss J Pringle, MBE	Rotherwood Royalist	Desarbre Folk Song*
1985		Miss C Kelway	Brierwood Rocket II*	Bengad Day Lily	L Partridge	Downland Goldleaf*	Millcroft Suzuya
1986		W Phillips	Revel Japhet*	Baledon Jubilation	Mrs M Morrison	Bunbury Mahogany	Nantcol Katrin*
1987		I J R Lloyd	Nerwyn Cadno	Cledwyn Seren Goch*	Miss L Hutchins	Millcroft Copper Lustre	Cwmwyre Samantha*
1988		E Bowen, MRCVS	Brierwood Rocket II*	Churchwood Promise	C Morse	Broadlands Coronet	Downland Edelweiss*
1989		Miss R Philipson-Stow	Breachwood Marwyn*	Baledon Verity	Mrs J Evans	Linksbury Celebration	Thornberry Demelza*
1990		Miss L Hutchins	Waitwith Romance*	Idyllic Pavlova	Mrs J Etheridge	Lemonshill Limelight*	Wynswood Zara
1991		S Jones	Silvester	Dyfrdwy Seren Arian*	Mrs D Williams	Paddock Camargue	Boston Bodicia*
1992		P Wilding-Davies	Winneydene Satellite	Tiffwyl Melodi*	Mrs R Mills	Mollegaards Spartacus*	Cottrell Charm
1993		D Blair	Gredington Calon Lan*	Blanche Mimic	Mrs M C Williams	Mollegaards Spartacus*	Thornberry Royal Gem
1994		D P Jones	Gredington Calon Lan	Dyfrdwy Seren Arian*	J Hendy	Mollegaards Spartacus*	Talhaearn Eirlys y Pasg
1995		D Prichard	Criccieth Arwr	Tiffwyl Melodi*	J T Davies	Shamrock Mr Oliver	Cottrell Aurora*
1996		P L Edwards	Revel Paul Jones	Eppynt Victoria*	Mrs J Mountain	Cwrtycadno Cadfridog*	Rotherwood Lorrikeet
1997		D S Davies, BSc, MPhil.	Synod The Colonel	Fronbach Crystal*	Mrs A Colbatch-Clark	Carwed Charmer*	Lemonshill Alarch
1998		Mrs C Jones	Eppynt Skyline*	Neuaddfach Skylark	T Best	Wortley Fisher King	Paddock Picture*
1999		Miss R Russell-Allen	Trefaes Guardsman	Betws Gweno*	Wm Jones	Griashall Kiwi*	Brenob Finch
2000		T J Jones	Lacy Justyn	Dyfrdwy Seren Fwyn*	L Bigley	Carwed Charmer*	Cottrell Royal Glance
2002		J Hendy	Friars Bonheddwr	Fouroaks Reanne*	Mrs E Mansfield	Carwed Charmer	Eyarth Windflower*
2003		Mrs J P Price	Gartconnel Shooting Star	Springbourne Elly*	Mrs K James	Lemonshill Top Note	Eyarth Windflower*
2004		W G Jones	Dyfrdwy Seren-y-Gogledd	Friars Goldilocks*	D Ll Evans	Polaris Elmer	Mintfield Songthrush*

Footnote: there were no shows from 1914 – 1922 and 1939 – 1945 due to the world wars, no Show in 1948 due to petrol rationing and no Show in 2001 due to FMD.

ROYAL WELSH CHAMPIONS SECTIONS C AND D 1904–2004

		Welsh Ponies of Cob Type			Welsh Cobs		
		Judge	Male Champion	Female Champion	Judge	Male Champion	Female Champion
Aberystwyth	1904	R Brydon	Klondyke	Llwyn Snowdrop*	R Brydon	Trustful*HSB	
Aberystwyth	1905	W Forrester Addie	Llwyn True Blue	Llwyn Snowdrop	W Forrester Addie	Trustful HSB	Treflys Blaze
Aberystwyth	1906	W S Miller	Golden Gleam	Bess	W S Miller	Melton Cadet HSB	Amman Empress
Aberystwyth	1907	J R Bache	Llew Llwyd	Llwyn Snowdrop*	J R Bache	Melton Cadet HSB	Amman Empress
Aberystwyth	1908	W Foster	Tissington Goss HSB	Naughty Naiad HSB	W Foster,Sir R Green-Price	Atwick Junior HSB	Pride of the Hills
Aberystwyth	1909	John Hill	Little Fire HSB	Tanrallt Paula HSB	John Hill	High Stepping Gambler II*	Sunflower
Llanelli	1910	J R Bache	Southworth Swell HSB	Tanrallt Paula HSB	J R Bache	Melton Cadet HSB	Groten Ddu*
Welshpool	1911	Tom James	Bobby Dazzler	Tanrallt Paula HSB	Tom James	Mark Well	Llwyn Flashlight*
Swansea	1912	Roger Howells, Ben Davies	Kismet	Lily of the Valley	Roger Howells, Ben Davies	Manoravon Flyer*	Norton Sceptre HSB
Porthmadoc	1913	Evan Jones,Rev John Owen	Temptation	Rosey	Evan Jones,Rev John Owen	King Flyer*	Lady Cenfina
Newport	1914	T J Evans, Bennett Owen	Temptation	Pinderfields Megania	T J Evans,Bennett Owen	King Flyer*	PingPong
Wrexham	1922	J R Bache	Baedeker	Llwyn Coralie	J R Bache	Llwynog Flyer	Pontfaen Lady Model*
Welshpool	1923	Tom James	Wingerworth Eiddwen*	Cilwen Lady Lilian	Tom James	Llwynog Flyer	Pontfaen Lady Model*
Bridgend	1924	Arthur Pughe	Criban Shot*	Teify Pride	Arthur Pughe	Mathrafal Brenin*	Wyre Lady
Carmarthen	1925	T H Vaughan	Cream Bun*	Kerry Queen	T H Vaughan	Mathrafal Brenin*	Polly of Pant
Bangor	1926	T Jones Evans	Baedeker*	Seren Ceulan	T Jones Evans	Mathrafal Eiddwen	Hwylog Peggy
Swansea	1927	Major Dugdale	Cefncoch Country Swell	Kerry Queen	Major Dugdale	Mathrafal Eiddwen*	Polly of Pant
Wrexham	1928	Edgar Herbert	Royal Welsh Jack	Seren Ceulan*	Edgar Herbert	Llethi Valiant	Pant Grey Star*
Cardiff	1929	J R Bache	Royal Welsh Jack*	Myrtle Rosina	J R Bache	Mathrafal Eiddwen*	Blaenwaun Flora Temple
Caernarfon	1930	T E Jenkins	Royal Welsh Jack	Cilwen Lady Lilian*	T E Jenkins	Mathrafal Eiddwen*	Cwmcau Lady Jet
Llanelli	1931	T J Jones	Ceulan Comet*	Flemish Cymraes	T J Jones	Llethi Valiant*	Pantlleinau Blodwen
Llandrindod	1932	Meyrick Jones	Ceulan Comet*	Cilwen Lady Lilian	Meyrick Jones	Caerseddfan Stepping Flyer*	Cwmcau Lady Jet
Aberystwyth	1933	Matthew Williams	Ceulan Comet	Cilwen Lady Lilian*	Matthew Williams	Myrtle Welsh Flyer*	Cwmcau Lady Jet
Llandudno	1934	T J Mathias	Ceulan Comet*	Cilwen Lady Lilian	T J Mathias	Craven Cymro*	Cwncau Lady Jet
Haverfordwest	1935	T E Jenkins	-	Croten Ddu O Tremain	T E Jenkins	Myrtle Welsh Flyer	Dewi Black Bess*
Abergele	1936	H Ll Richards MC	-	Vrondolau Chess	T J Jones	Myrtle Welsh Flyer	Teify of Hercws*
Monmouth	1937	T Jones Evans	-	Welsh Homage	T Jones Evans	Cystanog Trotting Comet	Teify of Hercws*
RASE	1938		-	-	-	-	-
Caernarfon	1939	Matthew Williams		Myrtle Rosina	Matthew Williams	Myrtle Welsh Flyer*	Meiarth Pride
Carmarthen	1947	J Morgan Evans MBE	Welsh Patriot	Queenie	J Morgan Evans MBE	Brenin Gwalia	Meiarth Welsh Maid*
Swansea	1949	Captain T A Howson	Welsh Echo	Queenie	Captain T A Howson	Llwynog-y-Garth	Meiarth Welsh Maid*
Abergele	1950	J M Havard	Gwenlli Valiant	Queenie*	J M Havard	Llwynog-y-Garth	Meiarth Welsh Maid*
Llanelwedd	1951	D O Morgan JP	-	Queenie*	D O Morgan JP	Pentre Eiddwen Comet*	Dewi Rosina
Caernarfon	1952	Gwilym Morris	-	Queenie*	Gwilym Morris	Mathrafal*	Sheila
Cardiff	1953	A L Williams	Teify Brightlight II	-	A L Williams	Pentre Eiddwen Comet	Dewi Rosina*
Machynlleth	1954	Douglas Meredith	Cymro Du	-	Douglas Meredith	Meiarth King Flyer	Meiarth Welsh Maid*
Haverfordwest	1955	J Edwards	Teify Brightlight II	-	J Edwards	Cefnparc Boy	Teify Welsh Maid*
Rhyl	1956	J O Davies	Teify Brightlight II	Dyffryn Rosina	J O Davies	Pentre Eiddwen Comet*	Parc Lady
Aberystwyth	1957	I Osborne Jones	-	Queenie*	I Osborne Jones	Pentre Eiddwen Comet	Princess*
Bangor	1958	T J Thomas	Teify Brightlight II	-	T J Thomas	Pentre Eiddwen Comet	Parc Lady*
Margam	1959	J R Berry	-	Pride of the Prairie	J R Berry	Pentre Eiddwen Comet	Parc Lady*
Welshpool	1960	Mrs I M Yeomans	Teify Brightlight II	-	Mrs I M Yeomans	Llwynog-y-Garth	Parc Lady*
Llandeilo	1961	D Edwardes	Teify Brightlight II	Queenie*	D Edwardes	Llanarth Braint	Parc Lady*
Wrexham	1962	H Ll Richards MC	Teify Brightlight II*	Pride of the Prairie	H Ll Richards MC	Pentre Rainbow*	Tyhen Mattie

		Welsh Ponies of Cob Type			Welsh Cobs		
		Judge	Male Champion	Female Champion	Judge	Male Champion	Female Champion
Llanelwedd	1963	E Evans	Gwynau Boy	Gwynau Puss*	E Evans	Tyngwndwn Cream Boy*	Pentre Eiddwen's Doll
1964		E G E Griffith	Teify Brightlight II*	Pride of the Prairie	E G E Griffith	Llanarth Brummel*	Geler Daisy
1965		J M Havard	Gwynau Boy	Llanarth Flying Saucer	J M Havard	Llanarth Brummel	Pentre Eiddwen's Doll*
1966		J F Lewis	Lyn Cwmcoed*	Lili Cwmcoed	J F Lewis	Tyhen Comet	Derwen Rosina*
1967		T G Llewellyn	Lyn Cwmcoed*	Brondesbury Welsh Maid	Miss A Wheatcroft	Honyton Michael ap Braint*	Derwen Rosina
1968		A L Williams	Lyn Cwmcoed	Lili Cwmcoed*	J H Davies	Rhystyd Prince	Derwen Rosina*
1969		W Jones	Lyn Cwmcoed*	Lili Cwmcoed	W Jones	Tyhen Comet*	Parc Rachel
1970		D J Thomas	Lyn Cwmcoed*	Brondesbury Welsh Maid	S D Morgan	Brenin Dafydd*	Cathedine Welsh Maid
1971		Miss B Saunders-Davies	Synod William*	Gwynau Dolly	J Lloyd	Nebo Black Magic	Parc Rachel*
1972		W Davies	Lyn Cwmcoed	Tydi Red Rose*	Mostyn Isaac	Llanarth Flying Comet	Parc Rachel*
1973		A L Williams	Lyn Cwmcoed	Lili Cwmcoed	Miss P Taylor	Nebo Black Magic*	Tyhen Mattie
1974		E L Mathias	Lyn Cwmcoed	Cefn Moonlight*	I J R Lloyd	Llanarth Flying Comet*	Cathedine Welsh Maid
1975		Mrs J Crotty	Isamman Dafydd	Cefn Moonlight*	T J Gwyn Price	Nebo Black Magic	Parc Rachel*
1976		J G Lloyd	Menai Fury	Lleuci Queen	Gareth Evans	Llanarth Flying Comet*	Parc Rachel
1977		S D Morgan	Synod William*	Lleuci Queen	Mrs C Richards	Llanarth Flying Comet*	Geler Neli
1978		Miss A Wheatcroft	Synod Roger	Chalkhill Dragonfly*	A L Williams	Llanarth Flying Comet*	Parc Rachel
1979		Miss P Taylor	Synod Roger*	Faelog Frolic	I James	Rhystyd Meredith	Ffoslas Black Lady*
1980		J M Jones	Synod William*	Paddock Dawn	J R Rees BA	Ffoslas Flying Rocket*	Porthvaynor Gold Dust
1981		M Isaac	Synod William*	Cefn Moonraise	Geraint Jones	Cyttir Telynor	Derwen Rosinda*
1982		D Meredith	Synod Roger*	Gurrey Brenhines	T B J Evans	Cyttir Telynor*	Derwen Princess
1983		D P Jones	Synod Reagan*	Coediog Dwynwen	W E Rowlands	Ebbw Victor	Derwen Princess*
1984		D J Jones	Synod Roger*	Gwylfa Joyce	D R Higgins	Ebbw Victor	Derwen Princess*
1985		R Robinson	Nebo Bouncer*	Rookery Flower Lady	W L Harris	Derwen Replica	Derwen Viscountess*
1986		Mrs J Hoskins	Nebo Bouncer*	Menai Rachelian	Gwil Evans	Nebo Daniel	Derwen Groten Goch*
1987		Mrs R Mills	Synod Roger*	Tyngwndwn Moonlight	T J Gwyn Price	Cyttir Telynor*	Penclose Rhian
1988		T A Lewis	Nebo Bouncer*	Neuaddparc Welsh Maid	Mrs G J Mountain	Nebo Daniel*	Northleach Duchess
1989		G Jenkins	Gwelfro Tywysog*	Tyngwndwn Moonlight	J E Jones	Nebo Daniel	Derwen Dameg*
1990		D Bushby	Bodwenarth Red Spark	Ty'reos Furietta	Ifan Phillips	Thorneyside The Boss	Derwen Groten Goch*
1991		Mrs D Jones	Waxwing Reward	Glynwyn Diamante*	Daff Davies	Pantanamlwg Red Fox*	Fronarth Welsh Model
1992		E J Evans	Synod Roy Rogers	Fronarth Red Rose*	D J Jones	Thorneyside Flyer	Derwen Groten Goch*
1993		G Hardacre	Nebo Bouncer*	Cwm Lowri	Mrs Ann Vestey	Horeb Euros*	Tydfil Magic Princess
1994		Mrs G Heppenstall	Synod Roy Rogers*	Ashgrove Abigail	Mrs Gladys Dale	Nebo Hywel*	Fronarth Welsh Model
1995		C T Davies	Synod Roy Rogers	Neuaddparc Rowena*	Miss R Philipson-Stow	Gellifach ap Dafydd*	Ynysfaen Lady Barneby
1996		Mrs M E Jones	Hengwys Tywysog	Hywi Moonlight*	William Lloyd FRAgS	Ebbw Victor	Fronarth Welsh Model*
1997		K Spenser	Nebo Bouncer	Ty'reos Lowri*	L Bigley FRAgS	Ebbw Victor	Trevallion Giorgio*
1998		S Everitt	Tyas Eiddwyn	Ty'reos Furietta*	Mrs M Edwards	Ebbw Victor*	Gwenllan Sali
1999		D Blair	Synod Rum Punch*	Menai Lady Conspicuous	J Thomas	Fronarth Victor	Fronarth Boneddiges*
2000		O Jones	Yarty Royal Bonus	Hywi Moonlight*	N Smith	Danaway Flashjack*	Elonwy Shooting Star
2002		G Jones	Thorneyside Bay Prince	Ashgrove Abigail*	P Gray	Gwynfaes Culhwch*	Fronarth Model Lady
2003		B Williams, AM	Hafodyrynys Welsh Crusader	Tyngwndwn Daylight*	D P Jones	Malnor Forest King	Gwenllan Sali*
2004		W Lloyd FRAgS	Tremymor Sportsman*	Hafodyrynys Cariad	K Spenser	Blaengwen Brenin*	Pantanamlwg Free Gift

ROYAL WELSH PART-BRED CHAMPIONS 1963–2004

Year	Judge	Champion	Reserve
1963	R J Richards	Henbury Bouquet	Promise II
1964	Mrs S Richards	Gaulden Gadabout	Henbury Bouquet
1965	Mrs Sellar	Miss Muffett	Henbury Bouquet
1966	Lady Myddelton	Choir Boy	Cusop Festivity
1967	Mrs N Pennell	Downland Starletta	Bracken
1968	T J G Price	Cusop Ringo	Simone of Henbury
1969	H Ll Richards	Sinton Samite	Rookery Grace
1970	R W H Jenkins	Towy Valley Simone	Bee's Wing
1971	J A Edwards	Small-Land Mayday	Bee's Wing
1972	R J Richards	Rosedale Questionnaire	Koh-I-Noor
1973	H Ll Richards	M'Lady	Small-Land Mayday
1974	Dr Wynne Davies	Chirk Cattleya	Rookery Graduate
1975	Mrs N Pennell	Small-Land Orsino	Small-Land Impala
1976	H Ll Richards	Coed Coch Windflower	Rotherwood Festival
1977	J A Edwards	Downland Woodpecker	Pendley Polka
1978	H C Chambers	Weston Chiffon	Rookery Grand Duchess
1979	R A Swain	Unicorn Zena	Glebedale Fieldmouse
1980	Mrs J Price	Costock Choir Boy	Cusop Joy
1981	Mrs C Richards	Small-Land Mascot	Rian
1982	Mrs R Mills	Small-Land Mascot	Trefaen Nemesis
1983	Mrs R S O White	Fairley Rembrandt	Sarnau Super Nova
1984	Lady Evans-Bevan	Carolinas Pussycat	Carolinas Kitten
1985	D Bushby	Carolinas Cat's Eye	Rotherwood Show Off
1986	T J G Price	Copybush Quotation	Carolinas Kitten
1987	T Best	Hodstock Catrina	Starlyte Royal Minstrel
1988	Mrs J Price	Copybush Quartermaster	Waxwing Dream Music
1989	H Roberts	Starlyte Royal Minstrel	Aberbrwynen Serenade
1990	Miss H Leggard	Mynach April Shower	Lapwater Gold Dawn
1991	Mrs A Bigley	Sianwood Star Turn	Duhonw Gwlith
1992	D E Bowen, MRCVS	Mynach Daffodil	Bromsden Flying Flute
1993	Mrs J Williams	Duntarvie Catamount	Courtway Victorious
1994	Mrs A Colbatch-Clark	Duntarvie Catamount	Llanarth Swansong
1995	Mrs C Rankin	Duntarvie Catamount	Shoreham Wilberforce
1996	D Jones	Rotherwood Peter Pan	Llanarth Quickstep
1997	Mrs J Gillespie	Rotherwood Peek a Boo	Goldsborough Morning Rose
1998	Miss A Wheatcroft	Aberbrwynen Superman	Calveley Mysterious
1999	M Bullen	Symondsbury Innocent	Sarnau Dragoon
2000	Mrs M-C Nimmo	Rosevale Only Fun	Keltic Gold
2002	Mrs M Edwards	Duntarvie Cat Burglar	Penstrumbly Popstar
2003	D E Puttock	Broadgrove Chatterbox	Blaenllain Doodleba
2004	Mrs A Bigley	Penstrumbly Lulu	Fenwick Lucy Glitters

ROYAL WELSH SECTION C IN-HAND ENTRIES 1947–2004

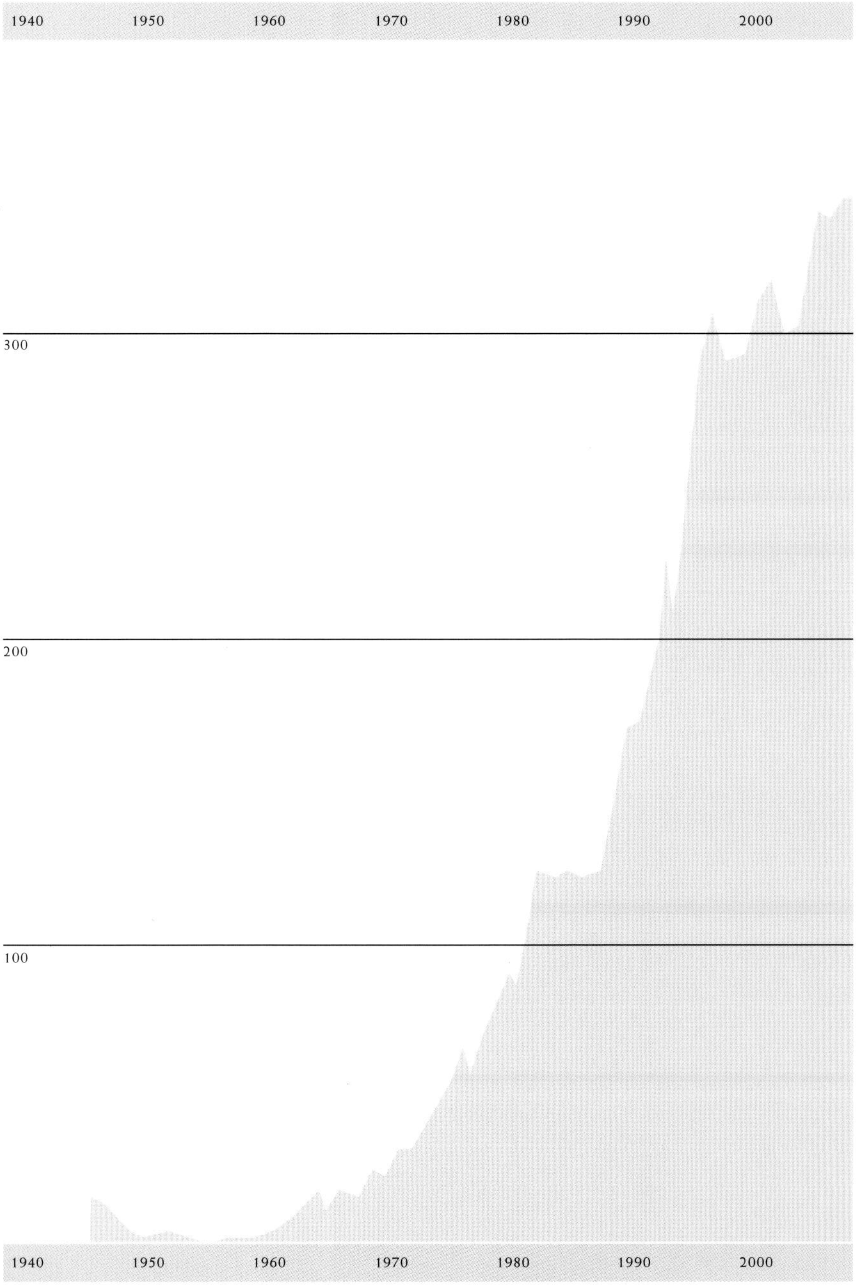

1940 1950 1960 1970 1980 1990 2000

300

200

100

1940 1950 1960 1970 1980 1990 2000

WPCS WELSH PART-BRED REGISTRATIONS AS A TOTAL OF REGISTRATIONS 1960–2004

WPCS PERFORMANCE SHOW CHAMPIONS 1993–2004

Year	Section A	Section B	Section C	Small WPB
1993	Peachfields Major	Small-Land Candyman	Watworth Bethany	Glebedale Pipsqueak**
1994	Cwmderw Puffin**	Small-Land Candyman	Leafycroft Merlyn*	Lacy Indiana
1995	Cwmderw Puffin	Small-Land Candyman	Synod Lord Charles	Pwllsarn Davey**
1996	Hollybush Cockade	Defaelog Rhiannon	Leafycroft Merlyn*	Pwllsarn Davey
1997	Hollybush Cockade	Skellorn Chevalier/ Cwmduad Vasami Fox/ Oakhouse Peregrine	Gellihaf Sant** Sackville Nicky*	Pwllsarn Davey
1998	Vinedale Vixen	Cwmduad Vasami Fox*	Sackville Nicky	Sarnau Medallion
1999	Bockmer Winston**	Cwmduad Vasami Fox*	Telynau Congressman	Chirk Fandango
2000	Just Roger*	Baverstock Talissa**	Gwyllan Tudur Prince/ Yarty Myfanwy	Chirk Fandango/ Blue Velvet
2001	No Show			
2002	Glenwood Caradog**	Cwmduad Vasami Fox	Gorfelyn Lucy Glitters	Sannanvalley Jester
2003	Penwayn Ryan**	Orielton Beamish	Gorfelyn Lucy Glitters*/ Hardys Ribbon*	Cefncoch Calon Lan
2004	Gorfelyn Busy Bee	Kirkhill Remembrance	Hardys Ribbon**	Sannanvalley Jester*

*(** supreme champion; * reserve champion)*

WPCS SIRE RATINGS 1965–2004

Year	Section A	Section B	Section C	Section D
1965	Coed C Madog 93	Criban Victor 26	-	-
1966	Coed C.Madog 79	Criban Victor 48		Cahn Dafydd 45
1967	Coed C Madog 64	Criban Victor 46	-	Cahn Dafydd 17
1968	Coed C Madog 94	Down Chevalier 82	-	Llanarth Braint 58
1969	Coed C Madog 68	Solway M Bronze 56	-	Pentre E Comet 48
1970	Coed C Madog 86	Solway M Bronze 56	-	Llanarth Braint 50
1971	Clan Pip 64	Down Chevalier 104	-	Pentre E Comet 60
1972	Coed C Madog 54	Brockwell Cobweb 44	-	Pentre E Comet 42
1973	Clan Pip 48	Down Chevalier 55	-	Pentre E Comet 47
1974	Coed C Madog 49	Down Chevalier 59	-	Pentre E Comet 51
1975	Coed C Norman 29	Down Chevalier 47	-	Pentre E Comet 34
1976	Clan Pip 94	Down Chevalier 116	Lyn Cwmcoed 46	D Rosina's Last 56
1977	Clan Pip 94	Down Chevalier 70	Lyn Cwmcoed 114	D Black Magic 82
1978	Clan Pip 102	Down Chevalier 88	Lyn Cwmcoed 70	Nebo Black Magic DRosina's Last 82
1979	Clan Pip 94	Down Chevalier Down Mandarin 70	Lyn Cwmcoed 84	Llanarth Meredith ap Braint 78
1980	Clan Pip 74	Kest R Occasion 92	Lyn Cwmcoed 66	Tyhen Comet 90
1981	Clan Pip 92	Down Chevalier 96	Synod William 96	Parc W Flyer 72
1982	Bengad Nepeta 74	Kest R Occasion 98	Nebo Brenin 108	Hewid Cardi 84
1983	Gred Simwnt 88	Kest R Occasion 160	Nebo Brenin 128	Hewid Cardi 86
1984	Bengad Nepeta 76	Kest R Occasion 106	Nebo Brenin 142	Nebo Daniel 74
1985	Gred Rabelais 58	Roth St Occasion 84	Nebo Brenin 108	Cyttir Telynor 98
1986	Penual Mark Penboeth Raffles 72	Roth St Occasion 118	Nebo Brenin 70	Nebo Brenin 96
1987	Penual Mark 100	Roth St Occasion 134	Nebo Brenin 78	Nebo Brenin 72
1988	Penual Mark 52	Roth St Occasion 204	Nebo Brenin 82	Nebo Brenin 116
1989	Penual Mark 98	Roth St Occasion 108	Nebo Brenin 86	Nebo Daniel 88
1990	Penual Mark 74	Abercrychan Spectator 86	Nebo Bouncer 140	Nebo Daniel 140
1991	Fuchsia Quince Spring Caraway 78	Roth St Occasion 136	Nebo Brenin 136	Nebo Prince 124
1992	Cefn Golden Glory Spring Caraway 108	Roth St Occasion 194	Nebo Bouncer 112	Nebo Brenin 102
1993	Spring Caraway 228	Roth St Occasion 132	Persie Ramrod 114	Nebo Brenin 120
1994	Spring Caraway 184	Roth St Occasion 120	Nebo Bouncer 138	Nebo Daniel 118
1995	Spring Caraway 134	Cottrell Artiste 194	Nebo Bouncer 154	Nebo Daniel 124
1996	(RW only)			
1997	Pendock Legend 84	Eyarth Rio 98	Nebo Bouncer 148	Nebo Brenin 117
1998	Spring Caraway 136	Eyarth Rio 139	Nebo Bouncer 114	Nebo Brenin 96
1999	Spring Caraway 133	Cottrell Artiste 153	Nebo Bouncer 150	Nebo Brenin 82
2000	Spring Caraway 159	Carwed Charmer 119	Nebo Bouncer 201	Ebbw Victor 128
2001	(no Shows)			
2002	Spring Caraway	Eyarth Rio	Nebo Bouncer	Ebbw Victor
2003	Pendock Legend 143	Carwed Charmer 129	Nebo Bouncer 141	Thorneyside Flyer 81
2004	Blackhill Picalo Pendock Legend 92	Carwed Charmer 184	Nebo Bouncer 163	Trevallion Harry 130

WPCS PERFORMANCE COMPETITION CHAMPIONS 1972–2004

Year	A	B	C	D	WPB
1972	Stoatley Rhosyn	Marston Mirage**	Stoatley Moonraker	Llanarth Firel	Housemaster*
1973	Revel Jon	Shimpling Mischief**	Cascob Cornet	Granby Gent	Twyford Gladeye*
1974	Sydenhurst Benedictine	Millcroft Aries**	Stoatley Moonstone	Caergwerlas Jago	Twyford Gladeye*
1975	Greenacres Thimble	Millcroft Aries**	Stoatley Moonstone	Scole Zircon, Scole Rebound	Catherston Telstar*
1976	Penlan Peanut	Millcroft Aries**	Mardy Pride	Turkdean Trouabdour	Catherston Telstar*
1977	Penlan Peanut**	Ceulan Sanderling*	Synod Cerdin	Turkdean Troubadour	Stoatley Venetia
1978	Highland Drummer Boy	Woodhouse Hoarfrost** Twyford Sportsman*	Synod Cerdin	Trefaes Dwyn	Stoatley Venetia
1979	Another Toy	Twyford Sportsman**	Llangeuord Cariadog	Caergwerlas Jago	Stoatley Venetia*
1980	Another Toy	Twyford Sportsman*	Llangeuord Cariadog	Brynymor Comet	Stoatley Venetia**
1981	Pencoedcae Gwilliam	Norwood Principal Boy**	Llangeuord Cariadog	Brynymor Comet	Quern Golden Pippin*
1982	Pencoedcae Gwilliam	Abercrychan Major	Clanfield Smokey	Kentchurch Commandant**	Quern Golden Pippin*
1983	Maxwelltown Moongirl	Hazelwood Shonet	Rhosfarch Andes	Trevallion Cadno*	Deildre Lyn**
1984	Caress of Rosslyn	Millcroft Aries	Glanteifi Nans	Trevallion Cadno**	Ashlands Amanda*
1985	Caress of Rosslyn	Quern Bay Jupiter** Haybury Othelo*	Glanteifi Nans	Cascob Druid	Ashlands Amanda
1986	Maxwelltown Moonbow	Deverell Sweepstake**	Glanteifi Nans	Scole Nora	Ashlands Amanda*
1987	Hawstead Mayflower	Millcroft Blazeaway**	Uplands Calypso Kinver Swallow	Scole Nora	Ashlands Amanda*
1988	Bengad Duranta	Coed Coch Pippin** Roundbush Sirius*	Kinver Swallow	Scole Nora	Carlden Fantasia
1989	Quickthorn Greylag*	Roundbush Sirius	Glanteifi Nans**	Scole Nora	Wylye Pink Panther
1990	Twyford Bobbie*	Windwhistle Curlew	Leyeswick Joe**	Parclletis Glyndwr	Benjamin
1991	Twyford Bobbie	Sunbridge Leslie	Glanteifi Nans	Parcllet Glyndwr*	Deeside Duke**
1992	Blackamoor Stevie	Langshot Toytown	Watworth Bethany	Parclletis Glyndwr** Ruxley Merlin*	Dartans Another Prince
1993	Twyford Bobbie	Towyvalley Corniche**	Watworth Bethany	Parclletis Glyndwr	Dartans Another Prince*
1994	Twyford Bobbie	Longriver Royal Venture*	Leafycroft Merlyn	Llanina Malgwyn	Dartans Another Prince**
1995	Wynswood Petronella*	Brants Moonlight Serenade	Leafycroft Merlyn	Calerux Boneddwr	Pwllsarn Davey**
1996	Wynswood Petronella	Kerromoar Dooiney Cheerey	Leafycroft Merlyn	Llanina Malgwyn*	Pwllsarn Davey**
1997	Roseisle Pannikin	Harwel Wizard**	Sackville Nicky*	Llanina Malgwyn	Llangeuord June
1998	Bockmer Winston	Harwel Wizard*	Sackville Nicky**	Llanina Malgwyn	Dewi
1999	Bockmer Winston**	Harwel Wizard*	Sackville Nicky	Calerux Boneddwr	Ridings Jeremy Fisher
2000	Cammac Drachma**	Feinion Figaro	Leyeswick Welsh Flyer, Leyeswick Bantam Cock*	Penycrug Rhodri	Llanarth Quickstep
2002	Glenwood Caradog**	Caroworth Pendant	Leyeswick Welsh Flyer, Leyeswick Bantam Cock	Raclog Mia Jess*	Sannanvalley Jester
2003	Erwfair Milwr Bach	Morwyn Bronze Knight	Leyeswick Welsh Flyer	Raclog Mia Jess** Curtismill Flyer*	Temmas Little Lancer
2004	Highland Jury	Cottrell Goldcrest	Leyeswick Welsh Flyer, Leyeswick Bantam Cock	Curtismill Flyer** Ruckham Henry*	Dewines-y-Mynydd

(*** supreme champion; * reserve champion*)

WPCS EXPORTS 1900–2000

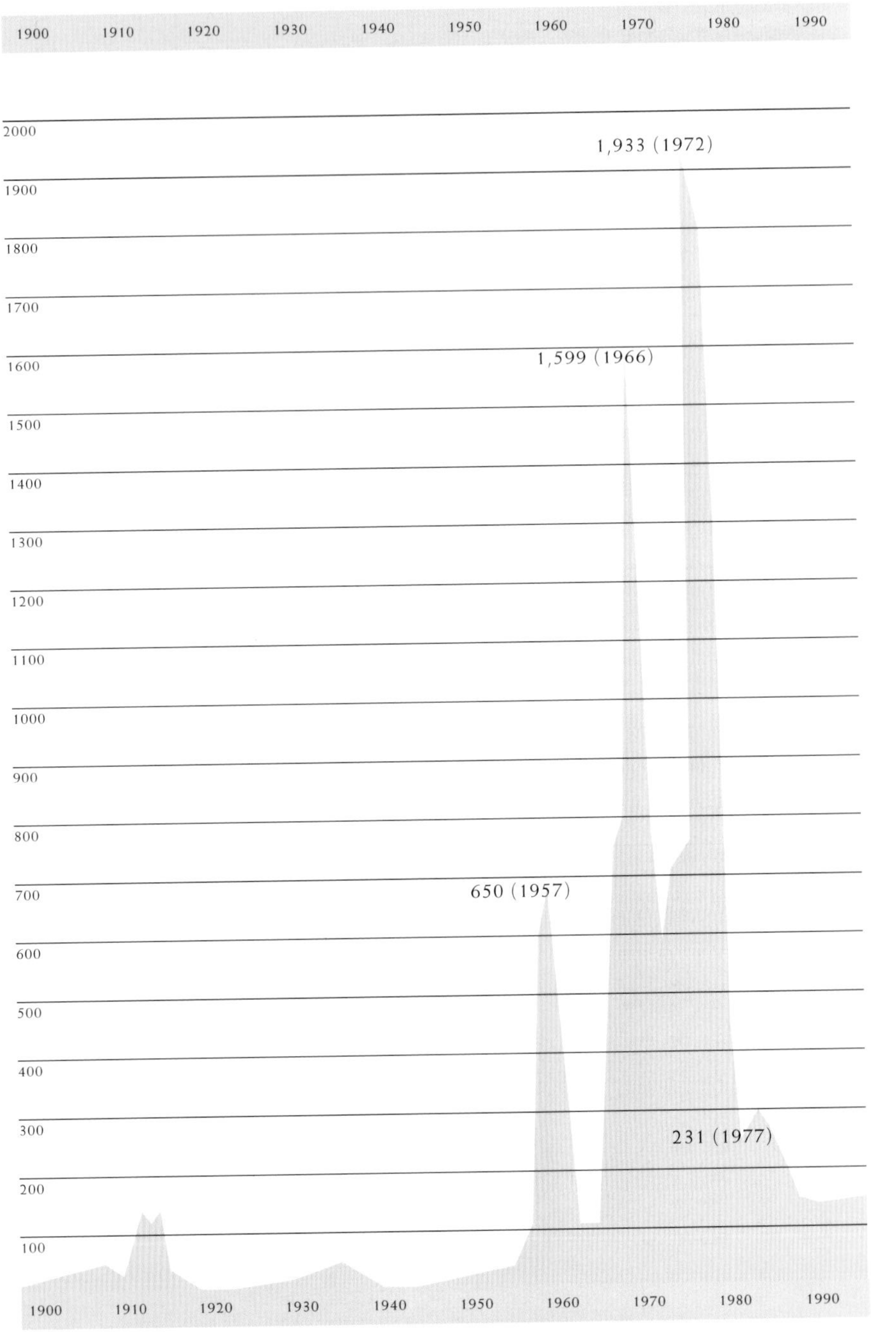

1900 1910 1920 1930 1940 1950 1960 1970 1980 1990

2000
1900
1800
1700
1600
1500
1400
1300
1200
1100
1000
900
800
700
600
500
400
300
200
100

1,933 (1972)
1,599 (1966)
650 (1957)
231 (1977)

1900 1910 1920 1930 1940 1950 1960 1970 1980 1990

FAYRE OAKS SALES STATISTICS 1954–2004

Year	No. Ent	Sale total	Average price	Top Section A	Top Section B
1954	78	£1,669	£21	Fayre Black Dawn 40g	
1955	114	£2,876	£31	Sundana of Maen Gwynedd 90g	
1956	169			Llanarth Pimpernel 100 g	
1957	157	£7,973	£59	Revel Sugar Bun (foal) 250g	Fayre Ladybird 85g
1958	240	£12,269	£77	Criban Bantam Bird 460g	Coed Coch Pws 120g
1959	227	£10,609	£67	Temevalley Silver Rose 260g	Brockwell Victoria 240g
1960	492		£46	Betws Ebrill 330g	Kirby Cane Ringdove 210g
1961	445			Revel Solo 240g	Criban Ester 420g
1962	413			Revel Romance 350g	Coed Coch Pawl 380g
1963	432	£21,998	£80	Coed Coch Sofren 270g	Downland Sandalwood 360g
1964	411			Coed Coch Siglen Las 550g	Belvoir Tiger Lily 400g
1965	517	£61,375	£144	Twyford Mayday 400g	Trefesgob Flush 700g
1966	657			Coed Coch Seren Wen 440g	Weston Carabella 500g
1967	581	£80,061	£169	Revel Springbok 1,000g	Kirby Cane Vogue 480g
1968	632	£101,571	£196	Coed Coch Perot 950g	Rotherwood Crocus 900g
				Twyford Matador 925g	Downland Demiure 900g
1969	841	£83,353	£158	Coed Coch Cadnant 750g	Lydstep Blondie 1,350g
1970	910	£57,035	£136	Coed Coch Nodyn 800g	Chirk Crogan 850g
1971	842	£64,845	£120	Aston Garway 900g	Bryn Shaundi 725g
				Synod Fairy Tale (foal) 340g	
1972	739	£98,947	£177	Fieldcote Vivandiere 420g	Weston Rita 850g
					Small-Land Otto(WPB) 900g
1973	982	£135,015	£230	Penant Lili o Benfro 720g	Downland Justina 1,300g
					Tetworth Tinkerbell 1,300g
1974	961	£95,974	£162(A);£242(B)	Coed Coch Darlun 780g	Downland Rosewood 1,700g
				Synod Nap (colt foal) 320g	Downland Dresden 1,700g
1975	600	£62,256	£118(A);£181(B)	Carnalw Hyderus 880g	Rotherwood Snowdrop 850
				Synod Ju Ju (filly foal) 680g	Small-Land Orsino (WPB) 1,450g
1976	646	£58,249	£153	Rowfant Seal 1,400g	Rosedale Falcon 1,600g
1977	578	£69,900	£200(A);£255(B)	Bengad Hercules 1,000g	Downland Kestrel 1,800g
				Weston Porcelain 1,000g	Baylayrel Mark Antony 1,000g
1978	605	£86,037	£217(A);£260(B)	Drym Arbennig 1,100g	Downland Dabchick 1,800g
				Synod Milky Way (foal) 550g	Orielton Aristocrat (1yr) 1,600g
1979	615	£76,421	£169(A);£253(B)	Synod Scamp 1,000g	Downland Goldleaf 2,000g
				Ceulan Lady May (foal) 500g	Tetworth Dancing Bronze 1,150g
1980	558	£62,038	£191(A);£221(B)	Weston Anniversary 1,900g	Sunbridge Tiger Tamer 1,900g
				Derwen Eclipse (foal) 900g	
1981	600	£64,836	£183(A);£209(B)	Hisland Hyderus 900g	Rotherwood Cavalier 1,300g
				Bowdler Bowstring 900g	Weston Moll Flanders 1,200g
1982	475	£52,439	£174(A);£209(B)	Weston Pearly Necklace 1,500g	Rotherwood Tomahwk 1,080g
				Fronbach Dyma Hi (foal) 1,500g	Sunbridge Aquarius 800g
1983	470	£46,268	£141(A);£255(B)	Maindiff Cock Robyn 750g	Cusop Sunset 1,250g
1984	411	£48,830	£202	Cwmsyfiog Trisca 980g	Chirk Corn Bunting 1,250g
1985	489	£64,998	£207	Coed Coch Bleddyn 2,500g	Gredington Lily 1,200g
1986	551	£69,948	£201	Vimpenny Chamomile 1,500g	Pennwood Eldorado 2,100g
1987	460			Dryfe Sheer Heaven 1,400g	Brookhall Shuttlecock 1,800g
1988	549	£102,315	£285	Sunwillow Monte Rosa 2,400g	Lemonshill Little Emperor 2,200g
1989	491	£121,705	£393	Foxhunter Parakeet 2,200g	Cennen Signature Tune 2,400g
				Fronbach Hello Dandy (c foal) 1,400g	Colbeach Minette 2,000g
1990	649	£153,699	£364	Gwynrhosyn Emerline 1,400g	Baledon Czarina 2,600g
				Bengad Wallfower 1,400g	Orielton Rumour 1,300g
1991	574	£182,856	£456	Lippens Dolly 3,600g	Colbeach Prince Consort 3,700g
1992	595	£204,628	£489	Springbourne Cameo 4,000g	Bureside Baron 2,500g
				Fronbach Shady Lady (foal) 4,000g	Pennwood Milan 2,500g
1993	594	£218,197	£526	Silvester 3,700g	Ashwel Diamond 3,200g
1994	737	£219,929	£492	Sunwillow Quest 4,500g	Cottrell Celebration 3,200g
1995	801	£192,131	£406	Fronbach Velvet Lady (foal) 2,400g	Priestwood Oberon 2,500g
1996	664	£198,845	£481	Springbourne Crocus 2,800g	Cottrell Rose of China 3,600g
1997	556	£160,292	£449	Springbourne Carmen 3,100g	Downland Pirouette 1,400g
1998	675	£136,676	£375	Friars Sweet Rose 2,200g	Priestwood Punchinello 2,500g
1999	534	£144,228	£418	Springbourne Clara 3,700g	Leucarum Poppy 3,000g
2000	530	£166,385	£490	Fronbach Carys 2,800g	Rhoson Carmen 4,000g
2001	524	£143,405	£418	Sarum Cadw Mi Gei £3,200	Downland Eventide £4,000
2002	425	£160,728	£543	Drumphin Trinket £3,200	Lemonshill Royal Flight £2,200
2003	506	£334,615	£862	Synod The Colonel £7,000	Orielton Beamish £10,500
2004	652	£339,341	£824	Castellau Valetta £7,000	Moelgarnedd Calipso £5,300
				Yaverland Cherry Blossom £7,000	

SECTION C SALES

Year	Sale	No. Cat	Sale Total (£)	Section C Average	Overall Average	Top Animals
1964	Llanarth	63	3,744	104		Gwynau Boy, 5yrs, RW Champ 1963, 1965, £200 / Faelog Frolic, 2yrs, RW Champ 1979, £100.
1965	Llanarth	64				Llanarth Philomena, 1yr, 135g
1966	Llanarth	98				Llanarth Marvel, 10yrs, 320g
1967	Llanarth	89			113	Ceiriog Caravelle, 5yrs, 150g
1968	Llanarth	75	5,779		123	Parc Dorothy, 3yrs, 155g
1969	Llanarth	115	7,828		119	Menai Cariadus, 2yrs, 160g
1970	Llanarth	130	9,311		116	Synod Bauble, f f, 300g
1971	Llanarth	191	23,117	120	164	Ross Lady Valiant, 2yrs, 250g / Synod Gerry, 1yr, 210g
1972	Llanarth	219	39,500	137	218	Faelog Fashion, 13yrs, 420g / Dwyfor Peter Pan, 3yrs, 400g
1973	Llanarth	298	58,537	166	260	Tydi Golden Shadow, 8yrs, 420g / Chalkhill Dragonfly, 2yrs, RW Champ 1973, 350g
1974	Llanarth	291	38,902	104	219	Synod Gerry, 4yrs, 500g
1975	Llanarth	285	42,968	135	199	Cynghordy Cream, 4 yrs, 540g
1975	RW	161				Ceulan (J) Tara, 5yrs, 150g
1976	Llanarth	344	46,237		195	Synod Glenda, 2yrs, 400g
1976	RW	189				Synod Gaynor, f f, 170g
1977	Llanarth	283	58,327	210	295	Parc Llinos, f f, 720g
1977	RW	143	18,942	143	188	Cefncoch Lady Grey, 4yrs, 320g
1978	Llanarth	284	76,755	243	348	Synod Princess Charming, f f, 900g
1978	RW	162	35,794	158	310	Khan Bronwen, 4yrs, 320g
1979	Llanarth	299	82,010		364	Ross Valiant, 4yrs, 600g / Synod Greetings, f f, 520g
1979	RW	325	62,055		287	Synod Liliddu, f f, 500g / Persie Ramrod, 1yr, 420g
1980	Llanarth	326	68,187	216	379	Synod Rondino, f f, 360g
1980	RW	400	66,176	181	274	Synod Gossip, 8yrs, 680g / Synod Rosita, 3yrs, 550g
1981	Llanarth	253	55,893	229	360	Cwnlle Lily, 11yrs, 600g / Neuaddparc Lady Diana, f f, 600g
1981	RW	348	74,035	254	311	Aston Breakaway, 4yrs, 1,600g
1982	Llanarth	171	22,097	251	272	Glanarthen Cardi Bach, 9yrs, 800g
1982	RW	409	82,251	202	300	Rhosymeirch Samaritan, 3yrs, 800g
1983	Derwen	138	19,305		250	Synod Gossip, 11yrs, 370g
1983	RW	423	86,388		313	Synod Rachelian, 13yrs, 650g
1984	RW	437	118,800		400	Talley Fusilier, 5yrs, 700g / Fronarth True Briton, 8yrs, 700g / Synod Reprint, f f, 700g
1985	RW	600	132,216		363	Leyeswick Tywysog, 3yrs, 650g / Peris Tiwlip, 10yrs, 580g
1986	RW	580	125,658		349	Bodelian ap Celt, 2yrs, 1,100g / Flemish Jane, 8yrs, 800g
1987	RW	476	156,463		504	Menai Sparkler, 4yrs, 1,200g / Menai Coryn, 7yrs, 1,100g
1988	RW	551	225,000		586	Synod Romantica, f f, 1,500g / Neuaddparc Monica, f f, 1,000g / Betws Enfys, 1yr, 900g
1989	RW	634	358,200		791	Neuaddparc Welsh Model, f f, 1,700g / Cilybebyll Dafydd Du, 3yrs, 1,650g / Taybog Lynne, 7yrs, 1,600g / Parvadean Rebecca, f f, 1,550g
1990	RW	918	531,027		912	Gorfelyn Swallow, 6yrs, 2,600g / Fronarth Step High, 4yrs, 2,000g / Aberarth Tanwen, f f, 1,600g / Parc Harry, c f, 1,300g
1991	RW	970	512,419		780	Cwm Lowri, 9yrs, 3,800g / Parcybedw Boy George, 3yrs, 2,000g / Glynwyn Dartanian, c f, 1,300g / Parc Heledd, f f, 1,000g
1992	RW	865	460,827		789	Persie Rosaleen, 11yrs, 3,200g / Parc Huw, c f, 2,000g / Synod Lady Penelope, f f, 1,000g
1993	RW	926	495,351		814	Paddock Lightning, 17yrs, 3,000g / Synod Rosie O'Neil, f f, 2,050g / Synod Glamour Chick, f f, 2,000g / Tyreos Adrian, c f, 1,000g
1994	RW	996	443,356		788	Tireinon Fashionette, 9yrs, 2,000g / Aberaeron Arbenigwr, 8yrs, 1,600g / Synod Raindrop, f f, 1,500g / Synod Glitter, f f, 1,400g
1995	RW	949	360,360		715	Dyrfal Red Rose, f f, 4,500g / Parvadean Report, c f, 2,200g / Persie Rainbow, 8yrs, 2,100g
1996	RW	861	334,790		702	Synod Maggie Poppins, f f, 2,700g / Parvadean Reload, 3yrs, 2,000g
1997	RW	757	333,055		711	Neuaddparc Dancing Queen, f f, 3,100g / Synod Raimunda, f f, 2,800g / Telynau Cantores, 7yrs, 1,800g
1998	RW	862	315,042		617	Synod Nutkin, 6yrs, 6,000g / Synod Rozalina, f f, 3,000g / Parvadean Golden Dawn, f f, 2,850g
1999	RW	786	324,784		683	Synod Rufflette, f f, 3,000g / Synod Rosa Blanca, f f, 2,000g
2000	RW	735	327,518		685	Synod Athina, 12yrs, 6,000g / Triad Ricochet, c f, 3,800g / Blaengwen Macy Gray, f f, 2,400g
2001	RW	757	358,937		719	Synod Relegance, f f, 11,000g / Synod Georgette, f f, 2,800g
2002	RW	709	485,979		911	Uphill Tom Thumb, 4yrs, 14,500g / Synod Ruby Gem, f f, 4,800g / Felinmor Grand Slam, 3yrs, 3,400g / Synod Rosie Ribbons, f f, 2,800g
2003	RW	739	530,600		977	Synod Rosie's Angel, 7yrs, 6,500g / Laurtom Gold Spark, 7yrs, 4,500g / Synod Sweet Celina, f f, 3,100g
2004	RW	779	620,128		1,071	Parvadean The General, 9yrs, 13,000g / Donys Gwrda, 3yrs, 5,500g / Parvadean Pom Pom, 13yrs, 4,000g / Synod Sweet Jessica, f f, 3,200g

Index of horse and pony names